LABOR PRODUCTIVITY IN
SOVIET AND AMERICAN INDUSTRY

A RESEARCH STUDY
BY THE RAND CORPORATION

LABOR PRODUCTIVITY IN SOVIET AND AMERICAN INDUSTRY

By WALTER GALENSON

PROFESSOR OF INDUSTRIAL RELATIONS
UNIVERSITY OF CALIFORNIA, BERKELEY
CONSULTANT, THE RAND CORPORATION

1955

COLUMBIA UNIVERSITY PRESS, NEW YORK

THE TRANSLITERATION SYSTEM
USED IN THIS SERIES
IS BASED ON
THE LIBRARY OF CONGRESS SYSTEM
WITH SOME MODIFICATIONS

AUTHOR'S NOTE

IT IS a pleasure to acknowledge my great indebtedness to Mr. Joseph A. Kershaw, who helped formulate this project as a part of a program of research by The RAND Corporation for the United States Air Force, and who guided it to completion with a benevolent but firm hand. Messrs. Hans Heymann, Jr., Oleg Hoeffding, Norman M. Kaplan, and A. D. Redding, of the staff of The RAND Corporation; Professor Abram Bergson, of Columbia University; Professor Alexander Gerschenkron, of Harvard University; and Professor Donald R. Hodgman, of the University of California, were kind enough to read critically all or portions of the manuscript. Mrs. Helena G. Williams of the RAND editorial staff has been most helpful in preparing the manuscript for publication. Whatever shortcomings the volume may contain are my sole responsibility, however.

I should also like to acknowledge the assistance of the Institute of Industrial Relations at the University of California, Berkeley, of which I have been a staff member while engaged in preparing the manuscript.

WALTER GALENSON

Berkeley, January, 1954

ACKNOWLEDGMENTS

THE AUTHOR wishes to thank the following publishers for permission to quote from the books and monographs listed:

American Slavic and East European Review: "Soviet Machinery Output," by Donald R. Hodgman. Copyright, 1953, by the *American Slavic and East European Review,* New York.

British Productivity Council: *Simplification in Industry,* London, 1939; *Cotton Weaving,* London, 1950.

Cambridge University Press: *Comparative Productivity in British and American Industry,* by L. Rostas. Copyright, 1948, by the Cambridge University Press, Cambridge, England.

International Labor Office: *Methods of Labor Productivity Statistics,* Studies and Reports, New Series, No. 18, Geneva, 1951.

National Bureau of Economic Research: *Employment in Manufacturing, 1899–1939,* by Solomon Fabricant. Copyright, 1942, by the National Bureau of Economic Research, New York.

Prentice-Hall, Inc.: *Russia's Soviet Economy,* by Harry Schwartz. Copyright, 1950, by Prentice-Hall, Inc., New York.

Row, Peterson, and Company: *Soviet Economic Growth,* by Abram Bergson (ed.). Copyright, 1953, by Row, Peterson, and Company, Evanston, Illinois.

Royal Economic Society: "The Influence of Productivity on Economic Welfare," by J. Tinbergen, *The Economic Journal,* March, 1952.

Royal Statistical Society: "The International Comparison of Industrial Output," by E. C. Snow. Copyright, 1944, by the Royal Statistical Society, London.

United Nations: *Labour Productivity of the Cotton Textile Industry in Five Latin-American Countries,* New York, 1951.

U.S. Department of Commerce, Bureau of the Census: *Census of Manufactures,* Washington, 1939, 1947; *Mineral Industries,* Washington, 1939.

CONTENTS

TABLES

INTRODUCTION

THE present study has three major purposes: to trace the development of labor productivity in a number of Soviet industries since 1928; to compare productivity in these industries with that in their U.S. counterparts; and to arrive at some general conclusions on comparative labor productivity in Soviet and American industry.

To these ends, output and employment data are obtained for a number of individual industries in both the USSR and the United States. With the exception of machinery, the industries covered are those for which a relatively homogeneous output can be identified and, thus, expressed in physical units. In the case of machinery, it is Professor Gerschenkron's revaluation of Soviet machinery output in dollars which permits its inclusion in the present study.[1]

For present purposes, an industry approach is believed to offer distinct advantages over alternative, more aggregative approaches. In the study of changes in Soviet industrial productivity over time, we can utilize Soviet data on physical volume of output in the industries examined, data believed to be much more reliable than the official Soviet index of industrial production in so-called constant 1926/27 prices, which is generally acknowledged to be subject to a strong upward bias.

For the purpose of comparing Soviet and American productivity levels, the industry study approach makes it possible to by-pass the twin obstacles imposed by the lack of dependable Soviet value-of-output data and by the currency-exchange-rate problem.

The chief drawback of our approach is its lack of comprehensiveness. It is impossible to express productivity in physical output terms unless an industry has a fairly homogeneous product structure. In many cases—e.g., in that of chemicals—output would have to be sub-

---

[1] Alexander Gerschenkron, *A Dollar Index of Soviet Machinery Output, 1927–28 to 1937*.

divided very finely for such an approach to be attempted. The sheer magnitude of the task required to approach completeness dictates some selectivity. In the present study there are further limitations of incomplete Soviet data for many industries.

In spite of these difficulties, the industries examined in this volume amount to a substantial segment of Soviet mining and manufacturing. Mining is represented by coal, iron ore, and crude oil production; capital goods, by the iron and steel industry and five branches of machinery production; and consumer goods, by cotton textile, shoe, and beet sugar manufacturing. The degree of coverage thus obtained is discussed in Part III, below. Suffice it to say here that from one fifth to one half of all mining and manufacturing is included, depending on the year and measure of coverage employed. It should be emphasized that this list includes all major Soviet industries for which adequate production and employment data are available. Some enlargement of the consumer goods sector could have been obtained by adding relatively minor industries, but the amount of work required would have been disproportionate to the resultant added coverage. The degree to which productivity within this sample is representative of all manufacturing and mining must remain a moot question.

The plan of the study is as follows: Part I contains a discussion of the productivity concepts employed and of the problems involved in the statistical comparisons. Part II consists of the separate industry studies, with the U.S.-USSR productivity comparisons. Part III includes a summary and generalization of the industry studies, an evaluation of some factors that may explain observed differences in productivity between the two countries, and some speculation regarding future trends in Soviet productivity.

PART I
THE CONCEPTS AND METHODOLOGY
OF PRODUCTIVITY MEASUREMENT

I

THE SIGNIFICANCE AND LIMITATIONS OF THE PRODUCTIVITY CONCEPT

INTEREST in the productivity of labor, as one of the factors of production, tends to increase as labor power becomes relatively scarce during the course of industrialization. Where labor is in abundant supply, as in nations in a preindustrial stage of development, the productivity of capital is likely to be of more concern: labor productivity acquires greater meaning as an economic indicator to the degree that labor must be economized. In a country such as India, where the major manufacturing industry, cotton textiles, has two qualified workers for every job and where wages are often below the Malthusian minimum, one would expect an exceedingly low level of labor productivity not susceptible of radical alteration through technological change within the cotton industry alone.

There is implicit in the concern with labor productivity comparisons, over time, within a country as well as between countries, the notion of a positive relationship between labor productivity and welfare, and the belief that a nation with a greater output per wage earner is likely to be in a position superior to one with lower productivity. The stated purpose of the Anglo-American Council on Productivity, which has produced many British-U.S. industry productivity studies, is "to promote economic well-being by a free exchange of knowledge in the realm of industrial organization, method and techniques, and thereby to assist British industry to raise the level of its productivity." However, it has become perfectly clear that magnitude of industrial output and consumer well-being are by no means synonymous. Labor productivity is now regarded as an important element in economic capabilities generally, in that it helps in the assessment of the ability of a nation to produce with a given quantity of manpower a combination of civilian and military goods sufficient at the same time to satisfy the material aspirations of various groups in society and to provide the military means necessary for national defense.

The labor productivity ratio[1] can tell us a good deal that is meaningful in this area. Even Rostas's bald statement that "in the pre-war period of 1935–9 average productivity—as measured by physical output per worker—was at least twice (about 2.2 times) as high in the U.S. as in Britain"[2] permits the formation of certain initial judgments both with respect to consumer welfare and to military capabilities in the two countries. When we are concerned, as we are increasingly, with conditions of full-employment production, statistically observable differences in the productivity of labor at least raise questions that may lead to the generally desirable goal of more effective labor utilization. Nor is it necessarily true that questions are raised only with respect to the productively inferior country. Even if every industry in Country A displays greater absolute productivity than the corresponding industry in Country B, there still remains to be explained the problem of the comparative productivity advantages enjoyed by particular industries in Country A.[3]

Special interest attaches to the determination of the level of labor productivity prevailing in the Soviet Union. Such a measure may help to shed light on the all-important question of that nation's economic capabilities.[4] Moreover, the process of Russian industrialization, which

[1] For a discussion of the various forms the ratio can take, as well as of certain basic conceptual problems, see Irving H. Siegel, *Concepts and Measurement of Production and Productivity*, Chap. 2; Hiram S. Davis, "The Meaning and Measurement of Productivity," in Industrial Relations Research Association, *Industrial Productivity*, p. 1.

[2] L. Rostas, *Comparative Productivity in British and American Industry*, p. 27.

[3] For example, the ratio of output per worker in the United States to that of Great Britain (1937) was 94 percent in cement manufacture and 130–140 percent in woolen and worsted manufacture compared with 364 percent in pig iron and 525 percent in tin can manufacture. See *ibid.*, p. 36.

[4] With respect to Russian labor productivity, there is much diversity of opinion. Colin Clark has estimated that real net income per employee man-hour in the USSR in 1936 was only 20 percent of the U.S. level. See *Review of Economic Progress*, August and September, 1949. Demitri B. Shimkin has stated that Soviet labor productivity at the present time may be 25 percent of the U.S. level. See *Fortune*, May, 1951, p. 106. A recent textbook on Soviet economics contents itself with quoting a Russian assertion that in 1937 Soviet labor productivity was 40.5 percent of the U.S. level, 103.1 percent of the British level, and 97 percent of the German level and observing: ". . . the conclusion that in 1937 Soviet industrial productivity per worker was still well below

is reflected in changes in labor productivity, is of considerable importance as a possible model for the industrialization of other backward
areas. Soviet economists themselves have placed great importance on
labor productivity measurements both for purposes of planning and
control[5] and as indexes of economic "backwardness" in comparison
with the United States.[6]

While comparative labor productivity measurements can be of considerable value, it is essential that their limitations be recognized. It
is scarcely necessary to point out that the labor productivity ratio is
in no sense a measure of the effort and contribution of labor alone
but is the joint result of labor and capital inputs expressed in terms
of a labor denominator.[7]

Nor is it necessarily true that productivity gains are equivalent to
increases in economic welfare.[8] It is sometimes forgotten that high

---

half that in the United States seems unquestionable. The comparisons with Great
Britain and Germany seem more open to doubt." Harry Schwartz, *Russia's Soviet
Economy*, p. 471.

[5] Treatises and textbooks on industrial statistics normally devote considerable attention to the construction and use of labor productivity indexes. The best recent treatment is A. I. Rotshtein, *Problemy promyshlennoi statistiki v SSSR*, Vol. III. The
Stakhanov movement and its many variants tend to center attention on labor productivity as a means of measuring worker achievement. The economic plans normally
contain a section setting forth for each industry and plant, and for the entire economy,
a goal for labor productivity. (English translations of Russian titles will not be given
in the footnotes. They may be found in the Bibliography.)

[6] Such comparisons were common before the war. See Ia. A. Ioffe, *SSSR i kapitalisticheskie strany*, pp. 75–80; E. L. Granovskii and B. L. Markus, *Ekonomika
sotsialisticheskoi promyshlennosti*, pp. 460–61. Since the war, Russian spokesmen have
concentrated on the comparison of productivity trends rather than absolute levels,
e.g., A. Cherniak, *O tempakh razvitiia sotsialisticheskoi promyshlennosti*, pp. 33–34.

[7] For a catalogue of the various factors that may affect the productivity of labor,
see International Labor Office, *Methods of Labor Productivity Statistics*, Chap. 2.
Some of the statistical problems encountered in attempting to account for the contribution of the several factors separately are considered in Sigmund P. Zobel, "On
the Measurement of the Productivity of Labor," *Journal of the American Statistical
Association*, XLV (June, 1950), 218. An excellent discussion is also to be found in
V. L. Belenkii, *Indeksy proizvoditel'nosti truda*.

[8] Professor Tinbergen has concluded, on the basis of several theoretical models
which involve the effects of changes in productivity upon the terms of trade: "The
old thesis that an increase in productivity leads to an increase in welfare should not
be misunderstood. Not under all circumstances does it lead to consequences that are
in all respects attractive. In a number of cases the consequences are definitely mixed;
some of them favorable, others unfavorable. It does not always entail an increase in
total real expenditure; nor does it always yield an increase in real workers' income.

labor productivity is neither a universal panacea nor an index of social progress. Maximizing output is not the same thing as achieving the highest possible level of labor productivity; a country with a high ratio of labor to capital might well prefer to employ a relatively large admixture of labor in the productive process. The same might be true of a highly industrialized nation in the throes of depression; it is conceivable that lowering the national labor productivity level by putting unemployed workers to work at low-capital-using tasks would raise the national product. Unless comparable levels of industrialization, employment, and economic activity are at the basis of labor productivity comparisons, completely erroneous conclusions may be drawn from unqualified international statistics on productivity.

The approach to global productivity comparison through industry studies, as compared with estimates of gross national product or total industrial output per head, has the inevitable disadvantage of limited coverage. The fact that labor productivity in the iron and steel industry of Country *A* is greater than that of Country *B* tells us nothing of relative economic welfare, or even of relative military capabilities, in the two countries. But, as is pointed out below, productivity comparisons made at the level, say, of total industrial output have certain defects which reduce their significance considerably—principally the currency conversion problem, which can be avoided by building up to a total figure from individual industry studies. Moreover, relative productivity by industry is not without interest as illustrating, for example, differences in industrial development and in industrial organization.[9]

Often it reduces the volume of employment." J. Tinbergen, "The Influence of Productivity on Economic Welfare," *The Economic Journal,* LXII (March, 1952), 85.

[9] See *infra,* Chap. XIV.

II

SOVIET LABOR PRODUCTIVITY STATISTICS

SOVIET statisticians have long been preoccupied with the methodological problems involved in the construction of an index of labor productivity. From the early twenties, this subject was the occasion for considerable discussion inspired by the central position of the labor theory of value in Marxist thought. A more practical reason for Soviet interest in the measurement of labor productivity was the necessity of maintaining statistical control over the mass of manpower flowing into industry. Rational allocation of labor resources might be furthered by watching comparative labor productivity trends among the various branches of industry and by setting productivity as well as production goals and inquiring into the causes of their nonfulfillment.

The following discussion is limited to the problems involved in constructing an aggregate labor productivity index for all industry, though the Russians developed various types of indexes to measure the performance of smaller economic units and to segregate the several factors that lie behind the general concept of labor productivity.[1] For the past thirty years, Soviet statisticians have been engaged in a debate over the appropriate form of an aggregate index. The official index of labor productivity, calculated and published by the Central Statistical Office of the State Planning Commission, has simply been "the percentage relationship between average output per wage earner in gross value of product and the analogous index for the base period."[2] This index may be represented as follows:[3]

[1] The reader interested in the details of Russian labor productivity index construction is referred particularly to V. L. Belenkii, *Indeksy proizvoditel'nosti truda,* and A. I. Rotshtein, *Problemy promyshlennoi statistiki v SSSR,* Vol. III.

[2] Tsentral'noe Statisticheskoe Upravlenie Gosplan SSSR, *Slovar'-spravochnik po sotsial'no-ekonomicheskoi statistike,* 1944, p. 218 (hereinafter cited as *Slovar'-spravochnik*). Beginning in 1949, a different pricing system was employed. See *infra,* p. 261.

[3] The symbols employed follow the colloquial practice of the International Labor Office in *Methods of Labor Productivity Statistics,* Appendix I.

(1)
$$I_{LP} = \frac{\sum q_1 p_c}{\sum m_1} \bigg/ \frac{\sum q_0 p_c}{\sum m_0}$$

where $q_1 p_c$ and $q_0 p_c$ represent, respectively, gross value of output, in constant prices, of all industry in the current and base periods, and m_1 and m_0 represent the corresponding industrial employment in the current and base periods. Essentially, this scheme represents comparison of an index of production with an index of employment.

This formulation was severely criticized by S. G. Strumilin,[4] the well-known Soviet economist, and others. The burden of the charges levied against it was that because of the implicit industry weighting by gross value of product, the resultant index was subject to severe fluctuation without any necessary correlation in underlying unit labor requirements. An example from Rotshtein (Vol. III, p. 78) may help to clarify this point:

TYPE OF PRODUCT	VALUE OF PRODUCT IN 1926/27 PRICES (MILLIONS OF RUBLES)		NUMBER OF WAGE EARNERS (THOUSANDS)		AVERAGE ANNUAL OUTPUT PER WAGE EARNER (RUBLES)		PERCENT CHANGE IN PRODUC- TIVITY 1927/28 TO 1932/33
	1927/28	1932/33	1927/28	1932/33	1927/28	1932/33	
Group A	4,393	12,027	1,036	1,463	4,240	8,221	+93.3
Group B	6,516	13,606	1,067	1,177	6,106	11,555	+89.2
All In- dustry	10,909	25,633	2,103	2,640	5,187	9,706	+87.2

In this example, Group A products, which were primarily raw materials and capital goods with a relatively low value of output per wage earner, increased as a percentage of the total volume of goods produced, whereas Group B products, consumer goods characterized by a higher value of output per wage earner, showed a relative decline. In consequence, the labor productivity increase calculated according to the official formula would be less than the separate increase of each of the two industrial groups.

Strumilin argued that the only theoretically unexceptionable meas- ure of labor productivity trend was one which answered the following question: What would be the total labor cost of a fixed complex of

[4] In the introduction to Belenkii, *op. cit.*

products in the current as compared with the base period?[5] However, the calculation of such an index on an aggregate basis presupposes the availibility of precise unit labor requirements data for a broadly representative group of products, a condition which did not prevail in 1930, when Strumilin wrote, and which still apparently remains an obstacle.[6] Therefore, he suggested that the aggregate index be constructed as an arithmetic mean of indexes calculated separately for each industry as a ratio of current to base period value of output per wage earner, weighted by current employment. Thus, following this suggestion, Savinskii proposed an index of the following form for each industry:[7]

$$(2) \qquad i_{LP} = \frac{\sum \left(\frac{q_1 p_c}{m_1} : \frac{q_0 p_c}{m_0} \right) m_1}{\sum m_1}$$

$$\frac{60.6}{13.9}$$
$$123$$

where q_1 and q_0 represent total output of each enterprise for the current and base periods, m_1 and m_0 the corresponding employment, and p_0 represents the constant unit prices.

The separate industry indexes are in turn summarized to construct an aggregate index for all industry, as follows:

$$(3) \qquad I_{LP} = \frac{\sum i m_1}{\sum m_1}$$

where i is the industry index of labor productivity, and m_1 is the current employment in each industry.

[5] This may be represented symbolically as follows:

$$I_{LP} = \frac{\sum q_x l_1}{\sum q_x l_0}$$

where q_x represents a fixed complex of goods, l_1 unit labor requirements in the current period, and l_0 unit labor requirements in the base period. Strumilin suggested using the base period complex, i.e., $q_x = q_0$.

[6] Rotshtein noted in 1947: ". . . the construction of indexes of the dynamics of labor productivity on a national scale by the 'labor' [Strumilin] method is work for the future . . . it would be possible to construct an index of production on the basis of a constant (for both periods) composite of products, of the greatest significance to the economy . . . the most complicated problem, however, is that of the denominator of the productivity fraction, i.e., the amount of labor time expended on the product. . . . An accurate estimate of this expenditure, adequate for each given unit of product in the national economy, requires an estimate of the expenditure of labor at all stages of production." Rotshtein, *op. cit.*, III, 153, 164.

[7] D. Savinskii, *Kurs promyshlennoi statistiki*, p. 195.

It may be noted that an index constructed according to formulae (2) and (3) does not correspond to the concept of labor productivity "considered as a specific characteristic of the product, undertaking or industry for which it is measured; in this case, averages for a group of components should remain unchanged if the individual productivity for each component remains unchanged."[8] On the contrary, it is quite possible for the index to change without any change in unit labor requirements, as a consequence of the shifting employment weights. However, the latter index does put all industries on a par insofar as the absolute level of the gross value (price) of their products is concerned, thus preventing changes in labor productivity in high value-of-product industries from dominating the index and concealing productivity changes in low value-of-product industries.

In May, 1943, the Central Statistical Office began to calculate an index of labor productivity along the lines of formulae (2) and (3), parallel to the traditional one shown in formula (1). The technique of construction has been described as follows:

... the ministries calculated partial indexes of labor productivity by factory, and then weighted them by the number of wage earners in the current period. The result was industrial branch indexes, from which the Central Statistical Office secured an all-industry index by weighting the ministry indexes by the number of wage earners in the current period. At the present time this index ... has been discontinued, and the only dynamic index of labor productivity in national economic statistics is the [old] index of shifting complexes.[9]

Since no public discussion accompanied the adoption and the subsequent discontinuance of the new type index, we can only speculate as to the motives behind the short-lived experiment. It cannot be said that the new type index offered any insurmountable computational problems. It may have been that the Soviet statistical authorities belatedly recognized that the new type index was not inherently superior to the old one, as evidenced by the following argument:

For the economy as a whole the dynamics of the quantity of material values produced in a unit of time is essentially independent of precisely how much particular groups of workers increased or decreased their productivity. The economy as a whole is interested in an increase in average labor

[8] International Labor Office, *Methods of Labor Productivity Statistics*, p. 57.
[9] Savinskii, *op. cit.*, p. 208.

productivity, i.e., in the growth of average output of material values in units of working time for the aggregate of enterprises or production. . . .

The correctness of this thesis may be illustrated by the following simple example. In a factory a worker on an automatic machine produces 100 units of a given type of product in a day, while another worker produces only 10 units by hand. It is clear that the enterprise is producing an average output (of the given product) equal to $(100 + 10) \div 2 = 55$ units per worker per day. If the output per worker in the mechanized department per unit of time increases by 50%, and in the hand department by 100%, this would mean that with the same labor force the enterprise produced $150 + 20 = 170$ units in two working days, i.e., $170 \div 2 = 85$ units per working day, against 55 units produced earlier. The increase in output would be

$$\frac{85 - 55}{55} \cdot 100 = 54\%$$

The "index" method of calculation . . . would yield as the index of labor productivity:

$$\frac{\dfrac{150}{100} + \dfrac{20}{10}}{2} = 1.75, \text{ i.e., an increase of } 75\%$$

From this example (and similar ones) the conclusion emerges that for measuring the dynamics of labor productivity, not only the rate of growth of output, but the absolute level of productivity in the base period, is important. Weighting the individual indexes of labor productivity by the number of wage earners or some other index of working time in a given department or enterprise is therefore insufficient, since essentially this assumes that equal rates of change in various enterprises are of equal significance. To put it differently, this means that the absolute levels of labor productivity in the base period in various departments or enterprises are assumed to be equal, i.e., that the mass of values created per unit of time are in all cases equal.[10]

Perhaps even more compelling was the realization that, except over long periods, the results obtained through use of the two indexes were not likely to differ greatly.[11] This was conceded many years ago by

[10] Rotshtein, *op. cit.,* III, 88.

[11] The results would differ significantly in the short run only if there were a systematic difference in the dynamics of productivity between industries characterized by low absolute value of product per wage earner (e.g., extractive industries) and those of high absolute value of output per wage earner (e.g., fabricating industries). In this event, productivity changes in the latter would tend to obscure those in the former under the old type index, whereas the new type index would reflect the

Belenkii, an advocate of the Strumilin index, on the basis of a comparison of the behavior of the two indexes during the period from 1913 to 1918.[12]

Table 1 contains the official Soviet labor productivity index for large-scale industry from 1928 to 1952, omitting the years 1941 to 1945, computed in accordance with the foregoing method. It should be emphasized that this index is based on the Soviet production index in 1926–27 prices, the inflationary bias of which is well known. The figures indicate an average annual rate of growth (compounded annually) of 10.3 percent in man-year productivity from 1928 to 1940 and of 11.6 percent from 1946 to 1952. While precise index figures for the war years 1941–45 cannot be derived from published data, it is quite clear that the German attack in 1941 resulted in a catastrophic decline in labor productivity. The average annual rate of productivity increase during the four years was put at 9 percent,[13] and this, together with the index figure for 1946 (which was derived by working backward from 1950) indicates that 1941 productivity must have been in the neighborhood of 200, based on 1928. Table 1 also shows, for the years 1928 to 1937, an index of output per man-hour. No subsequent data are available for this series.

The man-year productivity series shown in Table 1 is compared in Table 2 with indexes secured by dividing the published production index (a) by the "labor section" wage earner series of the Central Administration of Social-Economic Accounting (TSUNKHU) and (b) by the "industry section" wage earner series of TSUNKHU.[14]

---

influence of both in proportion to current employment. For the 1930's, when there were sharp interindustry productivity trend differences, it is impossible to say a priori which of the two indexes would have yielded a higher rate of productivity increase, since some of the high value per wage earner industries (e.g., shoes, textiles) had relatively small productivity gains, whereas others (e.g., machinery) experienced higher productivity gains than the low value per wage earner extractive industries.

[12] Belenkii, *op. cit.*, pp. 117–18.

[13] Sh. Turetskii, *Proizvoditel'nost truda*, p. 49.

[14] For the distinction between the "labor section" and "industry section" statistics, see *infra*, p. 38. There is some evidence that the Russians employed the "industry section" series in calculating labor productivity. For example, the figures on annual output per wage earner in rubles given in Ia. Ioffe, *SSSR i kapitalisticheskie strany*, p. 76, which approximate the official index when reduced to index form, were obviously calculated through the use of the "industry section" data.

TABLE 1

INDEX OF LABOR PRODUCTIVITY IN SOVIET LARGE-SCALE
INDUSTRY,[a] 1928–52

YEAR	INDEX OF OUTPUT PER MAN-YEAR (1928 = 100)[b]	ANNUAL PRODUCTIVITY INCREASE (PERCENT)	INDEX OF OUTPUT PER MAN-HOUR (1928 = 100)[f]
1928	100		100
1929	112.9	12.9	112.1
1930	123.9	9.7	128.7
1931	133.3	7.6	140.4
1932	136.8	2.6	150.7
1933	148.7	8.7	166.7
1934	164.6	10.7	189.1
1935	186.0	13.0	214.3
1936	225.8	21.4	254.4
1937	245.9	8.9	269.4
1938	272.9	11.0	....
1939	318.5	16.7	....
1940	324.6[c]	1.9	....
1946	270.4[d]		....
1947	305.6[d]	13.0	....
1948	351.4[d]	15.0	....
1949	397.1[d]	13.0	....
1950	444.7[d]	12.0	....
1951	489.2[e]	10.0	....
1952	523.4[g]	7.0	....

[a] Based on the Soviet index of industrial production in 1926–27 ruble prices.

[b] *1928–39:* N. S. Maslova, *Proizvoditel'nost' truda v promyshlennosti SSSR,* p. 42. Up to 1934, these figures are consistent with those contained in Ia. A. Ioffe, *SSSR i kapitalisticheskie Strany,* p. 75, and in *Trud v SSSR,* 1936, p. 91. For subsequent years, the following data appear in these sources: 1935—191.1; 1936—233.9; 1937—249.9. The figure in the table is accepted as coming from a later and apparently revised source.

[c] *1940:* Gosudarstvennyi Nauchnyi Institut, *Bolshaia sovetskaia entsiklopediia,* Moscow, 1948, p. 1092, where it is stated: ". . . for the first three years of the third five year plan [1938, 1939, 1940] [annual output per industrial wage earner] increased by an additional 32 percent." This figure also appears in Sh. Turetskii, *Vnutripromyshlennoe nakoplenie v SSSR,* p. 30: "For 1938–40, labor productivity in industry rose by 32%, which means an average annual increase of 10%." See also M. Spiridonov, *Proizvoditel'nost' truda v sotsialisticheskom obshtchestve,* p. 5. Turetskii, *op cit.,* also states: "For the years of the first three Stalin five year plans, for 13 prewar years (1928–1940) labor productivity in socialized industry rose more than 3.5 times." This figure, which would mean an index of 350 for 1940 instead of the 324.6 in the table, cannot be reconciled with other statements except on the hypothesis that

Notes to Table 1 *(Continued)*

Turetskii was referring to the socialized sector of industry, excluding cooperatives, rather than the more usual category of large-scale industry.

Nor can the index in the table be reconciled with the asserted labor productivity increases for each of the plans: 41 percent from 1929–32; 82 percent from 1933–37; and 32 percent from 1938–40, which yield a 1940 index figure of 339.

The 1940 estimate in the table, 324.6, allows for only a small productivity increase over 1939. This may explain, however, why published Soviet sources contain no separate productivity figure for 1940, referring always instead to the 32 percent increase from 1938 to 1940, inclusive.

d *1946–50:* calculated from *Voprosy ekonomiki,* 1950, No. 6, p. 39.

e *Trud,* January 29, 1952, p. 2. For a discussion of the production index basis of productivity data since 1950, see *infra,* p. 261.

f *1928–31:* B. L. Markus, "The Stakhanov Movement," *International Labor Review,* July, 1936, p. 5.

1932–37: Ioffe, *op. cit.,* p. 75. The figures in this source for 1932–34 are somewhat higher than those contained in the article by B. L. Markus.

g *Trud,* January 23, 1953, p. 1. See note *e*

Up to 1930, there was close correspondence between the published and calculated indexes; from 1930 to 1931, the published index jumped into the lead; and from 1932 to 1935, when the comparison ends, the gap continued to widen slowly.[15]

This behavior of the indexes, however, is to be expected in view of the following Soviet statement with respect to the computation of the published index:

A comparison of the data for the number of wage earners and production for large scale industry does not yield a correct statement of changes in labor productivity, because the enterprises satisfying the large scale industry

[15] In E. Varga, *Two Systems,* p. 66, the following series on annual output per wage earner is presented, covering "only those branches of industry which were comprised in the statistics of 1913," but which included 80 percent of all wage earners in large-scale industry in 1934:

YEAR	ANNUAL OUTPUT PER WAGE EARNER
1928	100
1929	111.8
1930	121.0
1931	120.3
1932	116.0
1934	145.6

Varga's figure for 1934 is quite close to the index in Table 2 computed by the use of the "industry section" series.

TABLE 2

A COMPARISON OF STATED AND CALCULATED SOVIET LABOR
PRODUCTIVITY INDEXES, 1928–35

YEAR	OFFICIAL INDEX	COMPUTED INDEX (TSUNKHU "LABOR SECTION" SERIES)	COMPUTED INDEX (TSUNKHU "INDUSTRY SECTION" SERIES)
1928	100	100	100
1929	112.9	115	112
1930	123.9	122	121
1931	133.3	124	124
1932	136.8	127	122
1933	148.7	139	133
1934	164.6	155	149
1935	186.0	168	166

Sources: The underlying gross value of output data are from Naum Jasny, *The Soviet Price System*, p. 172. The "labor section" employment series were secured as follows: 1928–32, *Sotsialisticheskoe stroitel'stvo SSSR*, 1934, pp. 306, 332, the process being to subtract the average of the number of apprentices at the beginning and end of each year from the given total of the average number of wage earners and apprentices for the year; 1933–34, *Trud v SSSR*, 1935, p. 3; 1935, *Trud v SSSR*, 1936, p. 93. The "industry section" employment series are from *Sotsialisticheskoe stroitel'stvo SSSR*, 1936, p. 3.

census conditions were augmented, in recent years, particularly in connection with the process of socializing small scale industry, by a great number of comparatively small enterprises just scarcely fulfilling the census requirements for classification as large scale. Enlarging enterprises results in an increase in their productivity, but their absolute level of productivity, of course, is significantly lower than the average level in large scale industry. Therefore, the inclusion of a great number of small enterprises in large scale industry on the basis of formal census statistical requirements retards the tempo of growth of output per wage earner by comparison with the true dynamics of labor productivity. For this reason, the data on output are limited to enterprises of the industrial commissariats, the industrial composition of which is more narrow and homogeneous.[16]

It is possible that the Soviet statisticians, in thus employing only a segment of industry for the purpose of measuring productivity, were motivated primarily by the desire to make a better showing than

[16] Tsentral'noe Upravlenie Narodno-Khoziaistvennogo Ucheta, *Sotsialisticheskoe stroitel'stvo SSSR*, 1936, p. 704 (hereinafter cited as *Sotsialisticheskoe stroitel'stvo SSSR*).

might otherwise have been the case. On the face of it, however, the statistical device of maintaining a relatively stable population of enterprises for which to measure productivity at a time when census coverage was changing rapidly is not unreasonable. At any rate, the reader can satisfy himself, from Table 2, regarding the excess productivity gain resulting from this practice.

The Soviet index of production, on which the index of labor productivity depends, has been criticized for overstatement of the rise in "real" production.[17] Any inflationary bias would of course have a proportional effect upon the labor productivity index. It can be estimated, on the basis of an American-constructed production index, that Russian labor productivity rose at a rate from 4½ percent to 5½ percent, compounded annually, in the period from 1928 to 1936, compared with a figure of 10.8 percent derived from Table 1.[18] The official Soviet index of labor productivity must thus be regarded with considerable caution.[19]

[17] Alexander Gerschenkron, *A Dollar Index of Soviet Machinery Output, 1927–28 to 1937*, Chap. 1.

[18] The production index is from Donald R. Hodgman, "Industrial Production," in Abram Bergson (ed.), *Soviet Economic Growth*, p. 232. (A somewhat higher rate was erroneously attributed to Mr. Hodgman by the present author on p. 197 of the same publication.) The variation depends on whether one uses a "labor section" labor force series (Tsentral'noe Upravlenie Narodno-Khoziaistvennoga Ucheta, *Zhenshchina v SSSR*, p. 55 [hereinafter referred to as *Zhenshchina v SSSR*]), or an "industry section" labor force series (*Planovoe khoziaistvo*, 1936, No. 8).

[19] See Irving H. Siegel, "Labor Productivity in the Soviet Union," *Journal of the American Statistical Association*, March, 1953, p. 65.

III

PROCEDURE OF THE PRESENT STUDY

THIS study attempts to compare output per wage earner in a selected group of U.S. and Soviet mining and manufacturing industries for a pre-World War II year and to project to 1950 the comparative ratios thus derived on the basis of the productivity data available in each of the countries. Its scope is more limited, therefore, than Rostas's analysis of British-American labor productivity, in which comparative productivity was assessed for the entire national economy of each of the two nations and reconciled with differences in national income per head.[1] Nor does it aspire to the detail achieved in a recent United Nations study of textile labor productivity in five Latin-American Countries.[2]

A compromise solution, avoiding global generalization such as that essayed by Rostas and others[3] on the one hand and the meticulous depth of analysis represented by the United Nations textile study[4] on the other, is largely dictated by the specific problem at hand and by the material available. Global labor productivity comparisons must be made in value terms: gross value, value added, or some combination. Even for intranational studies this presents some exceedingly difficult statistical problems.[5] In the case of international comparisons, there is the additional difficulty of securing a common denominator for the different currencies in which the values are expressed. There are

[1] L. Rostas, *Comparative Productivity in British and American Industry.*

[2] United Nations, Department of Economic Affairs, *Labour Productivity of the Cotton Textile Industry in Five Latin-American Countries.*

[3] For example, A. W. Flux, "Industrial Productivity in Great Britain and the United States," *Quarterly Journal of Economics,* Vol. XLVIII (1933); T. Barna, "Note on the Productivity of Labor," *Bulletin of the Oxford University Institute of Statistics,* Vol. VIII, No. 7 (1946).

[4] See also United Kingdom, Ministry of Production, *Report of the Cotton Textile Mission to the United States.*

[5] For an excellent discussion of some of them, see Irving H. Siegel, *Concepts and Measurement of Production and Productivity,* especially Chap. 4.

various ways of meeting the problem, none completely satisfactory.
A prevailing or official rate of exchange may be employed as a conversion factor on the assumption that it equates the relative purchasing
power of the two currencies in a general way;[6] or the products of one
country may be valued in the prices of another country, either for
broad categories of products[7] or for individual products.[8] The use of
rates of exchange may yield significantly different results, even for
countries whose currencies are widely traded in international markets,
depending on whether the rate chosen is the official rate, a free rate
prevailing at some particular time, or some rate calculated to express
purchasing power parity more accurately.[9] In the case of the Russian
ruble, which was not traded abroad, and the foreign exchange value
of which was tied only very loosely, if at all, to domestic prices,[10] the
choice of an over-all rate for conversion purposes must be even more
problematic.

An obvious means of avoiding the conversion problem in international comparisons, and the one chiefly relied on in this study, is
to carry out the comparisons in terms of physical units. In view of
the manner in which statistics are customarily compiled, this implies
the industry study as the basic unit of investigation. However, the
limitation is that only those industries with fairly simple and homogeneous product structures can be included, thus endangering the
representative character of the work. Rostas's solution was to compute
productivity on the basis of physical product for the industries which
lent themselves to such treatment and then to fill in some of the
important gaps—machinery, chemicals, electronics, rubber tires—by
resort to productivity computed in value terms. I have ventured less

---

[6] Rostas, *op. cit.,* employs the official rate of exchange for his global comparisons,
as well as for some individual industries, e.g., machinery, where he concludes: "Insofar as the rate of exchange in terms of engineering products differs from the general
rate of exchange, this comparison is arbitrary." (p. 108.)

[7] This method is usually employed by Colin Clark in his international comparisons
(see *A Critique of Russian Statistics*).

[8] The best example in the case of US—USSR comparisons is Alexander Gerschenkron,
A Dollar Index of Soviet Machinery Output, 1927–28 to 1937.

[9] See the example cited in International Labor Office, *Methods of Labor Productivity
Statistics,* p. 104.

[10] Marcin R. Wyczalkowski, "The Soviet Price System and the Ruble Exchange
Rate," *International Monetary Fund Staff Papers,* I, No. 2 (1950), 203.

far for the purely pragmatic reason that, with the exception of some machinery groups, I had no dollar-ruble conversion rate that had even the approximate validity of the official sterling-dollar rate employed by Rostas.

The indicated exception covered some important machinery groups —locomotives and railroad cars, tractors, automobiles, agricultural machinery, and construction machinery—specific conversion rates for which were available through Gerschenkron's recent valuation of Soviet machinery output in 1939 dollar prices.[11] This is by no means the precise equivalent of the expression of productivity in physical terms, for the use of U.S. prices carries with it U.S. market and scarcity relationships, which may be quite inappropriate to the Soviet Union. Nevertheless, since no alternative is available, it was felt that the importance of machinery to the entire picture warranted an exception.[12]

The approach to productivity comparisons through detailed engineering studies, while a highly desirable procedure, is of course out of the question for the American student where the Soviet Union is concerned. Several studies of this character made by Russian engineers and economists during the thirties are referred to in subsequent chapters.

It is not to be presumed that the restriction of comparisons to a physical output basis solves all the problems involved in international labor productivity comparisons. There are numerous questions that must be resolved, relating to the quality and structure of output and to the concepts employed in collecting and aggregating labor force statistics. However, these are statistical jungles which are passable if sufficient caution is exercised, which cannot be said of the alternative procedure involved in using global value data.

The precise years for which the productivity comparisons are made

---

[11] Gerschenkron, *op. cit.* Russian statisticians have made similar attempts to establish ruble-dollar rates for purposes of labor productivity comparisons, among others. For a critique of the widely cited rates developed by S. Yugenburg for the Russian machinery industry, see Gerschenkron, *op. cit.,* pp. 59–67, where it is suggested that the method used by Yugenburg may underlie other Soviet international labor productivity comparisons.

[12] In 1938, the gross value of Soviet machinery production constituted 26 percent of total gross value of industrial product. See *Sotsialisticheskoe stroitel'stvo SSSR,* 1939, p. 36.

have in large measure been dictated by the availability of data. Desirable though it might have been to use a postwar year, the paucity of Russian data made this impossible. The year 1939 appeared to be the next best alternative, for the following reasons:

a. It was the last year for which some reasonably accurate Russian employment estimates could be made. However, for most industries it proved necessary to revert to even earlier years for the Russian side of the comparison.

b. The year 1939 was the last prewar year in which the distorting effects of war production were still moderate in both countries. This is less true of Russia than the United States, for there are indications that considerable conversion to military production occurred at an earlier period.[13]

c. The prevailing level of economic activity exercises an important effect upon productivity. While a reduction in economic activity may lead to the employment of only the most efficient resources of labor and capital and thus tend to raise labor productivity, the net effect appears to be in the opposite direction. This is particularly true if productivity is measured in output per man-year, because of the element of short time.[14] It is thus desirable in international productivity comparisons to choose periods reflecting roughly comparable levels of economic activity in the countries compared. Ordinarily, where countries are involved in international trade and are subject to the impact of world market forces, this amounts roughly to choosing a single year. In the case of the Soviet Union, however, there is a further problem. A high degree of industrial activity appears to have been characteristic of its rapid industrialization in the 1930's, though undoubtedly there was some unemployment in terms of the nonemployment of available human and material resources throughout this period.[15]

[13] See Donald R. Hodgman, "Industrial Production," in Abram Bergson (ed.), *Soviet Economic Growth,* p. 238.

[14] Works Progress Administration National Research Project, *Production, Employment and Productivity in 59 Manufacturing Industries,* Part I, p. 65.

[15] For example, the loss in production due to presumably unnecessary seasonal fluctuation in 1937 was stated to be 12.7 percent in agricultural machinery manufacture; 20 percent in cement; 8.6 percent in coal mining; and 9.5 percent in cotton textiles. Idle time in paper production as a percentage of nominal working time was given at 24.1 percent for February, 1939; at 8.01 percent for cotton spinning during the first quarter of 1939; and at 7.71 percent in cotton weaving during the same period. See *Planovoe khoziaistvo,* 1939, No. 5, p. 54.

The Russians published no data on unemployment after 1930, and it is exceedingly difficult to judge fluctuations in the level of Russian economic activity from production data because of the great secular rise in output. The extent to which interstitial underutilization of facilities affected productivity cannot be determined with any degree of accuracy, though fragmentary material would make it appear that at least up to 1937 there were no startling fluctuations in this respect.[16] It seems safe to assume that year to year variations in Soviet industrial capacity utilization were less than those caused by business fluctuations in the United States.

This means that the choice of a particular year for purposes of making labor productivity comparisons constitutes less of a problem for Russia than for the United States, where there were sharp year to year variations during the thirties. As between the two years which suggest themselves for other reasons, i.e., 1937 and 1939, there appears to have been no great difference in U.S. economic activity,[17] so that the latter, more recent, year is given preference. However, the year 1939 was in no sense a year of full employment in the United States. Employment in manufacturing was 10 million in that year, and just two years later had risen to 15 million. The ratio of employment to population has been consistently higher since 1939 than in that year. The 1940 Census put unemployment at 7.5 million persons, slightly more than 14 percent of the labor force, and 1940 was, if anything, a year of fuller employment than 1939. We can only conjecture that the relative level of economic activity was higher in the Soviet Union than in the United States in 1939 (or in the Soviet Union in 1937 than in the United States in 1939), and that therefore the particular years chosen for comparison tend to overstate comparative Russian productivity by virtue of this inequality.

d. While 1939 appeared to be the best compromise, it was not possible to secure Russian employment data for most industries for that year,

[16] See the data on idle time and shift coefficients (the numbers of shifts worked per machine) in E. L. Granovskii and B. L. Markus, *Ekonomika sotsialisticheskoi promyshlennosti,* pp. 410–15.

[17] The gross national product, in constant dollars, was $87.9 billion in 1937 and $91.3 billion in 1939 (compared with $84 billion in 1938). Total wages and salaries paid out amounted to $45.9 billion in 1937 and $45.7 billion in 1939. The number of full-time equivalent employees was 36,187,000 in 1937 and 36,038,000 in 1939. See U.S. Department of Commerce, *National Income and Product of the United States.*

and it was therefore necessary to choose an earlier year, 1938 or 1937, for the Russian side of the comparison. To avoid intercensus definitional problems, it seemed preferable to adhere to 1939 uniformly for the United States. Depending on the particular circumstances of each industry, the resultant comparisons differ from those that would have been obtained if the same year had been used for the two countries in every case. The general trend in productivity in the two countries from 1937 to 1939 (manufacturing in the United States, manufacturing and mining in Russia) was as follows (1937=100):[18]

YEAR	UNITED STATES	SOVIET UNION (OFFICIAL STATISTICS)
1937	100	100
1938	94.4	110.9
1939	108.8	130.0

The conclusions that may be drawn from these figures must be strongly qualified by the probability of inflation in the Soviet data, which are the official Russian productivity series.[19] While Soviet productivity probably increased from 1937 to 1939, the index magnitude of 30 percent seems much too high. Nevertheless, there is a presumption that where a year earlier than 1939 is used to compare Russian productivity with that of the United States in 1939, relative Russian productivity tends to be understated.[20] This cannot be checked for individual industries by virtue of the same lack of data that led to departure from 1939 in the first place.

[18] Sources: For the United States, Rostas, *op. cit.*, p. 48; for the USSR, *supra*, p. 15.
[19] See the discussion *supra*, p. 18.
[20] The magnitude of the understatement depends on the "real" productivity increases in the two countries during the year in question. If, for example, it were established that Soviet output per worker rose by 15 percent from 1937 to 1939, and if the U.S. index were accepted as accurate, then a U.S. 1939–USSR 1937 comparison would tend to understate Soviet productivity by 13 percent compared with a straight 1939 comparison, and by 8 percent compared with a straight 1937 comparison.

IV

SOVIET STATISTICS AND THEIR COMPARABILITY WITH UNITED STATES STATISTICS

RELIABILITY OF SOVIET STATISTICS

ONE of the first questions asked of students of the Soviet economy is likely to be: Are Soviet statistics reliable, and are they adequate for working purposes? With respect to reliability, I should merely like to add my voice to the weight of expert opinion that Soviet statistics, though they may be deficient with respect to the techniques of collection and processing, are not pure fabrications and may be used for analytical purposes provided sufficient care is exercised.[1]

I have relied rather heavily on Russian technical journals published by the various industrial ministries and devoted mainly to articles on engineering and industrial engineering. Designed to assist operating personnel in the field, they contain a considerable amount of productivity information for entire industries, for plants, and for departments within plants. In no case have I found a major discrepancy between statistical material in these journals, in the more general journals devoted to economics and planning (*Planovoe khoziaistvo, Voprosy ekonomiki*), or in the various statistical handbooks published by the State Planning Commission. Apparent differences were usually traceable to the multiplicity of statistical units covered by Soviet data. To construct a fabricated system of statistics attaining such a degree of internal consistency would require herculean labor.

The adequacy of the Russian data is another matter. Up to 1936, a combination of State Planning Commission and industrial ministry (then commissariat) publications provides materials which are quite adequate for the assessment of labor productivity in most indus-

[1] See the articles by Abram Bergson and others, *The Review of Economics and Statistics,* XXIX (November, 1947), 213–46; *ibid.,* XXXIV (February, 1952), 75; the articles by Stuart Rice and others, *The American Statistician,* April-May and June-July, 1953; Abram Bergson, *Soviet National Income and Product in 1937,* pp. 7–9.

tries. In fact, the Russian labor statistics of this early period are in some ways superior to their U.S. contemporaries.[2] After 1936, however, a progressive decline in the volume of productivity data set in, until by 1950 virtually nothing was being published which would permit the independent calculation of labor productivity on an industry basis. Suppression rather than falsification appears to be the policy of the Russian authorities. Fortunately for our purposes, the worst suppression did not occur until after the war.

For the United States, principal reliance has been placed upon the 1939 Census of Manufactures, with the Works Progress Administration's industry productivity studies providing a valuable supplement. Since 1939, the most useful source of information on U.S. productivity trends is the studies of productivity and unit labor requirements undertaken by the Bureau of Labor Statistics. Unfortunately, the studies do not as yet embrace many important manufacturing industries, making some improvision necessary.

THE COMPARABILITY OF INDUSTRY AND PRODUCT CLASSES

Every country has a unique method of classifying industries, establishments, and products determined by industrial structure and custom and by the purposes of industrial censuses. There are therefore apt to be sharp differences with respect to the drawing of industrial boundaries and to the allocation of specific products among industries. The first step in attempting international productivity comparisons is to ensure identical product groupings for the countries being compared, as far as this is possible.[3]

[2] For example, the 1936 edition of the labor handbook, *Trud v SSSR*, contains labor force breakdowns by sex, skill, working time, etc., which were not matched by the U.S. Census of Manufactures, let alone by the employment data of the U.S. Bureau of Labor Statistics.

[3] An eminent British statistician has argued that differences in classification and concept between the American and British manufacturing censuses are so great—and this would presumably apply with at least equal force to American and Soviet censuses—that "they do not afford a reliable means for comparing industrial productivity per head in the two countries. . . . There is a mass of statistics available for both countries which should apparently be capable of providing a means of comparison, but the many points of difference in the fundamental features shown by the two countries create difficulties which cannot at present be properly overcome." E. C. Snow, "The International Comparison of Industrial Output," *Journal of the Royal Statistical Society*, Part I, 1944, p. 24.

A detailed comparison of the principles of classification employed in U.S. and Russian industrial censuses would be a useful undertaking, but it cannot be attempted here. On the whole, the standards employed to delineate the major industrial groups do not seem to differ greatly. The 1939 U.S. Census of Manufactures distributed industries into groups "each embracing those industries that are related, in most cases by the character of the principal materials used, although several of the groups are constituted on the basis of the purpose or use of the chief products."[4] When the U.S. Census industry groups are compared with those used in Russia since 1936[5] (see Table 3), the Russian criteria would seem to approximate the American.

However, there are numerous classification differences on the individual industry level. The 1939 U.S. Census lists about 450 industries, which are in turn subdivided into products, many of which are themselves aggregates. The Russians employ fewer industry classifications, but their product breakdown is exceedingly detailed[6] and by no means identical with the American. The basic classification principles are often at variance; e.g., the Russians classify shoes on the basis of the type of materials used, whereas in the United States the breakdown is by sex and age group of the consumer. Nevertheless, it appears possible by careful scrutiny of the physical products that make up product and industry groups to secure sufficient U.S.–USSR uniformity to make productivity comparison possible. It has been remarked that in the case of one of the most important industries, machinery, the divergences between the two countries are minor.[7] The same would appear to be true of coal and iron ore mining, petroleum extraction, and basic iron and steel production. Complications are

[4] U.S. Department of Commerce, Bureau of the Census, *Census of Manufactures,* 1939, II, Part II, 2 (hereinafter cited as the U.S. *Census of Manufactures*).

[5] Minor modifications in the Russian groups were made sometime between 1946 and 1948. For the 1936 classification, see A. I. Ezhov, *Kurs promyshlennoi statistiki,* pp. 16–17. The current grouping is to be found in *Slovar'-spravochnik,* 1948, pp. 106–7. For the classification system in effect prior to 1936, see A. I. Rotshtein, *Problemy promyshlennoi statistiki v SSSR,* I, 96–104.

[6] The last available detailed classification of Russian industry is that contained in *Gosudarstvennyi plan razvitiia narodnogo khoziaistva SSSR na 1941 god* (hereinafter cited as *1941 Plan*), which lists, for example, 22 different types of cotton cloth and 9 types of cigarettes.

[7] Alexander Gerschenkron, *A Dollar Index of Soviet Machinery Output, 1927–28 to 1937,* p. 13.

TABLE 3

A COMPARISON OF UNITED STATES (1939) AND SOVIET (1948)
MAJOR INDUSTRIAL CENSUS GROUPS

UNITED STATES		SOVIET UNION	
Group No.	*Group Name*	*Group No.*	*Group Name*
1.	Food and kindred products	25.	Foods, beverages, and tobacco products
2.	Tobacco manufactures		
3.	Textile-mill products	21.	Textile products
4.	Apparel	22.	Needle trades
5.	Lumber and timber basic products	7.	Lumber and timber
6.	Furniture and finished lumber products	18.	Wood manufacturing
		19.	Matches
7.	Paper and allied products	20.	Paper (including cellulose)
8.	Printing and publishing	27.	Printing trades
9.	Chemicals and allied products	9.	Chemical products
		24.	Fats, soap, cosmetics
		26.	Salt
10.	Products of petroleum and coal	8.	Manufacture of fuels
11.	Rubber products	17.	Rubber—asbestos products
12.	Leather and leather products	23.	Fur, leather, shoes
13.	Stone, clay, and glass products	10.	Construction materials
		11.	Glass
		12.	Ceramics and pottery
		16.	Abrasives
14.	Iron and steel and their products, except machinery	13.	Ferrous metallurgy
		15b.	Metal products
15.	Nonferrous metals and their products	14.	Nonferrous metallurgy (metal products of nonferrous metals in Group 15b)
16.	Electrical machinery	15a.	Machinery
17.	Machinery (except electrical)		
18.	Automobiles and automobile equipment		
19.	Transportation equipment, except automobiles		
20.	Miscellaneous industries	30.	Miscellaneous industries

Sources: United States: U.S. Department of Commerce, Bureau of the Census, *Census of Manufactures,* 1939, Vol. II, Part II.

Soviet Union: *Slovar'-spravochnik po sotsial'no—ekonomicheskoi statistike,* 1948, pp. 106–7.

The missing industry group numbers for the USSR represent mining and service industries not included in the U.S. *Census of Manufactures.*

greater, but not impossibly so, in consumer goods industries. To cite a few examples: The U.S. equivalent of the Soviet boot and shoe industry was subdivided into two major industries, "Boot and Shoe Cut Stock and Finding," and "Footwear," because of the usual specialization in cut stock and findings in the United States. The converting and finishing of cotton cloth is a separate industry in the United States, whereas this operation is part of a general cotton textile industry in the Soviet Union, the difference in treatment again being due to differences in industrial integration.

One possible difference in Census classification techniques which could not be assessed involves the classification of individual enterprises. In most cases, the 1939 U.S. Census treated each establishment as a unit and assigned it to a particular industry on the basis of its product or group of products of principal value.[8] *Current* Russian practice would appear to be similar. According to recent regulations, multiproduct establishments are assigned as a unit "to that branch of industry, the products of which constitute the predominant output, compared with other products, on a value basis. For example, a brick and tile plant belongs to the brick industry or to the roofing materials industry depending upon which group of products has greater weight in the total value of product of the enterprise."[9] Where single enterprises are engaged in different stages of processing, e.g., the extraction and processing of minerals, they are classified according to the later process stage, unless such production plays a minor role in the total activity of the enterprises. It cannot be determined with any certainty, however, whether this system was followed in the past. In a nonofficial volume published before the war, it is indicated that in the case of a multiproduct establishment, if semifinished by-products or subsidiary processes did not exceed 10 percent of the total value of output of the establishment, or if finished by-products and final subsidiary processes did not exceed 20 percent, the enterprise was assigned as a unit on the basis of its major product or process; but that if these "limits of exclusion" were exceeded, the output of the

[8] U.S. *Census of Manufactures,* II, Part II, 2. Occasionally different lines of activity within a single enterprise were assigned to different industries, but the impression is given that this was not a frequent practice.

[9] *Slovar'-spravochnik,* 1948, p. 104.

enterprise might be allocated to several branches of industry.[10] Whether this was standard practice, and for what period of time it was employed, we are not told.

To anticipate the next section, there is no explicit definition of the manner in which the labor force of Russian multiproduct enterprises is divided with respect to industrial classification. It is likely that the current rules relating to product classification apply as well to the labor force, though this assertion cannot be documented.

Such differences in industrial practice as the system of maintaining plant and equipment also affect the possibility of making accurate productivity comparisons. It has been asserted that "Soviet firms tend to carry out a much larger part of their own repairs and maintenance than American firms."[11] Information relevant to this point has been cited in the following chapters wherever available, but it must be conceded that it has not been possible to make quantitative allowances for the difference. This means that Soviet productivity tends to be understated relative to that of the United States in those industries in which outside repair and maintenance bulks large among American plants.

Qualitative product differences raise problems of a different order. In some instances, qualitative differences can be translated into quantitative terms through the application of prices or some measurable aspect of the physical commodity itself.[12] A good example of the latter would be the expression of different grades of cotton yarn in a common count, or fineness. For the machinery industry, an adjustment of the former type would be implicit in the pricing of Russian goods in American prices and aggregating them. But in many cases quality differences, which usually (though not necessarily) reflect differences in labor input, are not susceptible of expression in a common standard, e.g., cotton cloth, which is produced in a myriad of types and weights. In the latter event, it is possible only to indicate the direction of the

[10] Rotshtein, *op. cit.,* I, 106.

[11] Joseph Berliner, "Comments", in Abram Bergson, (ed.), *Soviet Economic Growth,* p. 219.

[12] This in part obscures the basic physical productivity comparison and is to be avoided wherever possible. Of course, the measurement of productivity in value terms automatically solves the problem of quality differences, provided that there is a sufficient degree of relationship between the prices used and relative labor inputs.

labor productivity effect produced by the quality differences, without specifying any magnitude.

An even more difficult evaluation is involved in comparing product structure internationally. To take shoe manufacturing as an example, the American industry endeavors to satisfy consumer tastes to a much greater degree than does the Russian industry. The result, in the past at least, was the production of a much wider assortment of shoes in material, style, and size, although it does not necessarily follow that the intrinsic wearing qualities of American shoes, pair for pair, were superior to the Russian, particularly since the Russians were not inclined to produce women's light shoes in great quantity. Yet the composition of American shoe output undoubtedly reduced U.S. productivity in comparison with the level that might have been attained had the Russian product structure been adhered to. While this seems to be true of other consumer goods industries, the reverse may be true in capital goods production, where Russians have pointed to the standardization of component parts achieved in U.S. industries, e.g., machinery, as a model.[13]

Considerable savings in labor input per unit of product can be realized from product standardization and simplification. A British productivity team reported: "As a result of our visit to the United States we are convinced that one of the main reasons for the high productivity and low cost which are characteristic of industry there is the ruthless elimination of unnecessary variety and the resultant concentration of manufacturing resources."[14] However, the manner of determining whether one country has gone beyond another in this direction as a general proposition constitutes an as yet unsolved problem,[15] and fruitful results can be achieved only by comparing individual product groups.

There is a special problem in the case of extractive industries, where the character of natural resources may be the predominant productivity factor. Iron ore mining constitutes a good example. Both in the

[13] E. L. Granovskii and B. L. Markus, *Ekonomika sotsialisticheskoi promyshlennosti,* p. 262.

[14] Anglo-American Council on Productivity, *Simplification in Industry,* p. 11. See also Anglo-American Council on Productivity, *Simplification in British Industry.*

[15] See the inconclusive nature of the remarks on this subject in L. Rostas, *Comparative Productivity in British and American Industry,* pp. 62–63.

United States and Russia, labor productivity is much higher in open cut than in underground mining. The relatively larger share of total product mined by the former method in the United States results in much greater U.S. productivity superiority for the industry as a whole than for the open cut and underground sectors taken separately. Differences in the thickness and depth of seams play a more important role in coal mining, where underground work is the rule. While it is sometimes possible to express quantitatively the productivity advantages accruing from superior resources, ordinarily this factor cannot be separated from technological and social conditions.

THE COMPARABILITY OF LABOR FORCE STATISTICS

Productivity comparisons may run in terms of the entire labor force or of a portion of the labor force. It is a convention to restrict the comparisons to wage earners,[16] however, both because it is this portion of the labor force that can be most easily identified with specific products and because statistics covering wage earners have been fuller and more reliable than statistics of the labor force as a whole. Both the U.S. Bureau of Labor Statistics and the Russian Central Statistical Office are currently computing their productivity indexes on the basis of wage earners alone, and this procedure will be generally followed. However, an attempt is made below to evaluate the results that would have been obtained had a broader segment of the labor force been used.

The 1939 U.S. Census of Manufactures defines wage earners as "those who perform manual work, using tools, operating machines, handling materials and products, and caring for the plant and its equipment. Working foremen and 'gang and straw bosses' are treated as wage earners, but foremen whose duties are primarily supervisory are classified as salaried employees."[17] However, these were only wage earners *engaged in manufacturing;* in addition, some wage earners, together with salaried employees, were classified as engaged in "distribution,"

---

[16] The term "wage earner" as employed in this study is the equivalent of the term "production worker" used by the Bureau of Labor Statistics and the postwar Census of Manufactures and of the British term "operative." The International Labor Office employs the term "wage earner" (*Employment, Unemployment and Labor Force Statistics,* Studies and Reports, New Series, No. 7, 1948) and this usage is adhered to because it appears to be the most easily understood of the various similar terms in current use.

[17] U.S. *Census of Manufactures,* 1939, II, Part I, 4.

"construction," and "other," the precise number not being determinable because of failure to distinguish between the two categories. The criteria by which these occupational assignments were made are not entirely clear, but it appears from the definitions that wage earners engaged in the intraplant transport of products and those engaged in repair and maintenance construction would have been classified as manufacturing wage earners, whereas those engaged in out-of-plant deliveries and new construction would have been classified as transportation and construction wage earners.[18]

Each manufacturing establishment covered by the Census was asked to report the number of manufacturing wage earners receiving pay at any time within the normal payroll period ending nearest the fifteenth of each month in the year. The averages for the year were calculated by dividing the sums for the individual months by 12.

Certain establishments were not covered by the Census, the most important for our purposes being the following:

a. Those that manufactured during the year products valued at less than $5,000.

b. Those engaged principally in the performance of work for individual customers, such as repair shops.

c. Those engaged in the so-called neighborhood industries and hand trades in which little or no power machinery is used, such as carpentry, blacksmithing, harnessing, tinsmithing.

Turning to the Soviet statistics, we find that employees of Soviet industry are divided into the following major groups:[19]

a. Wage earners (*rabochie*), defined as persons "immediately participating in the creation of products through physical labor."

b. Trainees or apprentices (*ucheniki*), persons who have "not yet acquired their productive qualifications, but are receiving instruction at the establishment itself and are paid according to reduced wage scales."[20]

---

[18] The 1947 U.S. *Census of Manufactures* defines "force-account construction workers," said to be "comparable to 'construction employees' in the 1939 Census classification," as employees engaged in major additions or alterations, utilized as a separate work force. See Vol. II, p. 13.

[19] The Soviet classification system has changed over time. See Abram Bergson, *The Structure of Soviet Wages*, pp. 213–14. However, these changes do not appear to be significant for our purposes.

[20] *Slovar'-spravochnik*, 1944, p. 209.

c. Engineering and technical personnel (*inzhenerno-tekhnicheskie rabotniki*) performing duties involving "technical leadership," requiring qualified engineers or technicians. This includes specialized factory management and production supervisory personnel down to and including nonworking foremen.

d. Salaried employees (*sluzhashchie*), including the following:

(1) Higher administrative personnel not performing specialized technical functions—chiefs of commercial, finance, supply, sales, personnel, etc., departments, chief accountants, chiefs of statistical bureaus, transport departments, etc.

(2) Other administrative and accounting-control personnel— bookkeepers, statisticians, economists, material checkers, cashiers, controllers, business machine operators, payroll clerks, etc.

(3) Secretarial and retail personnel—secretaries, stenographers, typists, etc.[21]

e. Junior service personnel (*mladshii obsluzhivaiushchii personal*), comprising plant guards, doormen, messengers, office store keepers, cleaners (office), watchmen, wardrobe attendants, firemen (guards and stationary engineers).[22]

The principal differences between the wage earner classification in the United States and the Soviet Union are as follows:

a. Trainees and apprentices are included among wage earners in the United States, to the extent that they are drawing pay from manufacturing enterprises. Full-time industrial vocational students are not included among wage earners, except insofar as they may be employed outside of school hours. The ratio of full-time industrial vocational students in state-run schools to the total number of employed wage earners plus full-time vocational students may be estimated at around 2 percent in 1940.[23] Traditionally, most industrial training in the United States takes place on the job, with an increasing recent admixture of the part-time vocational school.[24]

[21] Rotshtein, *op. cit.*, p. 240.

[22] *Slovar'-spravochnik*, 1944, p. 209.

[23] There were 207,000 full-time students in state-run vocational schools in 1940, compared with 8,922,000 craftsmen, operatives, and laborers employed in manufacturing and mining in the same year. See *Statistical Abstract of the United States*, 1947, pp. 140, 178. The additional number of full-time trainees in privately run schools was probably small.

[24] In 1940 there were 168,000 evening school and 384,000 part-time industrial

In Soviet manpower statistics, trainees and apprentices are segregated into a separate category, whether they are receiving their training on the job or in vocational schools.[25] One gets the impression that, prior to the institution of the State Labor Reserve System in 1940, virtually all new entrants to the labor force received their training in vestibule schools attached to factories or directly on the job; full-time vocational schools are not mentioned as part of the scheme of vocational training.[26] On January 1, 1936, trainees constituted 4.1 percent of the total of wage earners, trainees, and junior service personnel in Soviet industry.[27]

It is apparent that to put the U.S. and USSR wage earner category on a comparable basis, trainees should be added to the Soviet wage earner figure. To the extent that there were in the Soviet Union industrial trainees who were receiving full-time schooling and contributing nothing to factory output (but who were included with productive trainees), corresponding to full-time vocational trainees in the United States, there is a relative overstatement of the Russian labor force. However, in view of the small percentage of nonproductive U.S. trainees indicated for 1940 and the apparent Russian practice of securing at least some production from every wage earner from the very beginning of his training, the error involved would appear to be small. Probably of greater significance is the comparative productivity of trainees in the two countries, which may well have differed substantially, thus making it desirable to exclude trainees entirely from the productivity comparisons. Since the U.S. labor statistics do not lend themselves to this treatment, there is no alternative to the procedure of including them for both countries.

---

vocational students in state-run schools. See *Statistical Abstract of the United States,* 1947, p. 140. These students occupy a working status comparable to that of students in the Russian State Labor Reserves, i.e., they are part of the productive labor force as well as being in training.

[25] Since 1940, a portion of the new entrants to the labor force are being trained through the State Labor Reserves. Students of the State Labor Reserves are not included in the payroll lists of enterprises. See D. Savinskii, *Kurs promyshlennoi statistiki,* p. 149. This does not necessarily mean, however, that they are excluded from aggregate employment data, for they may be added en bloc.

[26] The factory vestibule schools, after 1933, devoted 80 percent of the time to practical job training and 20 percent to theoretical education. See E. N. Medinskii, *Narodnoe obrazovanie v SSSR,* p. 145. These schools became part of the State Labor Reserve System after 1940.

[27] *Sotsialisticheskoe stroitel'stvo SSSR,* 1936, p. 518.

b. It appears that the great majority of those employees listed in Soviet statistics as "junior service personnel" were included among wage earners in the U.S. Census. The major criterion for admission to the U.S. wage earner group was the performance of manual labor, which would seem to embrace most of the occupations listed above under Soviet "junior service personnel."[28] However, some "junior service personnel" may for certain industries in the United States have been classified with salaried employees; the example has been cited of timekeepers and messenger boys having been treated in this manner.[29]

The Russian "junior service personnel" category was a fairly large one, comprising for all industry 5.5 percent of the total number of wage earners and "junior service personnel" combined on January 1, 1936.[30] Manifestly, simply to ignore it in the labor productivity comparison would result in significant understatement of the numbers of Russian wage earners (as the term is defined in the United States) and would consequently tend to overstate comparative Russian productivity. On the other hand, for neither country do we have a breakdown of the relevant classifications which would allow uniform handling of the doubtful occupations. Examination of the 1940 U.S. Census of Population, which is not directly comparable with the Census of Manufactures but does provide an occupational analysis of the labor force, indicates that only 6.6 percent of the *identifiable* Russian "junior service personnel" would have been classified as clerical workers for the purposes of the Census of Population.[31] While this does not provide us with a certain guide, both because classification of employees into clerical and

---

[28] The 1947 U.S. *Census of Manufactures* is more explicit in its definition of wage earners as "working foremen and all non-supervisory employees (including leadmen and trainees) engaged in fabricating, handling, packing, warehousing, shipping, maintenance, repair, janitorial and watchmen services, product development, auxiliary products for the plants' own use (e.g., power plant), record keeping. . . ."

[29] Solomon Fabricant, *Employment in Manufacturing, 1899–1939*, p. 180.

[30] *Sotsialisticheskoe stroitel'stvo SSSR*, 1936, p. 518.

[31] The identifiable groups are:

Messengers, errand and office boys and girls	54,360
Guards, watchmen, doorkeepers	195,957
Charwomen, janitors, porters	575,624
Total	825,941

Statistical Abstract of the United States, 1947, pp. 179–87. Only the first group was carried under clerical employees in the 1940 Census.

nonclerical categories was not uniform in the 1939 and 1940 Censuses and because it does not provide an exhaustive catalogue of Soviet "junior service personnel,"[32] it does strengthen the conviction gained from perusal of the various occupations under consideration that, as was stated at the outset, the great majority of "junior service personnel" would have been classified as wage earners by the 1939 U.S. Census of Manufactures, the error being on the order of certainly less than 20 percent of the "junior service personnel" group (to allow a wide margin) and therefore less than 1 percent of the number of wage earners. To place the labor forces of the two countries on a comparable basis, therefore, "junior service personnel" are added to wage earners to secure the denominator of the Soviet productivity ratio.

c. According to Russian practice, workers engaged in current repair and maintenance are usually included among manufacturing wage earners, whereas those engaged in capital construction and repair are excluded.[33] Generally speaking, construction work performed on contract with outside agencies would not be included in manufacturing, while work performed on the payroll account of the manufacturing enterprise itself might be included or excluded, depending on the nature of the job.[34] The 1939 U.S. Census of Manufactures segregated from wage earners all employees, wage earners and non-wage earners alike, who were engaged in "major construction and major repair work" in the plant.[35] While there is no means of judging precisely where the line was drawn in practice in both countries, the criteria, at least, are sufficiently alike to justify confidence in the conclusion that no adjustment need be made for this group. Therefore, the category "construction employee" which appears in the U.S. Census as a separate item will not be added to wage earners, on the assumption that the employees performing similar work in the Soviet Union are treated as construction rather than manufacturing wage earners.

d. The U.S. Census carries a separate entry for employees engaged in distribution—selling, advertising, sales promotion, credit, billing, install-

[32] For example, wardrobe attendants, factory elevator operators, office storekeepers.
[33] Ezhov, op. cit., p. 52; I. L. Kukulevitch and M. A. Rubin, Planirovanie i analiz trudovikh pokazatelei, pp. 8–12.
[34] Rotshtein, op. cit., II, 243.
[35] Fabricant, op. cit., p. 227.

ing or servicing goods sold, and other distribution activities. Few employees engaged in these occupations in the Soviet Union would be classified there as wage earners, and therefore the U.S. distribution group is also omitted from the productivity comparison.

e. As far as it is possible to judge, there is no major discrepancy between the wage earner concept in the two countries with respect to other occupational groups. United States employees engaged in outside transportation are separated from manufacturing wage earners. In Russia, "transport workers segregated in units with independent functions" are not included in the financial plan of the enterprise,[36] which means that they are not included among manufacturing wage earners.[37] This does not rule out the possibility, however, that some Russian teamsters may be included among manufacturing wage earners, depending on their organizational status. The various (particularly numerous in Russia) service employees manning restaurants, medical clinics, libraries, housing facilities, etc., attached to factories are not classified with manufacturing wage earners in either country.[38]

TYPES OF SOVIET LABOR STATISTICS

There are three major types of Soviet labor statistics: (a) those that appear in the annual labor statistical handbooks and in the labor section of general statistical handbooks; (b) those contained in the industry output section of general statistical handbooks; and (c) those compiled quarterly by the trade unions.

The third category, the trade-union statistics, differs markedly from the first two by virtue of classification based on trade-union jurisdiction in contrast to the functional lines drawn in industrial statistics. Trade-union jurisdiction has tended to conform to that of the corresponding commissariat (ministry).[39] There are important differences between the scope of a "commissariat" and an "industry" in Russian statistics, making direct comparison between the trade-union and the industrial statistics impossible.

The chief differences between the two first-named series, which will

[36] Rotshtein, op. cit., II, 243.
[37] Savinskii, op. cit., p. 147.
[38] Rotshtein, op. cit., II, 243.
[39] Isaac Deutscher, Soviet Trade Unions, p. 121.

be termed "labor section" and "industry section" labor force statistics, are as follows:

a. Members of industrial cooperatives appear in the industry section data but not in those of the labor section.[40] The resultant difference is greater for light industry, where the small workshop tradition persists, than for heavy industry, where cooperatives played an unimportant role.

b. The industry section statistics included, in addition to employees working directly in the industrial enterprises covered by the census of production, employees performing work of an industrial character in the employ of agricultural, construction, and transportation enterprises. For example, the industry section statistics (but not the labor section statistics) included as manufacturing employees persons engaged in machinery repair on state farms, tractor stations, and railroads.[41]

c. The labor section data, at least up to 1936, the last year for which they are available, were limited in their coverage to enterprises meeting the minimum census requirements of sixteen wage earners, if mechanical power were available, or of thirty wage earners, if there were no mechanical power. The industry section data included enterprises failing to meet these minimum requirements in certain specified industries.[42]

d. The industries included in the industrial total are not identical for the two series.

For most of the industries with which this study is concerned, the magnitude of the difference between the two types of labor force statistics is not significant. In the case of light industry, where cooperatives were an important element, the labor section data must be corrected, since the output of cooperatives was usually merged with that of state-owned industry in production statistics. As for the distinction noted in point b, above, the labor section statistics seem to be closer conceptually to the U.S. Census of Manufactures than do the industry section statistics. Both for this reason and the additional compelling one that they are available in more detailed form, the labor section statistics will be used in the following productivity comparisons, adjusted for the deficiencies noted above wherever appropriate.

[40] *Sotsialisticheskoe stroitel'stvo SSSR*, 1936, p. 708.
[41] *Ibid.*
[42] *Ibid.*, p. 703.

THE SCOPE OF THE CENSUS DATA

Russian production and labor statistics are broken down as between so-called large- and small-scale industry. Only the large-scale industry statistics contain sufficient detail by industry to permit of labor productivity determination. While the definitional scope of small-scale industry has varied in some details over the years, its general significance may be indicated by the fact that in 1933 it employed 11 percent of the total number of industrial wage earners,[43] and that in 1946 its production "did not exceed 10 percent" of total industrial output.[44] The exclusion of small-scale industry has the effect of raising the average level of productivity, since output per wage earner was significantly less in small-than in large-scale industry.[45]

The criteria for excluding small enterprises from the 1939 U.S. Census of Manufactures have already been enumerated.[46] Much of the Russian small-scale industry would not have met the U.S. Census requirements. For example, in 1933 the average gross value of product of that portion of small-scale industry subject administratively to agricultural enterprises and employing 55 percent of the total number of wage earners in all small-scale industry was only slightly more than 10,000 rubles per establishment, and there were only two wage earners per establishment. For all small-scale industry in the same year, annual gross value of product per establishment was only 13,000 rubles, and average employment was three wage earners. Without assigning any precise dollar-ruble conversion rate, it would appear that the $5,000 U.S. Census minimum output requirement for inclusion in the Census would have excluded the majority of Russian small-scale enterprises. Whether the portion of industry not covered by the U.S. Census is equal to that in the Russian small-scale sector is, of course, impossible of determination, but it seems clear that exclusion of Russian small-scale industry results in a closer approximation to the U.S. Census concept than would its inclusion.

[43] *Sotsialisticheskoe stroitel'stvo,* 1935, pp. 30–31.

[44] Ezhov, *op. cit.,* p. 19.

[45] Average annual output per wage earner was 6,000 rubles (1926/27 prices) for large-scale and 4,400 for small-scale industry in 1933. See *Sotsialisticheskoe stroitel'stvo,* 1935, pp. 30–31.

[46] See *supra,* p. 33.

EFFECT UPON COMPARABILITY OF THE METHODS
OF COMPILING LABOR STATISTICS

Russian labor statistics are compiled for all so-called listed personnel, i.e., "all categories of permanent, seasonal, and temporary employees for whom . . . the enterprise must keep labor books."[47] The labor books were introduced in 1938, and there are detailed regulations governing the obligation of establishments to maintain these books for employed individuals.[48] Though some specific changes were made,[49] it appears that much the same criteria were employed in the inclusion or exclusion of wage earners from the payroll count prior to 1938. Generally speaking, the payroll list is quite broad, excluding only such classes of personnel as workers on temporary assignment to other factories, university students receiving some factory training, and workers employed for periods of less than five days to perform tasks other than those basic to the work of the enterprise.

From daily payroll lists, which include persons absent from work as well as those present, monthly averages are obtained by dividing the sum of the daily totals (including Sundays and holidays, which are assigned the same number of personnel as the working day immediately preceding) by the number of calendar days in the month. Quarterly and annual payroll averages are secured by taking simple averages of the monthly averages. In the event that an enterprise works only part of a year due to seasonality, or for some other reason, "the sum of the average monthly averages for the period of work is divided by the number of calendar months, i.e., by 12, and not by the number of months worked,"[50] to secure the annual average. Thus, what is secured is not the average payroll labor force during the period actually worked, but the labor force reduced to a full year equivalent.[51]

[47] *Slovar'-spravochnik,* 1948, p. 387.

[48] *Ibid.,* and see *Slovar'-spravochnik,* 1944, pp. 208–9.

[49] For example, home workers were excluded prior to 1938 but included thereafter. See Rotshtein, *op. cit.,* II, 243.

[50] Ezhov, *op. cit.,* p. 52.

[51] A simple example may clarify this point. Assume that an enterprise employs 1,000 wage earners per month, on the average, but operates for only six months of the year. During the period of its operation, its average payroll employment is 1,000, but Soviet labor statistics would show average annual employment as $1000 \times 6/12 = 500$.

The 1939 U.S. Census of Manufactures required each reporting establishment to submit the number of wage earners receiving pay at any time within the normal payroll period ending nearest the fifteenth of each month (ordinarily a week), the annual employment average being secured by dividing the sum of the monthly averages by 12. Consequently, though a wage earner who had been absent, say, for one day a week would be treated in the same manner in both countries, a wage earner who had been absent for the entire census week and received no pay would be excluded from the U.S. labor force and included in the Russian. On the other hand, a wage earner employed for only a single day during a payroll week might be counted as working a full month in the United States, whereas in Russia, if his employment terminated and he ceased to be a "listed" wage earner, he would be counted for only the days actually worked.

To secure complete comparability, it would be necessary to convert both sets of data into what has been termed the equivalent full-time number of workers, i.e., "the numbers of persons that would have been on the payroll if the work actually done had been performed by workers who all enjoyed full and continuous employment."[52] While this cannot be done precisely, it is possible to make some approximations of the magnitude of error introduced by the different methods of aggregating employment in the two countries.

Table 4 compares, for the Soviet Union, the actual average number of days worked per wage earner[53] with the total number of scheduled working days, excluding holidays and vacation, for 1935 (for some industries, 1934). The ratio of actual to potential working time provides an index of the extent to which the inclusion of absentees in the payroll count overstates active employment. For the industries shown, the ratio of actual to potential working time ranged from 86 to 90 percent, except for beet sugar, which for statistical reasons is a special case.[54]

[52] Fabricant, op. cit., p. 175.

[53] This figure includes, in addition to actual full days worked, (a) part-time days due to production stoppages and (b) days worked by wage earners who were transferred to other than their basic work, for whatever cause. See Slovar'-spravochnik, 1944, p. 216.

[54] Employment in beet sugar manufacturing is highly seasonal. "Actual days worked per wage earner" is apparently calculated by dividing total man-days worked by the listed number of wage earners, and since the latter figure has been reduced to a full-

TABLE 4

ACTUAL AND POTENTIAL WORKING TIME IN SOVIET INDUSTRY, 1935

INDUSTRY	ACTUAL NUMBER OF DAYS WORKED PER ANNUM PER WAGE EARNER	POTENTIAL WORKING DAYS, EXCLUDING HOLIDAYS AND VACATIONS	RATIO OF ACTUAL TO POTENTIAL WORKING DAYS (PERCENT)
Coal mining (1934)	264.24	295.3	89.5
Oil extraction	257.16	286.9	89.6
Iron ore mining	259.06	289.3	89.5
Iron and steel	251.30	287.2	87.5
Machinery and metalworking	266.14	300.2	88.7
Cotton textiles	258.44	300.2	86.1
Shoes (1934)	264.41	301.7	87.6
Beet sugar refining[a]	294.04	300 (assumed)	98[a]

Source: *Trud v SSSR,* 1936, p. 78; *ibid.,* 1935, pp. 142–43.

[a] For comment on this industry, see text, p. 42, *n* 54.

A somewhat similar comparison is made for the United States in Table 5. Here, total man-hours worked during the year are compared, by industry, with full man-year equivalents estimated by assuming a standard working year of 2,000 hours (40 hours a week, 50 weeks).[55] The 2,000-hour full employment year is of course an arbitrary one, and in those cases where scheduled working hours of an industry were in excess of the assumed 40-hour standard, and a high level of employment was maintained throughout the year, the ratio of actual to potential hours exceeded 100 percent.

When the U.S. data for 1939 and the Soviet data for 1935 are compared, there seems to be no significant difference in the deviation of

time-equivalent basis, the resultant figure represents the number of days of work that would have been required if the establishment had had no seasonal stoppages and was staffed by a sufficient number of full-time wage earners to yield, on a full-time basis, the same total of man-days of work per annum as the number worked by a larger staff employed for a smaller number of days. For example, 1,000 men working 150 days would provide the same labor input as 500 men working 300 days. The calculation of "actual number of days worked per wage earner" was apparently made, for beet sugar, by dividing 150,000 man-days by 500 men, yielding 300 days.

[55] The data of the Bureau of Labor Statistics on weekly hours worked were calculated by dividing total weekly man-hours worked by the reported number of wage earners and thus differ from the data for scheduled hours because of absenteeism, turnover, part-time work, and stoppages.

TABLE 5

ACTUAL AND POTENTIAL MAN-HOURS WORKED IN SELECTED
UNITED STATES INDUSTRIES, 1939 AND 1947

INDUSTRY	1939			1947		
	ACTUAL MAN-HOURS WORKED (THOU-SANDS)	FULL-TIME POTEN-TIAL EMPLOY-MENT MAN-HOURS[a] (THOU-SANDS)	RATIO OF ACTUAL TO POTEN-TIAL (PER-CENT)	ACTUAL MAN-HOURS WORKED (THOU-SANDS)	FULL-TIME POTEN-TIAL EMPLOY-MENT MAN-HOURS[a] (THOU-SANDS)	RATIO OF ACTUAL TO POTEN-TIAL (PER-CENT)
Coal mining	669,096[c]	967,134	69	949,540[b,c]	980,712[b]	97[b]
Oil extraction	206,712[c]	231,026	89	n.a.[d]	n.a.	n.a.
Iron ore mining	38,187[c]	40,274	95	69,509[c]	60,750	114
Iron and steel	709,414	776,882	91	937,690	941,570	100
Railroad loco-motives and cars	59,745	61,986	96	151,861	151,418	100
Tractors	63,176	62,550	101	125,699	125,852	100
Agricultural machinery	44,650	55,612	80	158,781	153,406	104
Automobiles	695,808	797,926	87	1,102,482	1,117,386	99
Cotton textiles	752,018	818,634	92	937,084	938,484	100
Shoes	399,312	473,746	84	438,902	460,680	95

Sources: U.S. Department of Commerce, Bureau of the Census, *Census of Manufactures,* 1939 and 1947; U.S. Department of Commerce, *Minerals Yearbook,* 1949. For 1939, the data on actual man-hours worked for coal, oil, and iron ore were available directly, as were the data for all industries in 1947. For the remainder of the industries in 1939, hours worked per annum were estimated by dividing Census annual payroll data by Bureau of Labor Statistics figures on average hourly earnings.

[a] Estimated by multiplying actual employment by an assumed standard of 2,000 hours per annum.

[b] Bituminous coal only.

[c] Because of the manner in which average man-day and man-hour totals are computed, these figures are probably overstated. See Harold Barger and Sam H. Schurr, *The Mining Industries, 1899–1939; A Study of Output, Employment and Productivity,* p. 274, and the several industry studies, *infra.*

[d] n.a. = information not available.

actual from potential time worked, except for coal mining, which is explained by endemic short time in that industry in the United States. To take shoe manufacturing as an example, if labor input were measured in terms of man-days of actual work rather than census employ-ment, calculated either in the U.S. or the Soviet manner, the U.S. figure would be 84 percent and the Soviet figure 87.6 percent of reported employment.[56] Though the calculation is a rough one, we may con-clude with some confidence that the inflation in actual labor inputs resulting from the manner in which censuses of employment were taken in both the United States and the Soviet Union[57] does not differ between the two countries to such an extent as to affect significantly the labor productivity comparisons.[58]

The 1947 data for the United States have been included to show the effects of cyclical changes in employment upon the divergence between the ratio of actual to potential time worked. The U.S. Census employ-ment data for 1947 reflect with remarkable accuracy full-time labor inputs. In labor productivity comparisons over time, changes in the ratio can result in sharp differences between changes in output per man-year and per man-hour.

THE PROPORTION OF WAGE EARNERS IN THE LABOR FORCE

The measurement of labor productivity in terms of wage earners alone is not inherently superior to a measurement which takes all em-ployees into account. The customary restriction of the productivity ratio to wage earners has its rationale in the limitations imposed by available statistics and in the concept of "productive" labor as being closer to and more identifiable with a specific quantity of output. When com-paring two economies which are institutionally so different as those of the United States and the Soviet Union, there is an added reason for adhering to the customary procedure. The technological requirements characterizing a particular type of producing enterprise are likely to be

[56] This assumes what seems to be true from the above description of Soviet census methods, that potential working time reflects the actual number of days of work counted for each "listed" wage earner. The method of making the U.S. estimate of potential working time automatically allows for nonpaid absenteeism, and the only distorting factor would be for time paid for but not worked, such as vacations.

[57] We have no figures by industry on actual versus potential working time in Soviet industry after 1935. However, unexcused absenteeism, which was 0.67 days in 1934, varied only to 1.05 days in 1937. Idleness of labor and equipment due to faulty organ-ization does not appear to have been much reduced from 1935 to 1937. See Granovskii and Markus, *op. cit.*, pp. 410, 465.

[58] Coal mining does constitute an important exception, and it will be necessary to correct for the short time factor in this case.

much more rigid, and therefore more uniform, with respect to wage earners than other groups of employees. Regardless of how a steel mill is managed, there must be a certain minimum number of operatives, based on the type of equipment employed. This relationship becomes less stable as we move to indirect labor (repair work, for example, can be performed by outside contractors) and then further to the clerical, sales, and managerial labor force. There appears to be more pooling of the latter types of functions among Soviet enterprises attached to government ministries[59] than is true in the United States, where each firm must maintain a complete staff of its own. Where large sales staffs are maintained by American corporations, with only rudimentary counterparts in Soviet establishments, a labor productivity comparison inclusive of sales personnel might prove misleading.

Nevertheless, it is of interest to consider the impact upon productivity of differences in the ratio of wage earners to total labor force. Such differences must be taken into account when labor productivity is to be reconciled with national income differences, as well as for purposes of forecasting future labor requirements.

Table 6 compares, for manufacturing as a whole and for selected industries, the ratio of wage earners to total employment in the United States and the Soviet Union. It appears that while on the average the ratio is slightly higher in the United States, this relationship is not consistent for all industries. Soviet studies calling attention to the relative top-heaviness of Soviet staffs refer not to this ratio but rather to the ratio of direct to indirect labor *within* the wage earner group. A high ratio of wage earners to total labor force is by no means an invariable index of economic efficiency; in fact, industrialization may bring with it a reduction in this ratio.[60] The conclusion to be drawn from Table 6 is that, on the average, labor productivity measured for all employees would not diverge significantly from the results obtained by using wage earners alone, though for individual industries there would be significant differences, sometimes in favor of the United States, sometimes in favor of the Soviet Union.

[59] See Gregory Bienstock, Solomon M. Schwarz, and Aaron Yugow, *Management in Russian Industry and Agriculture,* especially Chaps. 1 and 5.

[60] E. H. Phelps Brown and P. E. Hart, "The Share of Wages in National Income," *The Economic Journal,* June, 1952, p. 253. It may be noted that the Russian *1941 Plan* called for a comparable ratio of 85.8 percent in that year for all industry.

RATIO OF WAGE EARNERS TO TOTAL LABOR FORCE, UNITED
STATES AND SOVIET UNION, FOR SELECTED INDUSTRIES
(*In percentage*)

INDUSTRY	UNITED STATES (1939)[a]	SOVIET UNION (JANUARY 1, 1936)[b]
All manufacturing	88.3	87.0[c]
Coal mining	94.5[d]	92.2
Iron mining	90.0[d]	88.6
Petroleum extraction	78.8	82.1
Iron and steel	91.4	90.6
Automobiles	89.6	83.5
Agricultural machinery	83.3	87.2
Tractors	83.3	83.9
Construction machinery	80.6	84.3
Locomotives	81.3	{ 85.8
Railroad cars	86.1	
Cotton textiles	96.3	92.6
Footwear	93.7	88.4
Beet sugar manufacture	87.6	90.1

Sources: United States: U.S. Department of Commerce, Bureau of the Census, *Census of Manufactures*, 1939, *passim*.
Soviet Union: *Trud v SSSR*, 1936, pp. 64–67.

[a] Figures represent the ratio of manufacturing wage earners to the total of manufacturing wage earners, salaried officers of corporations, and salaried employees. "Construction," "Distribution," and "other" employees were excluded because the Census fails to distinguish between wage earners and other categories for these groups.

[b] "Wage earners" includes wage earners, trainees, and junior service personnel.

[c] This figure is reduced to 86.7 if power stations and mining are eliminated to make it more comparable with U.S. "manufacturing."

[d] Includes proprietors performing manual labor.

Table 7 relates to another facet of labor force distribution, the division of the non-wage-earner labor force into managerial and clerical employees.[61] For all manufacturing, there was only a small difference in this respect, for the dates shown, between the United States and Russia. For individual industries, there were striking differences. Why such variation should be displayed, not only between the two countries, but among industries within the same country, is not immediately

[61] The available data are not sufficiently detailed to ensure that an identical line of division is employed in each country. However, there is no reason to believe that the dividing line is inconsistent among industries within each country.

Table 7

COMPOSITION OF NON-WAGE-EARNER GROUPS IN THE LABOR FORCE OF UNITED STATES AND SOVIET INDUSTRY

(*In percentage*)

INDUSTRY	UNITED STATES (1939)[a] Salaried officers and managerial employees	Clerical employees	SOVIET UNION (JANUARY 1, 1936)[a] Salaried officers and managerial employees	Clerical employees
All manufacturing	50.3	49.7	52.1[b,c]	47.9[c]
Coal mining	n.a.[d]	n.a.	63.9	36.1
Iron mining	n.a.	n.a.	50.9	49.1
Petroleum extraction	n.a.	n.a.	63.5	36.5
Iron and steel	43.1	56.9	58.6	41.4
Automobiles	48.8	51.2	59.8	40.2
Agricultural machinery	45.9	54.1	60.7	39.3
Tractors	45.4	54.6	60.0	40.0
Construction machinery	46.5	53.5	60.0	40.0
Locomotives	28.5	71.5	66.0	34.0
Railroad cars	48.3	51.7		
Cotton textiles	56.1	43.9	35.6	64.4
Footwear	51.3	48.7	48.4	51.6
Beet sugar manufacturing	44.5	55.5	53.7	46.3

Sources: United States: U.S. Department of Commerce, Bureau of the Census, *Census of Manufactures*, 1939, *passim*.

Soviet Union: *Trud v SSSR*, 1936, pp. 64–67.

[a] The U.S. Census breaks down non-wage-earner groups into (*a*) corporation officers; (*b*) managers, superintendents, and other supervisory employees, and responsible professional and technical employees; and (*c*) clerks, stenographers, and other clerical employees. The first two categories correspond to Soviet "engineering and technical personnel," except that the latter does not include chiefs of financial, supply, and sales departments, whereas the former does. The U.S. category (*c*) corresponds to Russian "salaried employees" (*sluzhashchie*). This correspondence must be regarded as a rough one at best, for individual occupational groups, e.g., accountants, may be handled differently in the two countries.

[b] This figure is 51.8 if power stations and mining are eliminated.

[c] The *1941 Plan* figures are: Salaried officers and managerial employees, 60.0; clerical employees, 40.0 (p. 512).

[d] n.a. = information not available.

apparent. If productivity comparisons relating to the entire labor force were undertaken, it would be a factor requiring careful examination.

STRUCTURE OF THE LABOR FORCE

A fundamental rationale of the labor productivity ratio as an index of change in the effectiveness of resource employment is the concept of the individual wage earner or the labor-hour as a homogeneous unit. The idea has of course only a very general validity, since there are many specific factors which produce a differentiation in the productivity of the individual or the working hour. Such differences are institutional, to a large extent, and are therefore apt to be particularly great in international comparisons. Here we consider three of the major factors influencing the inherent productivity of the average laborer in the United States and the Soviet Union: sex, age, and skill differences in the labor force.

Sex distribution. The Soviet industrial labor force is characterized by a relatively high proportion of female workers. On July 1, 1938, women constituted 42 percent of the industrial labor force;[62] in 1940, they were said to comprise "about 40%" of the labor force in industry, transport, and construction.[63] As a consequence of the war, this ratio increased sharply and at the beginning of 1949 was still about 50 percent.[64] By comparison, women constituted 24.7 percent of the U.S. manufacturing labor force in 1940 and 27.3 percent in 1950.[65]

Even more striking differences are revealed in the figures for some of the separate industries shown in Table 8. Many heavy industries which in the United States have virtually no female employment, such as coal mining, have substantial contingents of women workers in the Soviet Union.[66] In the trades traditionally employing females, such as textile

---

[62] *Planovoe khoziaistvo,* 1939, No. 10, p. 134. The proportion had grown steadily from 29 percent in 1928.

[63] N. Popova, *Zhenshchiny strany sotsializma,* p. 40. N. Voznesenskii, *Voennaia ekonomika SSSR,* gives the figure of 41 percent for the female ratio in industry (*promyshlennost'*) in 1940.

[64] *Professional'nye soiuzy,* March, 1949, No. 3, p. 9.

[65] The Conference Board, *The Economic Almanac 1951–52,* p. 267.

[66] This fact is always remarked by visitors to the Soviet Union. A British aircraft worker stated apropos of the large numbers of women he observed on the assembly line of the Stalin Auto Works in Moscow: "I was personally disturbed to see so many women taking part in these tasks, but apparently it was quite a normal matter

TABLE 8

WOMEN AS A PERCENTAGE OF ALL EMPLOYEES IN SELECTED
UNITED STATES AND SOVIET INDUSTRIES

INDUSTRY	UNITED STATES, 1940	SOVIET UNION, JULY 1, 1938
Coal mining	0.6	24.5
Metal mining	0.9	21.9
Crude petroleum production	2.8	8.4[a]
Iron and steel	7.4	23.9
Machinery	11.4	29.7
Cotton manufacturing	37.8	67.4
Shoe manufacturing	43.0	57.4
Food products	18.2	47.2

Sources: United States: *Statistical Abstract of the United States,* 1947, pp. 191–92.
Soviet Union: *Planovoe khoziaistvo,* 1939, No. 10, p. 114.
[a] As of July 1, 1936. From *Zhenshchina v SSSR,* p. 62.

manufacturing, the proportion of women working in the Soviet Union far exceeds that in the United States.

It is generally assumed that the annual productivity of a female worker is less than that of a male worker, but precise measurements are lacking. Rostas[67] assumed that 60 percent expressed the ratio of female to male productivity, based on the relationship in earnings, whereas Barna[68] similarly derived a ratio of 66 percent. However, relative wages can hardly be regarded as an index of relative productivity,[69] and these ratios must be considered as being quite arbitrary. In the absence of reliable relative productivity measurements, by industry, it is best to refrain from weighting the labor force quantitatively for this factor and simply to assert that the expression of the Soviet and U.S. labor forces in male worker equivalents would result in a relative labor force reduction for the Soviet Union and thus cause a relative increase in its comparative productivity.

here." Official Report of the Elected Delegation of Trade Unionists to the USSR, *Russia—The Truth,* p. 29. A group of British miners stated: "We were surprised to find women working on switches, tub runs, and screens." *Ibid.,* p. 32.

[67] Rostas, *op. cit.,* p. 32.

[68] T. Barna, "Note on the Productivity of Labor," *Bulletin of the Oxford University Institute of Statistics,* Vol. VIII, No. 7 (1946), p. 205.

[69] See John T. Dunlop, "Productivity and the Wage Structure," in Lloyd Metzler and others, *Income, Employment and Public Policy,* p. 351.

Age structure. The age distribution of the prime working age populations of the United States and the Soviet Union, as of 1939–40, is shown in Table 9. Apparently the Russian labor force was at that date pronouncedly younger than that of the United States, particularly among the males. It is arguable whether a younger labor force is more productive than an older one; at any rate, there are no standards by which to weight the various age groups.[70] Nothing conclusive can be said about the effect upon relative productivity of reducing the U.S. and Soviet labor forces to standard age equivalents.

Skill. At the beginning of the planning period, the Russian economy was at an enormous disadvantage compared with the American regarding available industrial skills. The great majority of new entrants to the labor force came from rural areas and were unfamiliar with factory routine and discipline. Most training was done directly on the job,[71] though technical training was expanded to meet the growing demands of industry.[72] Both because of the emphasis on quantity rather than

TABLE 9

PERCENTAGE DISTRIBUTION OF UNITED STATES AND SOVIET
POPULATIONS AGED 15 TO 59 YEARS, 1939–40

AGE GROUP	UNITED STATES (1940)			SOVIET UNION (1939)		
	Male	*Female*	*Total*	*Male*	*Female*	*Total*
15–19	14.5	14.5	14.5	17.2	16.0	16.6
20–24	13.4	13.9	13.7	15.2	13.9	14.5
25–29	12.8	13.3	13.1	17.3	16.0	16.6
30–34	11.9	12.2	12.1	14.3	13.6	13.9
35–39	11.2	11.3	11.2	11.6	12.1	11.9
40–44	10.4	10.3	10.3	8.2	9.0	8.6
45–49	9.9	9.5	9.7	6.5	7.2	6.9
50–54	8.8	8.3	8.5	5.3	6.7	6.0
55–59	7.1	6.7	6.9	4.4	5.5	5.0
	100.0	100.0	100.0	100.0	100.0	100.0

Sources: United States: 1940 *Census of Population.*
    Soviet Union: Warren W. Eason, "Trends and Prospects of the Soviet Population and Labor Force," p. 49.

[70] Barna, *op. cit.,* quite arbitrarily assigns the following age weights: persons under 16, 1/5; 16–19, 1/2; 20–64 (men), 1; 65 and over (men), 2/3.
[71] See Deutscher, *op. cit.,* pp. 93–96; *Voprosy ekonomiki,* 1952, No. 12, p. 19.
[72] From 1928 to 1937, technical schools graduated 942,800 persons. See *Sotsialisticheskoe*

quality, and of the insatiable requirements of industry, skilled labor remained in short supply in 1940. In consequence, the State Labor Reserves, a compulsory system for the training of young recruits to the labor force, was established. During the first decade of its operation, this training system turned out 6 million workers,[73] though on-the-job training continued to be the principal method of vocational education.[74]

This information is obviously insufficient to permit of any precise quantitative generalizations regarding the comparative skill levels of the U.S. and Soviet labor forces. It is a safe surmise that, in 1939, the average Soviet level of skill was well below that of the United States. The same statement would probably characterize the current situation, though certainly the systematic training of large numbers through the State Labor Reserves has tended to reduce the difference. As of 1939, however, the skill factor operated adversely on Soviet labor productivity, which would probably have been raised relative to U.S. labor productivity could all skill be reduced to a single, homogeneous unit of labor input.

HOURS WORKED

Labor productivity may be measured in any unit of time—the hour, week, month, year, etc. The choice of a unit depends on the purpose for which the measurement is made and the availability of data. The International Labor Office has pointed out that "when measuring productivity with the object of determining the changing volume of output in relation to the time actually worked, the productive capacity of labor, or the cost of production in labor units, it is better to use the man-hour concept; when measuring productivity with the object of estimating manpower requirements, employment possibilities, future national

---

stroitel'stvo SSSR, 1939, p. 124. Voznesenskii, *op. cit.,* p. 27, cites the following increases in the numbers of particular skills from 1926 to 1939: drill press operators, 570 percent; turners, 680 percent; milling machine operators, 1,300 percent; instrument makers, 1,230 percent; pressing and stamping machine operators, 630 percent; fitters and electricians, 640 percent; locomotive machinists, 330 percent; shipbuilding machinists, 320 percent.

[73] U.S. Department of Labor, *Notes on Labor Abroad,* January, 1951, No. 7, p. 14.

[74] For example, in 1946 and 1947 the State Labor Reserves turned out 1,172,000 persons, while 4,700,000 obtained training in other ways. See S. Gurevitch and S. Partigul, *The New Economic Upswing of the U.S.S.R. in the Postwar Five Year Plan,* pp. 55–56.

incomes, etc., the concept of output per man [year] is more appropriate."[75] For example, if output per man-hour is taken (realistically) as a diminishing function of hours worked per day over a certain minimum, an estimate of the potential output of two nations that could be achieved through an increase in working hours, if based on a comparative man-hour productivity relationship, would be erroneous by virtue of the implicit assumption, unless specifically corrected, that the marginal hourly increment in output was equal for the two countries. The output per man-year unit of measurement has the advantage, for such purposes, of having built into it all the institutional differences in working arrangements, such as hours worked per day, holidays, absenteeism, rest periods, which may change during a national emergency but otherwise tend to be inflexible.

The procedure followed by the U.S. Bureau of Labor Statistics in its current studies of productivity trends in American industry, that of presenting both man-hour and man-year measures, is the ideal one. Unfortunately, we are precluded by the limitations of available data from constructing man-hour productivity comparisons. To do this, it would first be necessary to equate, for the United States and Russia, actual working hours, including allowances for rest periods, meals, and activities not directly related to production (grievance meetings, trade-union business, welfare activities, etc.). Even if this degree of accuracy were eschewed, and all hours from the beginning to the end of the working day were to be counted, it would still be impossible to secure the requisite information for the Soviet Union after 1935.

The purpose of the following remarks is to indicate the general order of magnitude of the correction that would be required to convert man-year into man-hour productivity. Table 10 contains a limited comparison of hours worked in Soviet and American industry during the thirties. The Soviet figure for all manufacturing includes mining, whereas the American figure does not; if mining were included in the latter as well, the total figure for the two countries would be somewhat closer, due to the relatively small number of hours worked in U.S. coal mining. More important, however, is the fact that the Russian figures are mostly for a period prior to the armament drive, when overtime work was

[75] International Labor Office, *Methods of Labor Productivity Statistics,* p. 38.

relatively unimportant. By 1939, overtime work had become significant; we are informed, for example, that in shoe manufacturing, overtime work constituted about 1 percent of all working time in 1938; 2.7 percent in 1939; and 5.5 percent during the first half of 1940.[76] If this had

TABLE 10

ESTIMATED AVERAGE HOURS WORKED PER WEEK IN SELECTED UNITED STATES (1939) AND SOVIET (1934–35) INDUSTRIES

INDUSTRY	UNITED STATES	SOVIET UNION	PERCENTAGE OF EXCESS OR (DEFICIT) OF UNITED STATES OVER RUSSIAN HOURS
All manufacturing	37.6	35.7	5.3
Iron and steel	35.5	33.3	6.6
Machinery, excluding transport equipment	38.9	} 37.7	
Transport equipment	36.3		
Cotton goods	36.7	36.7	
Boots and shoes	35.7	38.1	(6.3)
Beet sugar	42.9	39.6	8.3
Coal mining	27.1	35.2	(23.0)
Crude petroleum producing	38.3	34.6	10.7

Sources: United States: The data are from the U.S. Department of Labor, Bureau of Labor Statistics, *Handbook of Labor Statistics,* 1941 edition, Bulletin 694, pp. 22–25. These figures are secured by dividing the total number of man-hours reported for an industry for the week ending nearest the fifteenth of the month by the total number of employees who worked any part of the same period. Therefore they represent actual average hours worked per week by each payroll wage earner, allowing for short time, overtime, and temporary layoffs.

Soviet Union: The data are from *Trud v SSSR,* 1936, p. 78. They were estimated by multiplying the actual number of days worked per annum per wage earner in 1935 by the *normal* working day for adult wage earners in 1934 and dividing the total by 52. There is therefore no allowance for short time reflected in less than a normal day's work. Temporary layoffs would be reflected in the number of days worked per annum, however. The Russian figure for all manufacturing includes mining as well.

been typical of industry as a whole, the excess of United States over Soviet hours worked per week would have been reduced to about 2 percent on the basis of the comparison in Table 10. It would not be implausible to assume more overtime work in heavy industry than in shoe

[76] *Kozhevenno-obuvnaia promyshlennosti,* 1940, No. 8, p. 12.

manufacturing, thus further reducing the difference. However, for individual industries, and for coal mining in particular, adjustment for overtime would not serve to obliterate the wide divergence revealed in Table 10.

One additional fact relating to the prewar period should be noted. The average working day in Russian industry, including overtime, fell from 7.37 hours in 1928 to 7.03 hours in 1936.[77] It presumably began to increase thereafter until 1940, when, in addition to overtime, the eight-hour scheduled day was reinstated.[78] Thus, assuming that all other factors remained constant, Russian annual labor productivity indexes based on 1928 would have to be raised by about 4 percent for 1936, if converted into man-hour productivity, and lowered increasingly thereafter.[79]

The comparative situation in 1950 was quite different from that in 1939. Average weekly hours in U.S. manufacturing in 1950 were 40.5, and in bituminous coal mining, 35.[80] In that year Russian workers were on a standard 48-hour week, but overtime was apparently quite common.[81] Thus, a minimum correction factor of 16 percent in favor of the United States would have been in order in 1950 to convert man-year into man-hour productivity relatives.

[77] B. L. Markus, "The Stakhanov Movement," *International Labor Review,* July, 1936, p. 5.

[78] Vladimir Gzovski, "Elements of Soviet Labor Law," *Monthly Labor Review,* March, 1951, p. 262.

[79] Beginning with 1929, there was experimentation with continuous work weeks, with various shift arrangements. By 1936, however, most workers had returned to the standard interrupted six-day week. See Solomon Schwarz, *Labor in the Soviet Union,* pp. 268–77.

[80] *Monthly Labor Review,* March, 1952, p. 345.

[81] Voznesenskii, *op. cit.,* p. 114, indicates that monthly hours worked rose by 22 percent from 1940 to 1943, and since there was considerable overtime in effect already by 1940, a minimum ten-hour working day during the war would appear to have been required. After the war, there was undoubtedly some shortening of working hours. A British trade-union delegation to Russia reported in 1950 that the Moscow building trades worked from 8 A.M. to 5 P.M. with no overtime unless management could show that it was "completely necessary." Report of the British Workers' Delegation, *Russia with Our Own Eyes,* p. 63. It was said by a similar delegation a year later that in the Stalin Auto Works "overtime is permitted with the consent of the union, but cannot exceed ten hours a month." Report of the Nineteen Americans on Their Visit to the USSR, *We Saw for Ourselves,* p. 26. These are propaganda statements, of course, and tend to minimize the extent of overtime worked.

PART II
INDUSTRY STUDIES

V

COAL MINING

SOVIET coal production from 1927 to 1952 is shown in Table 11.[1] The tentative character of the postwar data, which are estimates rather than firm production data, must be emphasized. Prior to the war, the Don Basin (Donbas) provided some 60 percent of total production, the Kuznetsk Basin (Kuzbas) and the Moscow fields being the only other major sources (see Table 12). Efforts to expand production at Kuznetsk, in the Urals (Kizel, Cheliabinsk), and at Karaganda, accentuated by the occupation and destruction of the Donbas facilities during the war, have resulted in an eastward shift in the center of gravity of coal production. It is estimated that in 1949 only 33 percent of coal output was mined in the Donbas and 11 percent at Moscow, the bulk of the remainder coming from the three major eastern areas.[2] However, the Donbas had regained its position as the foremost coal area of the Soviet Union,[3] and it is not likely that its share of the national output will increase by virtue of its superior resources and locational advantages.

There are significant differences in the quality of coal produced in the Soviet Union and in the United States, as the following data indicate:[4]

	PERCENTAGE OF TOTAL COAL OUTPUT, BY WEIGHT	
TYPE OF COAL	USSR (1934)	United States (1939)
Anthracite	24	12
Bituminous	64	87
Lignite	12	1

Subsequent to 1934, the proportion of Soviet anthracite declined with the shift of production away from the Donbas, the chief source of

---

[1] It is not known whether the Soviet coal output statistics are net of cleaning losses aboveground. United States output statistics represent marketable, i.e., cleaned coal, and are thus net of cleaning losses. It has been estimated that the Soviet output data would have to be reduced by 6 to 8 percent, if they are actually gross of cleaning losses, to put them on the same basis as the U.S. data. See Nancy Nimitz and Alexander

anthracite. By the same token, the proportion of lignite produced
increased, constituting 14 percent of all coal mined in 1937.[5]

Coal output may be compared either in natural units, disregarding

TABLE 11

COAL PRODUCTION IN THE SOVIET UNION, 1927/28 TO 1952

(In thousands of metric tons)

YEAR	AMOUNT	YEAR	AMOUNT
1927/28	35,510	1937	127,100[a]
1928/29	40,067	1938	132,900
1929/30	47,780	1939	n.a.[b]
1931	56,752	1940	166,000
1932	64,664	1945	149,300
1933	76,205	1948	213,500
1934	93,940	1949	236,900
1935	108,900[a]	1950	260,000
1936	126,400[a]	1951	285,000
		1952	300,000

Sources: 1927/28–1934: *Sotsialisticheskoe stroitel'stvo SSSR*, 1936, p. 101.
1935–37: Ia. A. Ioffe, *SSSR i kapitalisticheskie strany*, p. 150.
1938: *Sotsialisticheskoe stroitel'stvo SSSR*, 1939, p. 40.
1940: Gosudarstvennyi Nauchnyi Institut, *Bolshaia Sovetskaia entsiklopediia*, 1948,
p. 810.
1945, 1949: Harry Schwartz, *Russia's Soviet Economy*, p. 214.
1948: New York Times, September 1, 1952, pp. 1, 3.
1949–52: *Ibid.*, September 1, 1952, pp. 1, 3; August 10, 1953, p. 7.

[a] For these years several alternative output figures are available from different sources.
However, only for 1937 is the difference between the high and low figures significant,
and for that year it is only 0.7 percent.

[b] n.a. = information not available.

Gerschenkron, "A Dollar Index of Soviet Coal Output" (unpublished). In both
countries, coal consumed by the mines themselves is included in the output statistics.
Ibid.; see also U.S. Department of Labor, Bureau of Labor Statistics, *Trends in Output
per Man-Hour: Mining*, p. 33.

[2] Harry Schwartz, *Russia's Soviet Economy*, p. 214.

[3] *Voprosy ekonomiki*, 1952, No. 2, p. 25.

[4] Sources: *Sotsialisticheskoe stroitel'stvo SSSR*, 1936, pp. 100–101. U.S. Department of
Commerce, Bureau of the Census, *Mineral Industries*, 1939, I, 225 (hereinafter cited as
U.S. Census, *Mineral Industries*). The anthracite total for the United States includes
only Pennsylvania anthracite, the small amount of other anthracite being included
with bituminous.

[5] *Planovoe khoziaistvo*, 1940, No. 12, p. 30. Virtually the entire output of the Moscow
fields consists of lignite, of economic importance only because of its proximity to a
large industrial market. Some 30 percent of the Ural coal is also lignite.

TABLE 12

PRODUCTION OF COAL IN THE SOVIET UNION, BY FIELD,
FOR TRUSTS OF THE COMMISSARIAT OF HEAVY INDUSTRY, 1937

FIELD AND TRUST	OUTPUT (THOUSANDS OF METRIC TONS)	PERCENTAGE OF TOTAL
Donbas	75,041	60.6
Kuzbas	17,340	13.9
Khakazugol	777	0.6
Kizelugol	3,714	3.0
Cheliabugol	3,467	2.8
Bogoslovsk and Egorshino	900	0.7
Karagandaugol	3,937	3.2
Podmoskovni	7,743	6.3
Vostsibugol	3,035	2.5
Kirugol and Shurab	903	0.7
Sakhalinugol	316	0.3
Tkvarchelugol	158	0.1
Tkvibulugol	240	0.4
Dalugol	4,356	3.5
Vostugol	1,792	1.4
	123,719[a]	100.0

Source: *Ugol'*, 1938, No. 1, p. 1.

[a] This total differs from that presented in Table 11 by virtue of the fact that it is limited to the output of the Commissariat of Heavy Industry, whereas Table 11 covers the entire output of the USSR.

quality differences, or in standard units. Against the latter practice the argument may be advanced that the statistics of Russian coal production are inadequate for accurate conversion into standard units, for within each major quality classification there is a wide variation in quality.[6] More important, however, is the consideration that there is no necessary relationship between quality of coal and labor productivity. It is true that in the United States, productivity has been much lower in anthra-

[6] For example, West Virginia bituminous averaged 14,200 British thermal units per pound produced in 1936, compared with 10,790 Btu for Iowa bituminous. In the same year Pennsylvania anthracite averaged 13,300 Btu. See Works Progress Administration, *Mechanization, Employment and Output per Man in Bituminous-Coal Mining*, p. 53 (hereinafter cited as WPA, *Bituminous-Coal Mining*). See, however, the careful attempt to classify Soviet coal output by quality in Nimitz and Gerschenkron, *op. cit.*

cite than in bituminous mining, but this may be due to the specific character of the U.S. anthracite resources rather than inherent in the quality of the coal itself.[7] There is no clear indication of whether the same productivity relationship prevails in the Donbas.[8] Under the circumstances, the productivity comparisons are best made in terms of natural units of coal, disregarding quality.[9]

Of greater relevance here is the division of coal output by the two basic methods of mining: underground and strip mining. Strip mining has been said to be from two and one-half to three times as productive as underground mining in Russia,[10] whereas in the United States the average output per man-hour at strip mines in 1939 was almost three times as great as at underground mines.[11] Coal mined by stripping constituted only 1.9 percent of all the coal mined in the Soviet Union in 1937, but the percentage rose to 3.8 in 1940 and to 11.9 in 1945.[12] The U.S. industry, on the other hand, had gone much further with strip mining: 9.7 percent of all coal produced in 1939 was mined by this method (9.6 percent of all bituminous and 10.6 percent of anthracite), while by 1950 the percentage had risen to 23.9 percent (bituminous).[13] It is not known what the Russian percentage was in 1950, but with

[7] Depletion of Pennsylvania anthracite resources because of the age of the industry and the difficulty of mechanizing owing to the dip of seams, faults, and other irregularities appear to be the major factors behind relatively low U.S. anthracite productivity. Harold Barger and Sam H. Schurr, *The Mining Industries 1899-1939: A Study of Output, Employment and Productivity,* Chap. 9.

[8] In November, 1935, monthly output per employee in the anthracite trust of the Donbas was 22.2 tons compared with 20.2 tons for the Donbas as a whole. *Ugol',* December, 1935, p. 2. In 1936, the average monthly productivity of a heavy cutting machine was greater in the anthracite than in the bituminous mines of the Donbas, but the opposite relationship prevailed with respect to the productivity per pick hammer. See *Gornyi zhurnal,* 1937, No. 17, pp. 37–38.

[9] As a further disadvantage of departing from natural unit measurement, it may be pointed out that quality and the economic importance of coal are quite different things. If one is interested in the economic effectiveness of output per man, locational and other factors will have to be taken into account, the result of which will be a productivity concept that differs from the conventional one.

[10] *Planovoe khoziaistvo,* 1940, No. 12, p. 30; *ibid.,* 1948, No. 4, p. 37.

[11] U.S. Census, *Mineral Industries,* 1939, I, 228.

[12] *Planovoe khoziaistvo,* 1948, No. 4, p. 37. Part of the increase in 1945 was due to low production in the Donbas, where the depth of the deposits makes strip mining impossible.

[13] Calculated from U.S. Department of Commerce, *Minerals Yearbook,* 1940, p. 821 (hereinafter cited as *Minerals Yearbook*), and U.S. Department of Labor, Bureau of Labor Statistics, *Productivity Trends, Bituminous-Coal Mining,* p. 2.

the resumption of large-scale production in the Donbas, it is not un-likely that the percentage diminished.

In order to indicate the effect upon productivity of differences in these mining techniques, the productivity comparisons will be supple-mented by data on productivity in underground mining alone. How-ever, one must not lose sight of the fact that the basic productivity comparison must cover the entire industry, regardless of mining methods; the availability of a relatively greater amount of coal that may be strip mined is an important but by no means the only resource factor conferring a mining productivity advantage upon a nation.

United States coal production in 1939 amounted to 446,572,000 short tons, or 405,130,000 metric tons.[14] The regional distribution of this out-put is not relevant for our purposes.

THE LABOR FORCE

The Soviet Union. The various series for coal mining employment that are directly available from Russian sources, covering persons em-ployed in that part of coal mining falling within large-scale industry,[15] are shown in Table 13. Employment on January 1 tended to exceed the average for the year because of some seasonality of employment.[16]

Table 14 presents statistics on that portion of the Russian coal mining labor force engaged in the "operation" of the mines (the Russian term is *po eksploatatsi*). I have not been able to find a precise definition of this term as it is used in Russian mining statistics. It seems clear, how-ever, that the transformation of coal into coke and the manufacture of products from coal are not considered as part of the coal industry, since they are generally classified separately in detailed production and em-

[14] U.S. Census, *Mineral Industries*, 1939, I, 225.

[15] This includes all but a very small portion of the industry. In 1938, about 95 percent of total coal produced in the Soviet Union came from trusts under the jurisdiction of the national coal commissariat. See *Planovoe khoziaistvo*, 1939, No. 2, p. 55. Moreover, most of the remaining 5 percent probably came from local industries or cooperatives that met the census qualifications for large-scale industry.

[16] For example, employment of wage earners in 1935 varied from 104.6 percent of the annual average on February 1 to 95.5 percent on September 1. See Tsentral'noe Upravlenie Narodno-Khoziaistvennogo Ucheta, *Trud v SSSR*, 1936, p. 107 (hereinafter cited as *Trud v SSSR*). The summer seasonal decline has been ascribed to the drawing off of miners into agriculture during the harvest. See *Gornyi zhurnal*, 1937, No. 11, p. 15.

TABLE 13

EMPLOYMENT IN SOVIET COAL MINING, 1928–39

(*In thousands of persons*)

YEAR	(1) TOTAL EMPLOYMENT ON JANUARY 1 (LABOR SECTION DATA)[a]	(2) WAGE EARNERS ON JANUARY 1 (LABOR SECTION DATA)[b]	(3) AVERAGE ANNUAL NUMBER OF WAGE EARNERS (LABOR SECTION DATA)[c]	(4) AVERAGE ANNUAL NUMBER OF WAGE EARNERS (INDUSTRY SECTION DATA)[d]
1928	281.3	246.0	n.a.[e]	212.9
1929	306.1	266.0	n.a.	222.5
1930	330.0	283.8	n.a.	225.1
1931	364.3	301.7	n.a.	272.9
1932	517.5	407.4	374.2	361.7
1933	499.6	388.3	398.9	397.7
1934	503.1	427.5	407.1	422.8
1935	492.9	427.6	412.3	n.a.
1936	494.0	427.6	n.a.	n.a.
1937	n.a.	n.a.	n.a.	403.5[f]
1938	n.a.	n.a.	n.a.	n.a.
1939	n.a.	n.a.	n.a.	392.1[f]

[a] *Trud v SSSR*, 1936, p. 106.

[b] *Sotsialisticheskoe stroitel'stvo SSSR*, 1934, pp. 326–27. The figures from 1934 to 1936 are from *Trud v SSSR*, 1936, p. 106, and *Sotsialisticheskoe stroitel'stvo SSSR*, 1936, p. 516.

[c] *Trud v SSSR*, 1936, p. 107; *ibid.*, 1935, p. 62.

[d] *Socialist Construction in the USSR*, 1936, p. 121.

[e] n.a. = information not available.

[f] These figures were obtained by dividing data on fixed capital by data on capital per wage earner. Sources: *Sotsialisticheskoe stroitel'stvo SSSR*, 1939, p. 37; L. M. Kantor, *Osnovnye fondy promyshlennosti i ikh ispol'zovanie*, p. 25; and an unpublished manuscript by Norman Kaplan. That the data are of the industry section type is indicated by the coincidence of labor force figures for 1929 and 1932, similarly calculated, with the published data derived from the source cited in footnote *d*, above.

ployment statistical tables. On the other hand, it is likely that such preparatory activities as washing and sizing are considered part of the coal mining industry in Russia, as they are in the United States.[17]

In the light of available material, the most plausible hypothesis is

[17] The technical journal of the coal industry, *Ugol'*, carried numerous articles dealing with these operations, and data were often attributed to the Coal Trust. For example, see *Ugol'*, June, 1936, p. 36.

TABLE 14

THE OPERATING LABOR FORCE IN SOVIET COAL MINING, 1928–40
(*In thousands of persons*)

YEAR	(1) AVERAGE ANNUAL NUMBER OF WAGE EARNERS (INDUSTRY SECTION DATA)	(2) AVERAGE ANNUAL EMPLOYMENT ESTIMATED FROM PRODUCTIVITY DATA	(3)
		Wage earners	*Total employment*
1928	212.9[a]	n.a.	n.a.
1929	222.5[a]	n.a.	n.a.
1930	225.1[a]	n.a.	n.a.
1931	272.9[a]	n.a.	n.a.
1932	323.5[a]	n.a.	n.a.
1933	339.1[b]	330.6[e]	412.0[l]
1934	n.a.[c]	367.0[e]	430.0[k]
1935	n.a.	386.2[e]	437.0[l]
1936	n.a.	387.2[e]	n.a.
1937 (January 1)	n.a.	398.8[f]	444.6[f]
1937	344.2[d]	404.0[g]	450.7[m]
1938	341.4[n]	406.6[h]	463.1[m]
1939	334.4[d]	n.a.	n.a.
1940	n.a.	468.1[j]	544.3[m]

[a] *Sotsialisticheskoe stroitel'stvo SSSR,* 1934, p. 76.

[b] S. G. Strumilin, *Chernaia metallurgiia v Rossii i v SSSR,* p. 91.

[c] n.a. = information not available.

[d] Estimated from Table 13, column (4), by assuming that the ratio of operating wage earners in 1938 and 1939 to 1933 followed the trend indicated for all wage earners.

[e] Estimated from published data on monthly output per operating wage earner in *Gornyi zhurnal,* 1937, No. 17, p. 62. These figures may be slightly understated by virtue of the fact that the productivity data relate to enterprises of the Coal Trust (Glavugol), which were probably characterized by somewhat higher productivity than the rest of the industry. However, since Glavugol produced 95 percent of total coal output (1938), the error cannot be great. For the year 1936, a figure of 386.5 thousand operating wage earners for the entire industry can be derived from Ia. A. Ioffe, *SSSR i kapitalisticheskie strany,* p. 78, very close to the estimate for that year.

The difference between the figures in columns (1) and (2) for 1933 may be due to conceptual differences, since the data in column (2) appear to be of the "labor section" type.

The ratio of operating wage earners to total operating employment for the years 1933 to 1935 were: 1933, 80.2 percent; 1934, 85.3 percent; 1935, 88.4 percent. The ratio on January 1 (published) was 89.7 percent. These percentages approximate the trend in a similar ratio for all wage earners on January 1 as shown in Table 13, and since the data for operating wage earners and total operating employment were calculated from separate sources, this fact serves to confirm the validity of both sets of estimates.

Notes to Table 14 (*Continued*)

ᶠ *Gornyi zhurnal*, 1937, No. 17, p. 15. Figures for earlier years found in the same source correspond to the labor section data published in *Trud v SSSR*, 1936.

ᵍ Estimated by applying to total operating employment in 1937 the ratio (published) prevailing on January 1, 1937, between operating wage earners and total operating employment. See *Ugol'*, 1941, No. 5, p. 5.

ʰ Estimated by applying to total operating employment in 1938 the average of the (published) ratios of operating wage earners to total operating employment prevailing on January 1, 1937, and January 1, 1940. See *Ugol'*, 1941, No. 5, p. 5.

ʲ Estimated by applying to total operating employment in 1940 the (published) ratio of operating wage earners to total operating employment on January 1, 1940. See *Ugol'*, 1941, No. 5, p. 5. Operating wage earner employment under the Commissariat for Heavy Industry may be estimated at 476.5 thousand for 1940 from the *1941 Plan*, p. 514. Since both estimates are approximate, this difference does not appear to be significant.

ᵏ *Ugol'*, January, 1935, p. 2. Of the total, 403 thousand employees were attributed to Glavugol.

ˡ Total operating employment for Glavugol was 386.8 thousand in 1933 and 410.3 thousand in 1935. The figures in the table were estimated by applying to these data the ratio of Glavugol to total industry employment, as per note *j*.

ᵐ Derived from the following data of coal output per operating employee (tons):

YEAR	MONTHLY OUTPUT PER EMPLOYEE (PUBLISHED)	ESTIMATED ANNUAL OUTPUT PER EMPLOYEE	ESTIMATED AVERAGE NUMBER OF EMPLOYEES
1937	23.5	282	450.7
1938	23.9	287	463.1
January–July, 1940	25.4	305	544.3

Source: *Ugol'*, November, 1940, p. 2.

The figure of 23.5 tons per month is identical with that in *Planovoe khoziaistvo*, 1939, No. 2, p. 60. However, the same source quotes a figure of 24.3 tons per month for 1938. The later source is preferred.

The 1940 employment figure is derived from average monthly output for the first seven months of the year only. No subsequent data are available.

ⁿ Estimated from *Sotsialisticheskoe stroitel'stvo SSSR*, 1939, pp. 36, 38.

that the Russian term *po eksploatatsii* refers to the operation of mines that are actually in production, as contrasted with the development of new mines. Wage earners engaged in developmental work in producing mines—e.g., timberers—are included in the operating labor force.[18] However, when large-scale development of new mines was undertaken under the five year plans, the Russians apparently decided to separate this process from normal operation of mines. Up to 1928, no distinction

[18] *Gornyi zhurnal*, 1937, No. 17, p. 62.

seems to have been made between total and operating employment,[19] and industry section labor statistics first show separate figures for operating and total employment in 1932.[20] It was in the early planning years that investment in new shafts first took on large proportions,[21] and one of the purposes of the distinction may have been to prevent the enlarged labor force engaged in development from exercising a depressing effect upon productivity indexes. Since 1932, virtually all direct labor productivity statements relate only to operating employment and not to the total labor force.

During 1932 and 1933, when industry section statistics were available both for operating and all wage earners, the ratios between the two were 89.4 percent and 85.3 percent for the respective years. For 1934 and 1935, a comparison of operating wage earners computed from productivity data with labor section statistics covering all wage earners yields ratios of 84.0 percent and 83.9 percent. Thus, after the initial decline from 1932 to 1933,[22] the ratio between the two groups seems to have remained fairly stable. For subsequent years one would expect an increase in the ratio, due to a reduction in new developmental work, but the appropriate data for testing this hypothesis are not available.

Both the U.S. Census and the U.S. Bureau of Mines have endeavored to separate from the producing or operating labor force those employees who were engaged in nonproducing operations.[23] In the United States,

[19] *Ibid.*

[20] This will be seen if column (4) of Table 13 is compared with column (1) of Table 14.

[21] The number of new mines put into operation, by year, was as follows:

1929: 9	1931: 78	1933: 35	1935: 43
1930: 13	1932: 40	1934: 20	1936: 19

Source: *Gornyi zhurnal,* 1937, No. 17, p. 12.

[22] As will be seen from Table 13, the labor force was undergoing tremendous fluctuation from 1930 to 1934, and variations in such a ratio as this are not unexpected.

[23] The 1939 Census carried separate employment figures for "general contract services for the coal industries" and "nonproducing operations," defined as follows:

"Contract service operations. These are operations conducted by contractors for the account of others and devoted principally to development of mineral properties. Operations conducted by contractors engaged principally in mineral production for the account of others (for example, operations of Pennsylvania anthracite strip-pit contractors) are not included with 'contract-service operations' but rather with 'producing operations.'

"Nonproducing operations (other than contract-service operations). The statistics for operations that neither produced minerals nor performed work for others are

however, operating wage earners constituted, according to the 1939 Census, 99.8 percent of total wage earner employment. In view of this great discrepancy between the Russian and the U.S. figures, can the U.S. operating concept be deemed the equivalent of the Russian?

During the 1930's, very little new developmental work was undertaken in the U.S. coal industry, due to chronic overcapacity. The U.S. coal industry reached a peak in 1923, and thereafter many mines were closed or abandoned because of falling demand.[24] The number of mines in operation decreased from 6,548 in 1938 to 6,324 in 1940,[25] and it may be presumed that virtually no new development was being performed.

In 1932 there were in the Soviet Union 441 mines with an annual capacity of more than 20 thousand metric tons each.[26] From 1929 to 1936, 257 new mines with an average annual capacity of 370 thousand tons each were newly put into operation (these would be Class 1 mines, by U.S. standards), 140 of them during and prior to 1932, and the remainder after 1932.[27] Thus, in 1928 there were roughly 300 Class 1 mines in operation in Russia, and from then until the year 1936 (inclusive) about 35 new mines of this size were added each year, on the average. Since these were all large mines requiring a large initial outlay of capital and labor, it is not implausible that roughly 15 percent of all coal mine wage earners should have been engaged in new development.

However, this problem cannot be resolved statistically, and it will simply be assumed that, for the purpose of comparing labor productivity, the Russian and U.S. operating concepts are roughly equivalent. This assumption may have the effect of overstating relative Russian productivity; but the only alternative, that of using all wage earners, would result in an understatement with respect to productivity in the actual mining of coal.[28]

---

always clearly distinguished throughout the volumes from statistics for producing operations. Many of the operations that had no products were engaged in development work. It should be noted, however, that mines undergoing development often produce some minerals; such mines were classed as producing mines, regardless of the quantity of minerals produced." U.S. Census, *Mineral Industries*, 1939, I, 6.

For Bureau of Mines practice, see WPA, *Bituminous-Coal Mining*, pp. 352–56.

[24] *Minerals Yearbook*, 1940, p. 777.

[25] *Ibid.*, 1948, p. 291.

[26] *Sotsialisticheskoe stroitel'stvo*, 1936, pp. 104–5.

[27] *Gornyi zhurnal*, 1937, No. 17, p. 12.

[28] Russian statisticians, in comparing U.S. and Soviet labor productivity, have

Table 14, which is limited to the operating labor force, shows two series for wage earners: one of these, column (1), is available directly from Soviet sources from 1928 to 1933 and is estimated from Soviet data on total fixed capital and capital per wage earner for 1937 and 1939; the other, column (2), has been estimated indirectly from a number of Soviet statements on output per wage earner. The difference between the two series for 1938 is seen to be of considerable magnitude, 341.4 thousand versus 406.6 thousand.

The reasons for this difference are not clear. A possible cause of discrepancy may lie in the fact that while the data in column (1) are industry section data, those in column (2) are probably of the labor section type.[29] However, for years for which both industry and labor section type statistics are available (1932–34), no difference of this magnitude appears.

The considerations which dictated the choice of the higher labor force figure for 1938, that in column (2) of Table 14, as the basis for our productivity comparison are as follows:

a. An article in *Planovoe khoziaistvo* indicated that the average monthly output per operating employee in coal mining was 24.3 tons in 1938.[30] A figure of 23.9 tons appeared in the journal of the coal industry.[31] Whichever of these two figures is accepted, the resultant total for operating employment is much higher in relation to operating *wage earner* employment than appears to be warranted by the magnitude of that ratio for known years.[32]

b. The number of operating wage earners as of January 1, 1937, is

followed the practice of using the total U.S. labor force (which is virtually identical with the operating labor force) and the Soviet *operating* labor force. For example, see P. D. Duzh, "Proizvoditel'nost' truda v promyshlennosti SSSR," in Akademiia Nauk, Institut Ekonomiki, *Proizvoditel'nost' truda v promyshlennosti SSSR*, p. 133.

[29] The figure for operating wage earners as of January 1, 1937, 398.8 thousand, which appears to be of the correct order of magnitude, comes from a series which for earlier years is clearly of the labor section type. *Gornyi zhurnal*, 1937, No. 17, p. 15, compared with *Sotsialisticheskoe stroitel'stvo SSSR*, 1934, p. 327.

[30] *Planovoe khoziaistvo*, 1939, No. 2, p. 60.

[31] *Ugol'*, November, 1940, p. 2.

[32] As of January 1, 1937, the ratio of operating wage earners to total operating employment was 89.7 percent. See *Gornyi zhurnal*, 1937, No. 17, p. 15. As of January 1, 1940, for all employees (operating and nonoperating) the ratio was 86.0 percent. See *Ugol'*, 1941, No. 5, p. 5. Acceptance of the lower wage earner figure for 1938 would imply a ratio in that year of less than 75 percent.

stated to be 398.8 thousand (labor section type figure).[33] It is difficult
to reconcile a figure of this magnitude with the industry section figure
of 341.4 thousand for 1938, since there were no indications of a sharp
decline in the coal labor force from 1937 to 1938.

c. An authoritative source put the output of coal per operating wage
earner at 327 tons in 1936.[34] On this basis, the number of operating wage
earners might be estimated at 386.5 thousand in 1936, which again
would imply a sharp decline in wage earner employment from 1936
to 1938 were the industry section wage earner figure for the latter year
accepted.

In summary, there would seem to be little doubt that Russian statisticians, in preparing productivity estimates for the years 1936 to 1939,
employed a labor force series which exceeded in magnitude that shown
in column (1) of Table 14 by a substantial amount; and that the latter
series was not inclusive of all coal miners, either because of the limitations imposed by the industry section labor force definitions or for some
unspecified reason.

Neither of the available distributions of labor force personnel by
major category, that for January 1, 1937, nor that for January 1, 1940,
has a separate entry for learners; the 1937 distribution has an entry of
"not available" in the "learner" column, while that for 1940 simply
omits the learner category, the others adding up to 100 percent.[35] In
view of this treatment, it is likely that learners were added to the wage
earner category. Junior service personnel, who must also be added to
wage earners for the purposes of the productivity comparison, bore the
following quantitative relationship to wage earners: 1937, 3.55 percent;
1939, 3.96 percent; and August, 1940, 3.92 percent. Using for 1938 the
average ratio for the years 1937 and 1939, which was 3.75 percent, results in the addition of 15.2 thousand junior service personnel to the
previously estimated figure of 406.6 thousand wage earners, bringing the
relevant labor force figure up to 421.8 thousand.

The United States. According to the concept employed in the U.S.
Census, the average number of operating (producing) wage earners
in U.S. coal mining was 453.5 thousand in 1939. To this figure should

[33] *Gornyi zhurnal,* 1937, No. 17, p. 15.
[34] Ia. A. Ioffe, *SSSR i kapitalisticheske strany,* p. 78.
[35] *Ugol',* January, 1941, p. 16.

be added 3.5 thousand proprietors and firm members performing manual labor (mainly in small cooperatives), raising the total to 457.0 thousand.[36]

For the same year the Census also compiled an alternative employment average, "the average number of wage earners on active days (excluding shutdown periods)." This was obtained "by aggregating figures reported by individual operators for the average number of wage earners employed on active days. The industry average thus obtained is usually greater than the [Census] average of the 12 monthly figures, since the former is not influenced by low levels of employment on days when the respective operations were inactive."[37] The average number of wage earners in 1939, under this concept, appears to have been 510.6 thousand.[38]

Finally, the Bureau of Mines published for 1939 a figure of 514.9 thousand wage earner and working proprietors employed on active days (not including shutdown periods), conceptually akin to the second Census figure.[39]

In determining which of the two concepts is appropriate for the purpose at hand, it must first be recalled that the Russian employment figure is for average "listed" or payroll wage earners, compiled on a daily basis and including all wage earners attached to the enterprise, whether or not they actually appear for work. A monthly average is secured by dividing the sum of the daily payroll counts by the number of calendar days in the month; when the enterprise is shut down, as on holidays, the payroll count of the preceding day is imputed to the holiday. Because of absenteeism, this results in an overstatement of actual labor inputs, which may be estimated for 1938 to have been on the order of 9 percent.[40]

The two employment concepts in the United States have been aptly

[36] U.S. Census, *Mineral Industries,* 1939, I, 225.

[37] *Ibid.,* p. 4.

[38] Estimated from the data on the number of man-hours worked by wage earners on active days, average days of operation, and average hours per shift, in U.S. Census, *Mineral Industries,* 1939, I, 225.

[39] This figure represents the addition of separate data for bituminous and anthracite employment. See *Minerals Yearbook,* 1940, p. 821; *ibid.,* 1941, p. 824.

[40] This is the ratio of actual annual days worked per wage earner in coal mining in 1937, 270 days, to total potential working days, excluding holidays, in 1934 (the last year for which such a figure is available), 295.3 days.

termed "full year" and "active year" averages.[41] If one were interested in securing the most accurate expression of annual labor input in man-days, the "active year" (Bureau of Mines) concept would appear to be the more appropriate starting point; multiplying average employment under this concept by the annual active days worked per mine should yield total man-days worked per annum, if man-days worked on in-active days were added.[42] If the "full year" (Census) concept were adopted as the starting point, however, labor input would tend to be understated, since the lower annual average employment resulting from the averaging in of periods of inactivity, multiplied by active days worked per mine, would impute to active mining days a smaller labor force than that which actually obtained.

To derive man-day inputs for Russia similar to those secured from the U.S. "active year" average, the official daily payroll count averages should merely be multiplied by the number of active days per annum (which under Russian conditions in the late thirties would presumably have approximated total potential working days). Thus, the Russian average would appear to be closer to the Bureau of Mines concept than to that of the Census, rendering the former the appropriate one for U.S.-Soviet productivity comparisons.

As already noted, the Russian wage earner data were inflated over actual labor inputs by roughly 9 percent by virtue of the inclusion of absentees in the payroll count. However, because of the manner of keeping records and reporting employment to the Bureau of Mines, the employment data published by the latter also tended to overstate labor inputs on account of the absenteeism factor, though the probable magnitude of the overstatement appears to have been somewhat smaller than in the Russian data.[43] For both countries man-day inputs would

[41] Barger and Schurr, op. cit., p. 274. The quantitative divergence between the two concepts would only be significant in the case of industries having considerable shut-down periods, either for cyclical or seasonal reasons.

[42] The correction factor for the latter is about 4 percent, on the basis of Census man-hour data. See U.S. Census, Mineral Industries, 1939, I, 225.

[43] U.S. overstatement was due to the fact that no time records were kept for piece workers, who may have been on the payroll on the reporting day but not actually at work. About 60 percent of the working crew was on piece work, and absenteeism among this group was found to average 10 percent. There may have also been a small additional overstatement because of turnover. See WPA, Bituminous-Coal Mining, pp. 192, 196.

be overstated because of the failure to account for lost time within the working day;[44] there is no way of telling, however, whether there was any significant difference between the countries in this respect.

It may be concluded that, for our purposes, the 1939 Bureau of Mines employment figure of 514.9 thousand wage earners,[45] while by no means the precise equivalent of the Soviet employment concept, is the most appropriate figure for comparing labor productivity.

COMPARATIVE PRODUCTIVITY

The foregoing material on output and employment may now be brought together in the following summary:

	RUSSIA, 1938	UNITED STATES, 1939
Output of coal (thousands of metric tons)	132,900	405,130
Number of operating wage earners (thousands)	421.8	514.9
Annual output per wage earner (metric tons)	315	787
Russian productivity as a percentage of U.S. productivity (per annum)	40	

There are Russian data indicating that the average monthly output of coal per employee (not per wage earner) rose from 23.9 tons in 1938 to 25.1 tons during the first seven months of 1939.[46] From these it may be estimated roughly that Russian 1939 productivity as a percentage of that of the United States for the same year was 42 percent.

If underground mining (omitting strip mining) is compared, Russian

[44] In Russia, partial man-days of work were tabulated as full man-days. *Slovar'-spravochnik*, 1944, p. 216. In the United States, piece workers may leave early because they have completed their allotted task for the day, or for personal reasons. No record of actual time worked is kept. See WPA, *Bituminous-Coal Mining*, p. 200.

[45] We are told that "mine employees not producing coal, such as maintenance men and watchmen," are excluded from the Bureau of Mines totals. See WPA, *Bituminous-Coal Mining*, p. 352. This might be taken to mean that junior service personnel should be excluded from the Russian employment total. However, wage earner employment under the alternative ("active year") Census concept, in which watchmen and maintenance personnel were included among wage earners, was so close in 1939 to the Bureau of Mines total as to throw some doubt upon the consistency of reporting practices in this respect, or, in the alternative, to indicate that the excluded U.S. category was insignificant in magnitude. Under the circumstances, we are justified in following the customary practice in this study of including junior service personnel in the Russian employment total.

[46] *Ugol'*, November, 1940, p. 2.

1938 productivity as a percentage of U.S. 1939 productivity can be estimated at 42 percent.[47] Adjusting the Russian figure for the productivity
increase there from 1938 to 1939 raises the comparative ratio, on a
straight 1939 basis, to 44 percent.

These ratios fail to reflect the significant differences in the number
of days worked per annum in Soviet and U.S. coal mining.[48] The following data indicate the extent of this discrepancy:

	RUSSIA, 1938	UNITED STATES, 1939
Number of days[49] worked per annum by wage earners (thousands)	113,886[50]	95,738[51]
Daily output per wage earner (metric tons)	1.17	4.23
Russian productivity as a percentage of U.S. productivity (daily)	28	

Adjusting this figure for the estimated increase in Russian productivity from 1938 to 1939 raises the comparison to 29 percent. For underground mining alone, the percentage is 29 percent for Russia in 1938

[47] The adjustment is made as follows: It is assumed that in both countries strip
mining is three times as productive as underground mining. The percentages of coal
mined underground are available for both countries, resulting in an estimate of 310
tons per wage earner for Russia (1938) and 736 tons for the United States (1939).

[48] There appears to have been little difference in the length of the immediate
prewar shift, the seven-hour shift having been standard in both countries. However,
there may have been overtime, particularly in Russia, not reflected in the standard
working day.

[49] To the extent that multiple shifts were worked by Soviet coal mines in 1938,
the payroll figure would exceed that for the full one-shift labor force. However, the
labor input data are not affected thereby, since it is presumed that each miner worked
only one shift per day and that a man-shift was considered the equivalent of a
man-day of work.

[50] Estimated from the information that in 1935, the actual number of days worked
per wage earner, on the average, was 269 (*Trud v SSSR,* 1936, p. 110) and that in
1937 the average number of days worked each month per wage earner was 22.5 or
270 per annum (*Problemy ekonomiki,* 1939, No. 5, p. 47). Application of the figure
of 270 to the 1938 labor force estimate yields the figure in the text. The foregoing
discussion has made it clear that the man-day estimate is inflated by virtue of the
inclusion of absentees in the labor force.

[51] Estimated by dividing the census figure of total man-hours worked by wage
earners, during both active and inactive periods, by the average number of hours worked
per day, 7. The census data on man-days worked, if divided by the Bureau of Mines
employment total of 514.9 thousand, yields 186 active mining days per annum,
compared with 180 days estimated by the Census. The difference appears to be due
primarily to the inclusion of the number of man-days worked on inactive days.

as compared with the United States in 1939, and 31 percent for the two countries in 1939.

The various estimates in this section are summarized in Table 15.[52]

CHANGES IN SOVIET PRODUCTIVITY, 1928 TO 1940

The available data on trends in Soviet coal mining productivity are summarized in Tables 16 and 17. The data in Table 16 are subject to certain limitations, as indicated in a footnote thereto, but nevertheless present a reasonable approximation to trends in productivity during the years covered. The indexes in columns (2) and (3) of Table 17 were taken, with a minimum of independent calculation, from published Russian productivity statements and represent productivity trends expressed in physical and value units of measurement, respectively.

While Table 17 displays some puzzling features, notably the tendency of the physical indexes of labor productivity to outrun the value index from 1933 to 1935, the main outlines of the productivity trends are quite clear. Measured in physical units, labor productivity in Soviet coal mining more than doubled from 1928 to 1940, the increase in value terms (up to 1938) having been somewhat greater. The physical and

---

TABLE 15

COMPARISONS OF SOVIET AND UNITED STATES PRODUCTIVITY IN COAL MINING

(Soviet productivity as a percentage of U.S. productivity)

	SOVIET UNION, 1938– UNITED STATES, 1939	SOVIET UNION, 1939– UNITED STATES, 1939[a]
Annual output per wage earner	40	42
Daily output per wage earner	28	29
Annual output per wage earner in underground mining	42	44
Daily output per wage earner in underground mining	29	31

[a] The comparisons for the year 1939 are based on a single rough reported figure of productivity rise in Soviet mining from 1938 to 1939 and must be regarded merely as supplementary to the basic 1938–39 productivity comparison.

[52] On the basis of an unpublished study (Nimitz and Gerschenkron, *op. cit.*), in which Soviet coal output was valued in 1939 U.S. dollars, Soviet productivity in 1937 may be estimated at 41 percent of U.S. 1939 productivity.

TABLE 16

ESTIMATED OUTPUT PER WAGE EARNER IN SOVIET COAL MINE OPERATION, 1928–40[a]

YEAR	AVERAGE ANNUAL NUMBER OF WAGE EARNERS (THOUSANDS)[b]	ANNUAL PRODUCTION OF COAL (THOUSANDS OF METRIC TONS)[c]	OUTPUT PER WAGE EARNER (METRIC TONS)	INDEX OF OUTPUT PER WAGE EARNER (1928 = 100)
1928	212.9	35,510	167	100
1929	222.5	40,067	180	107.8
1930	225.1	47,780	212	126.9
1931	272.9	56,752	208	124.6
1932	323.5	64,664	200	119.8
1933	339.1	76,205	225	134.7
1934	367.0	93,940	256	153.3
1935	386.2	108,900	282	168.9
1936	387.2	126,400	326	195.2
1937	404.0	127,100	315	188.6
1938	406.6	132,900	327	195.8
1939	n.a.[d]	n.a.	n.a.	n.a.
1940	468.1	166,000	355	212.6

[a] The productivity series is based on a labor force series which is subject to ambiguities and must therefore be used with caution. Specifically, the industry section data for the years 1928 to 1931 show identical figures for total and operating wage earners. From 1934 on, employment is estimated from statistics of output and labor productivity, and probably conforms to the labor section concept rather than to that of the industry section. For the year 1937 and thereafter, learners are probably included, which would have the effect of understating productivity.

[b] Source: Table 14.

[c] Source: Table 11. The data for the years 1928–30 inclusive cover the economic rather than the calendar year, the effect of which is slightly to understate productivity because of the rising trend of output during the period.

[d] n.a. = information not available.

value unit indexes follow one another much more closely than similar indexes for other industries.

A more detailed picture of Soviet productivity development, broken down by individual coal fields, is shown in Table 18. The rise of Donbas productivity approximated that for the industry as a whole, the index in 1939 standing at 207 based on 1928. In absolute terms, the Donbas was low in productivity as compared with the other major fields, which

TABLE 17

COMPARISON OF ESTIMATED AND PUBLISHED INDEXES OF
LABOR PRODUCTIVITY IN SOVIET COAL MINING, 1928–40
(1928 = 100)

YEAR	(1) ESTIMATED IN PHYSICAL UNITS[a]	(2) PUBLISHED IN PHYSICAL UNITS[b]	(3) PUBLISHED IN VALUE UNITS[c]
1928	100	100	100
1929	107.8	109.6	112.4
1930	126.9	127.9	128.2
1931	124.6	120.0	120.6
1932	119.8	119.9	117.1
1933	134.7	127.2	122.8
1934	153.3	147.7	140.7
1935	168.9	172.8	163.9
1936	195.2	200.0	n.a.
1937	188.6	n.a.	193.7
1938	195.8	200.0	220.7
1939	n.a.[d]	n.a.	n.a.
1940	212.6	n.a.	n.a.

[a] Source: Table 16.

[b] Sources: 1928–36, *Gornyi zhurnal*, 1937, No. 17, p. 62. These index numbers are based on a series representing the average monthly output of coal per operating wage earner.

1938: *Ugol'*, 1938, No. 11, p. 1. The underlying unit output figure represents the average monthly output for the first seven months of 1938.

[c] Sources: 1928–35, *Trud v SSSR*, 1936, p. 106.

1937: E. L. Granovskii and B. L. Markus, *Ekonomika sotsialisticheskoi promyshlennosti*, p. 461.

1938: *Sotsialisticheskoe stroitel'stvo SSSR*, 1939, p. 38.

The value units were expressed in 1926/27 rubles.

[d] n.a. = information not available.

has been attributed to its relatively poor resource conditions.[53] The high level of productivity shown for the mines of the Far East, which were not large coal producers, was due chiefly to a high proportion of strip mining in those areas.

PRODUCTIVITY TRENDS SINCE 1939

The effect of the German invasion of Russia was to lower coal labor productivity, notwithstanding the fact that the occupied coal fields were

[53] *Voprosy ekonomiki*, 1950, No. 6, p. 32.

TABLE 18

MONTHLY OUTPUT PER OPERATING WAGE EARNER IN
SOVIET COAL MINING, BY COAL FIELD, 1928–39
(*In metric tons*)

YEAR	USSR	DONBAS	KUZNETSK BASIN	MOSCOW BASIN	URAL FIELDS	KARA- GANDA	FAR EAST	CEN- TRAL ASIA
1928	13.6	12.6	19.7	15.6	18.7	n.a.[a]	15.0	n.a.
1929	14.9	13.9	21.3	18.3	19.5	n.a.	15.0	n.a.
1930	17.4	16.2	21.7	21.2	22.8	n.a.	23.8	n.a.
1931	16.3	14.9	23.2	19.7	19.7	n.a.	32.2	n.a.
1932	16.2	14.5	24.0	20.4	17.9	10.2	31.4	12.0
1933	17.3	15.6	26.8	21.3	17.6	13.5	35.3	13.5
1934	20.1	18.1	29.9	22.3	20.4	16.1	44.5	15.9
1935	23.5	20.8	35.1	25.6	25.6	22.0	54.5	27.3
1936	27.2	23.6	43.1	28.6	31.2	31.3	72.0	19.9
1937	n.a.	23.7	n.a.	n.a.	n.a.	n.a.	n.a.	n.a.
1938	n.a.	24.7	38.4	27.7	n.a.	34.3	n.a.	n.a.
1939	n.a.	26.1	n.a.	n.a.	n.a.	n.a.	n.a.	n.a.

Sources: 1928–36: *Gornyi zhurnal*, 1937, No. 17, p. 59.

1938: P. D. Duzh, "Proizvoditel'nost' truda v kammennougol'noi promyshlennost' SSSR," in Akademiia Nauk, Institut Ekonomiki, *Proizvoditel'nost' truda v promyshlennost' SSSR*, p. 110.

1939: *Ugol*, August, 1940, p. 1.

[a] n.a. = information not available.

relatively low productivity areas.[54] The labor force was diluted by withdrawals for military service, compensated for largely by the use of more female labor, which even before the war had played a significant role in coal mining.[55]

The subsequent movement of coal output to the east, occasioned by the devastation of the Donbas mines, tended to raise average productivity.[56] Nevertheless, annual labor productivity in coal mining in 1950

[54] N. Voznesenskii, *Voennaia ekonomika SSSR*, p. 114. The two major areas occupied were the Donbas and the Moscow Basin.

[55] In 1938 about one-quarter of the labor force in coal mining consisted of women. See N. Popova, *Zhenshchiny strany sotsializma*, p. 39.

[56] The planned 1950 productivity levels of the major fields, taking the Donbas as 100, was:

Kuznetsk	120.0
Karaganda	111.4
Cheremkhov	180.0
Kizel (Urals)	114.3

Source: *Voprosy ekonomiki*, 1950, No. 6, p. 33.

had not yet risen to the 1940 level.[57] During the years of the first postwar five year plan, the labor productivity rise in coal mining was 26 percent, under the Soviet method of calculation,[58] which means that at the beginning of 1946 productivity was something less than three-quarters of the 1940 level.

By the third quarter of 1949, the 1940 annual rate of output was said to have been reached in the Donbas,[59] though labor productivity remained below the 1940 level. The Rostov Trust in the Donbas reported in May, 1950, a rate of labor productivity equal to 90.8 percent of 1940, while Karaganda stood at 89.2 percent.[60] The Donbas mines were to reach the 1940 productivity level in March, 1951, according to plan.[61] If these two fields, one occupied during the war and the other not occupied, are assumed to represent the entire industry, the productivity index shown in Table 19 can be constructed for the postwar years. These data must be regarded as tentative in nature, for all that is actually known for certain is that 1950 productivity was below the 1940 level.[62]

Output per wage earner in U.S. bituminous-coal mining increased 38.5 percent from 1939 to 1950; the comparable increase in anthracite-coal mining was only 1.1 percent. The comparable figures for man-hour output are 24.4 percent and minus 12.8 percent.[63] If the two industries are weighted by 1950 output, the 1950 index for bituminous and anthracite combined is as follows: per annum, 135.5 percent; per man-hour, 121.4 percent. From these figures and the data in Table 19, the follow-

---

Comparing these relationships with those prevailing in 1936 (see Table 18), it appears that the productivity advantage of these fields over the Donbas diminished from 1936 to 1950, probably because of the more intensive exploitation of the eastern fields and depletion of the most accessible resources.

[57] *Voprosy ekonomiki,* 1951, No. 8, p. 47.

[58] *Trud,* December 30, 1951, p. 2.

[59] *Ibid.,* December 28, 1949, p. 1.

[60] *Voprosy ekonomiki,* 1951, No. 8, p. 47.

[61] *Trud,* June 21, 1952, p. 2.

[62] A productivity rise of 8 percent was claimed for 1951 and of only 4 percent for 1952. *Trud,* January 29, 1952, p. 1; *ibid.,* January 23, 1953, p. 1.

[63] U.S. Department of Labor, Bureau of Labor Statistics, *Productivity Trends in Selected Industries,* Bulletin No. 1046, p. 18; U.S. Department of Labor, Bureau of Labor Statistics, *Productivity Trends, Bituminous-Coal Mining,* (hereinafter cited as Bureau of Labor Statistics, *Bituminous-Coal Mining*). The divergence between output per annum and per man-hour is due to the increase in active days worked by mines since 1939.

TABLE 19

ESTIMATED INDEX OF LABOR PRODUCTIVITY IN SOVIET
COAL MINING, 1940–52
(1940 = 100)

END OF YEAR	INDEX
1940	100
1945	75[a]
1948	80[b]
1949	85[c]
1950	95[d]
1951	103[e]
1952	107[f]

[a] Based on the statement that productivity rose by 26 percent during the years of the postwar plan. See *Trud,* December 30, 1951, p. 2.

[b] Labor productivity rose by 6 percent during 1948. See *Trud,* May 12, 1949, p. 2. This figure was estimated by going back from 1949.

[c] Labor productivity rose by 12 percent during 1949. See *Voprosy ekonomiki,* 1951, No. 8, p. 47. Estimated by going back from 1950.

[d] Based on the assumption that as of May, 1950, the current rate of labor productivity in the Rostov Coal Trust and at Karaganda, 90 percent of that of 1940, represented the status of the entire coal industry. An additional 5 percent was added to represent half of the claimed productivity increase during 1950. See *Trud,* January 27, 1951, p. 1.

[e] Based on the reported productivity increase during 1951. See *Trud,* January 29, 1952, p. 1.

[f] Based on the reported productivity increase during 1952. See *Trud,* January 23, 1953, p. 1.

ing approximations of relative Soviet-U.S. productivity in 1950 may be derived (Russian productivity as a percentage of U.S. productivity):[64]

	PERCENTAGE
Output per man-year	30
Output per man-day	23

These figures must not be taken as anything more than very general approximations. They do, however, indicate one fact of which we may be fairly certain: that between 1939 and 1950, Russian coal mining labor productivity declined significantly as a percentage of the level in the United States.

[64] It is assumed that, for the Soviet Union, the index in Table 19 applies equally to man-year and man-hour productivity; and for the United States, that the published man-hour productivity index represents the trend in man-day productivity.

FACTORS BEHIND THE PRODUCTIVITY DIFFERENCES[65]

Resource conditions. Labor productivity in mining is greatly dependent on the character of the natural resource. Adverse resource conditions in a mine can be overcome in part by technology, but the initial handicap persists as compared with a more richly endowed mine. In general, the coal resources of the United States are more favorably situated, from the standpoint of the mechanics of mining them, than those of the Soviet Union. An exhaustive analysis of the subject cannot be undertaken here, but a few remarks on some of the salient differences are in order.[66]

Depth of mine cover is an important factor in coal mining. "For underground mining it is largely immaterial whether the cover is 150 or 350 feet. Between 350 and 600 feet consideration must be given to ample pillars, and between 600 and 1,000 feet proper roof control is imperative."[67] As mine shafts grow deeper, rock pressure, ventilation, hoisting, and pumping ground water become increasingly difficult problems. The average depth of cover of all underground bituminous mines in the United States was 321 feet in 1926;[68] this figure overstates the depth of shafts, since many mines can be tunneled horizontally into hillsides rather than vertically from the surface. In 1939, Donbas coal was mined at an average depth of about 1,400 feet. Some of the newer fields had shallower mines: 450 feet average at Kuznetsk, 200 to 300 feet at Karaganda.[69] But the overshadowing importance of the Donbas meant that for the industry as a whole, Russian resources were considerably less favorable than those of the United States in this respect.

"Ordinarily, thickness of seam ranks with character of roof as one of the most important resource conditions affecting unit labor requirements."[70] The average seam thickness of U.S. bituminous mines in 1920, the last date for which statistics are available, was about 5 feet.[71] The

---

[65] A good analysis of the relevant factors may be found in International Labor Office, Coal Mines Committee, Fourth Session, *Productivity in Coal Mines.*

[66] An excellent discussion of the relationship between coal resources and productivity may be found in WPA, *Bituminous-Coal Mining,* Vol. I, Chap. 3.

[67] *Ibid.,* p. 58.

[68] *Ibid.* There appears to have been little change since 1939 in this respect.

[69] *Voprosy ekonomiki,* 1950, No. 6, p. 32.

[70] WPA, *Bituminous-Coal Mining,* p. 59.

[71] *Ibid.,* p. 62.

figure for the Donbas before the war was 3 feet; for the Kuznetsk Basin, 12 feet; and for Karaganda, 7 feet.[72] In this respect, the Russian industry does not appear to be badly endowed, though the Donbas was clearly on the low side in comparison with the United States.

Among other resource factors that have been cited as favoring U.S. productivity are a greater pitch of seam in the United States, permitting to a greater extent the use of gravity in the delivery of coal[73] and better roofing, ventilation, and floor and water conditions.[74] The last group of factors is related to depth of cover.

/Technology. The relationship between resources and technology has been summarized aptly as follows:

> . . . in the main, conditions surrounding coal resources in their natural state exert an influence upon labor output that is relative to several other factors. Mining technology had advanced to a point at which low output resulting from adverse physical factors can be raised materially by the use of suitable machinery. When installation of machinery is accompanied by other favorable elements, including a high degree of managerial skill, its effects on output are greatly enhanced, but whatever the results obtained, their ultimate limits are determined by the resource conditions under which all the other factors operate.[75]

Soviet planners have given high priority to advancing the technology of coal mining; particularly since the war, but during the prewar plans as well, coal mining was favored with a relatively high rate of capital investment.[76] Even before the war, the Russians alleged that the cutting of coal was highly mechanized. The data in Table 20 indicate the means used to cut coal in December, 1936. These figures purport to indicate

[72] *Voprosy ekonomiki,* 1950, No. 6, p. 33.

[73] The few available facts do not bear out this assertion. It has been stated by an authoritative U.S. source that in the United States, "utilization of gravity is possible only to a limited extent in bituminous mining, whereas in anthracite and in metal mining it is not an uncommon practice." WPA, *Bituminous-Coal Mining,* p. 70. On the other hand, we are told that in the Donbas in 1940, 29.5 percent of the coal produced was delivered by its own weight; in the Kuzbas, 40.7 percent; in the Urals, 54.2 percent. See *Voprosy ekonomiki,* 1950, No. 6, p. 33. It would seem from this that the USSR enjoyed an advantage over the United States. However, excessive pitch of seam may constitute a productivity disadvantage, adding to the burden of underground hauling.

[74] Duzh, *op. cit.,* p. 134.

[75] WPA, *Bituminous-Coal Mining,* p. 57.

[76] See Norman Kaplan, "Capital Formation and Allocation," in Abram Bergson (ed.), *Soviet Economic Growth,* p. 66.

TABLE 20

MECHANIZATION OF CUTTING OPERATIONS IN SOVIET
COAL MINING, DECEMBER, 1936
(*In percentage of total coal mined*)

TYPE OF MACHINERY	USSR	DONBAS	KUZNETSK BASIN	MOSCOW BASIN	URALS	KARAGANDA
Heavy cutting machines	42.5	57.4	13.0	10.5	26.3	49.2
Light cutting machines	0.8	0.2	0.1	0.4	4.2	0.3
Pick hammers (pneumatic)	15.6	14.8	10.2	38.6	38.7	......
Electric drills	19.9	4.7	66.5	19.8	9.7	28.4
Without cutting (blasting)	6.2	7.8	2.5	0.8	18.3	6.9
Hand	15.0	15.1	7.7	29.9	2.8	15.2
Total	100.0	100.0	100.0	100.0	100.0	100.0

Source: *Gornyi zhurnal*, 1937, No. 17, p. 34.

85.0 percent mechanization at that time, with subsequent advances to 89.5 percent in 1937, 94.8 percent in 1940, and 98.1 percent in 1949.[77] In the United States, 87.9 percent of bituminous coal was mechanically cut in 1939[78] and over 90 percent since 1943.[79]

The Russian data, however, are not directly comparable with the American. It will be seen from Table 20 that the Russian mechanization total is secured by adding cutting, drilling, and shooting from the solid (blasting), whereas, in the United States, the percentage mechanically cut is the ratio of coal cut by mechanical means to total coal mined by cutting, drilling being regarded as a separate and nonadditive process and shooting from the solid as a nonmechanized process.[80] Measured according to U.S. concepts, the Soviet mechanization percentage prior to the war would undoubtedly have been lower than the American.[81]

The greater use of the pneumatic hammer in the Soviet Union has

[77] A. I. Pashkov, *Voprosy sotsialisticheskoi ekonomiki*, p. 55.
[78] Barger and Schurr, *op. cit.*, p. 174.
[79] Bureau of Labor Statistics, *Bituminous-Coal Mining*, p. 2.
[80] WPA, *Bituminous-Coal Mining*, pp. 13–24.
[81] This applies to American bituminous coal only. The mechanical cutter is rarely employed in U.S. anthracite mines because of the nature of the resources. In 1939, only 4.4 percent of U.S. anthracite was cut by machine. See Barger and Schurr, *op. cit.*, p. 185.

been attributed to the presence of sloping and faulty seams, the lack of heavy cutting machines suitable for such seams, and the unavailability of electric pick hammers.[82] Russian engineers have indicated a distinct preference for the cutting machine whenever available.

One of the most labor-consuming processes in coal mining is the underground loading of coal into mine cars. In 1939, about 70 percent of all bituminous coal mined in the United States was loaded by hand, accounting for more than half the total volume of employment in bituminous mining.[83] Since then there has been a virtual technological revolution, for in 1950, 69 percent of all bituminous coal mined was mechanically loaded, explaining a large part of the productivity advance from 1939 to 1950.[84]

In 1938, underground loading was said to have been mechanized to the extent of 24 percent in the Donbas, 50 percent in Kuznetsk, but not at all in Moscow.[85] In 1946–47 this operation was regarded as being in a "rudimentary" state of mechanization generally,[86] though it reached 40 percent in some trusts of the Donbas by 1950.[87] Though no precise Soviet mechanization percentage can be derived, two conclusions may be drawn: that in 1939 the productivity advantage of the United States in this respect was not great, owing to its own lack of mechanization, but that by 1950 the United States had pulled far ahead of the Soviet Union. This factor played a major role in widening the productivity gap between the two countries during the decade.

Russian statistics indicate that other mining operations have been fairly well mechanized. Underground transportation advanced from 59.6 percent in 1941 to 95.5 percent in 1949, while the percentage of coal mechanically loaded on the surface rose from 91 percent to 98.6 percent.[88] In the United States, "mechanical power has now [1939] superseded animal power for mainline haulage in all but the very small mines, and motorized gathering haulage is rapidly advancing."[89]

[82] *Gornyi zhurnal,* 1937, No. 17, pp. 34–35.

[83] WPA, *Bituminous-Coal Mining,* p. 2.

[84] Bureau of Labor Statistics, *Bituminous-Coal Mining,* p. 2.

[85] *Planovoe khoziaistvo,* 1940, No. 3, p. 60.

[86] *Ibid.,* 1950, No. 2, p. 16. In 1951, the average for the Donbas was put at 25 percent. *Ibid.,* 1951, No. 2, p. 52.

[87] *Ibid.,* 1950, No. 2, p. 36.

[88] Pashkov, *op. cit.,* p. 55.

[89] WPA, *Bituminous-Coal Mining,* p. 29.

✓ *Organization.* The Soviet authorities themselves have repeatedly called attention to organizational deficiencies as a factor in low relative productivity. Table 21, which comes from a study by a Russian mining

---

TABLE 21

COMPARISON OF LABOR FORCE IN A MINE OF THE PITTSBURGH COAL COMPANY IN PENNSYLVANIA AND THE LENIN MINE OF THE KIZEL TRUST IN THE USSR, FOR AN UNSPECIFIED PREWAR YEAR

	PERCENTAGE OF TOTAL LABOR FORCE	
OPERATION	USSR	United States
Cutting, loading, blasting, timbering	27.2	49.6
Underground transport	13.8	17.5
Machinery servicing	11.0	4.8
Draining	2.3	1.2
Ventilation and safety	4.1	5.1
Repair, cleaning, etc.	6.7	4.3
Hoisting, surface loading	4.8	6.2
All other surface work, including office staff	30.1	11.3
	100.0	100.0

Source: *Industriia,* July 18, 1940, p. 2.

---

engineer who had worked in the United States, and which compares the occupational distribution of a Soviet mine with that of an American mine of comparable size, presents one facet of poor Soviet organization. In this, as in similar comparisons, the Russian staff is smaller at the face and larger in overhead. The author of the comparisons indicated that there were 165 administrative and technical personnel in the Russian mine compared with 15 in the U.S. mine, and that there were 8 office workers in the U.S. mine compared with 67 employed by the Russian mine.

The following comparison from another source for the year 1940, for the entire industry, makes the same point:[90]

[90] *Ugol',* March, 1940, p. 3. For a similar comparison, see *Planovoe khoziaistvo,* 1938, No. 2, p. 71. A British miner on a visit to a mine at Tula (Moscow fields) in 1950 had this to say: "The output of coal from the mine was approximately 1,500 tons per day, two shifts. There were 1,000 employees, including non-producers. The output per man-shift was therefore 1½ tons per man. This figure was pretty low bearing in mind the seam's thickness, its depth from the surface and the fact that the pit was free from gas.

PERCENTAGE OF TOTAL WAGE EARNERS

	USSR	United States
Face workers	36	63
Other underground workers	41	23
Surface workers	23	14
	100	100

Among other organizational lacks that have been cited are high labor turnover,[91] excessive specialization and insufficient versatility among repair personnel, and lack of coordination among the factors of production.[92]

The small output per man-shift was due to the large number of employees other than actual producers or miners at the coal face." Report of the British Workers' Delegation, *Russia with Our Own Eyes,* pp. 67–68.

[91] Labor turnover reached fantastic heights during the early thirties. In 1933, for example, for every 100 payroll wage earners during the year, 129.2 miners were hired and 120.7 left their jobs. See *Trud v SSSR,* 1935, pp. 136–37. Turnover was subsequently reduced considerably, but even after the war there were numerous press accounts of excessive turnover, particularly among younger workers.

[92] *Ugol',* January, 1941, p. 9.

VI

IRON ORE MINING

THE PRODUCT

THE output of iron ore in the Soviet Union from 1928 to 1940 is shown in Table 22. No adjustment will be attempted for differences in quality between the ore produced in the United States and that produced in

TABLE 22

IRON ORE PRODUCTION IN THE SOVIET UNION, 1928–40

YEAR	OUTPUT (THOUSANDS OF METRIC TONS)
1928	6,133.0[a]
1929	7,997.1
1930	10,663.4
1931	10,591.3
1932	12,085.7
1933	14,454.5
1934	21,508.8
1935	27,078.0
1936	27,762.9
1937	27,770.0
1938	26,529.7[b]
1939	27,400.0[c]
1940	29,800.0[c]

[a] Data for the year 1928–37 from S. I. Shul'kin, "Proizvoditel'nost' truda v zhele-zorudnoi promyshlennosti SSSR", in Akademiia Nauk, Institut Ekonomiki, *Proizvoditel'nost' truda v promyshlennosti SSSR*, p. 92. These figures were taken from *Sotsialisticheskoe stroitel'stvo SSSR*, 1936, p. 152, for the years for which the data are given in the latter source.

[b] *Sotsialisticheskoe stroitel'stvo SSSR*, 1939, p. 55. Marked "preliminary" in the source.

[c] Demitri B. Shimkin, *Minerals—A Key to Soviet Power*, pp. 43–44.

Russia. However, to the extent that ore of poor quality requires some form of beneficiation,[1] there is an effect upon productivity, since bene-

[1] For a description of the beneficiating process, see Harold Barger and Sam H. Schurr, *The Mining Industries, 1899–1939*, pp. 148–49.

ficiation performed at the mine is part of the mining industry.[2] In the United States, 17.2 percent of the ore produced in 1939 was beneficiated before shipping,[3] while a comparable figure for the Soviet Union in 1940 has been estimated at 18 percent.[4]

Output statistics also indicate a roughly comparable proportion of beneficiating activity in the two countries before World War II. Production statistics for the United States are available for both "crude" and "merchantable" ore, the latter figure reflecting the shrinkage of tonnage for that portion of the ore subjected to beneficiation. The U.S. ratio of merchantable to crude ore in 1939 was 90.2 percent.[5] A comparable Soviet ratio between merchantable (*gotovaia*) and crude (*syraia*) iron ore may be estimated at 90 percent for the year 1940.[6]

Of greater importance for the purpose of measuring productivity is the distinction between open cut and underground mining. In the first, the ore is removed from open diggings by power shovels, without any need for subterranean tunneling. This is feasible only when the ore is near the surface, for if the overburden of earth and rock is too thick, it becomes cheaper to resort to underground mining. "The average output of merchantable ore per man-hour at open-pit operations during the 23 years from 1915 to 1937 [in the United States] for which data are available was 1.32 gross tons as compared with 0.44 gross tons for underground mines."[7] That is, productivity in open cut mining was three times as great as in underground mining.

[2] For the United States, the Census stated: ". . . the iron-ore industry embraces mines and beneficiating plants at mines producing ores valued chiefly for their iron content." U.S. Census, *Mineral Industries*, 1939, I, 320. For Russia, the evidence that ore beneficiation was treated as part of mining is indirect. For example, statistics of iron and steel manufacture specifically exclude iron ore departments of integrated enterprises. See *Sotsialisticheskoe stroitel'stvo SSSR*, 1936, p. 7. The technical journal for the mining industry, *Gornyi zhurnal*, regularly carried a section on ore beneficiation.

[3] Barger and Schurr, *op. cit.*, p. 215. This excludes ore that was subjected merely to crushing and screening.

[4] Demitri B. Shimkin, *Minerals—A Key to Soviet Power*, p. 44.

[5] *Minerals Yearbook*, 1940, p. 551.

[6] *Stal'*, 1947, No. 11, p. 974, and Shimkin, *op. cit.*, p. 44. It is assumed that the data in Table 22 represent output of merchantable ore. This seems likely from the relative magnitudes of merchantable and crude ore in 1940, 29.8 versus 33 million tons. The former figure, specifically labeled merchantable ore, represents a more plausible extension of the earlier series than does the latter.

[7] Works Progress Administration, National Research Project, *Technology, Employment and Output per Man in Iron Mining*, pp. 14–15.

The proportion of U.S. ore mined by each of these methods has been subject to considerable year to year fluctuation.[8] Open cut mining reached a high of 65.8 percent in 1937, fell to 48.9 percent the following year, and rose again to 63.3 percent in 1939.[9] Because of the close relationship between the open cut mining percentage and productivity, the latter was rather volatile from year to year, though the long-run trend has been upward.

No precise statistics on the extent of open cut mining in the Soviet Union are available. However, an estimate may be secured on the basis of scattered material. The geographical distribution of iron ore in the Soviet Union in 1937 and 1941 appears in Table 23. The pre-

TABLE 23

GEOGRAPHICAL DISTRIBUTION OF SOVIET IRON ORE OUTPUT, 1937 AND 1941

FIELD	1937[a]	1941[b]
Krivoi Rog	59.0	54.1
Magnitogorsk	23.9	22.5
Kerch	2.8	5.5
Kushvinsk and Nizhne Tagil	4.5	7.2
Tula	2.4	1.8
Lipetsk	2.5	1.4
Bakal	1.9	1.8
Telbes	1.8	2.0
Other	1.2	3.7
	100.0	100.0

[a] Harry Schwartz, *Russia's Soviet Economy*, p. 20. The source combines the data for Magnitogorsk and Bakal. Separate figures were estimated on the basis of the relative shares of the two fields in 1940.

[b] Gosudarstvennyi Nauchnyi Institut, *Bolshaia sovetskaia entsiklopediia*, p. 250.

dominant source of iron ore in the prewar period was Krivoi Rog, accounting for 59 percent and 54 percent of total output in 1937 and 1941, respectively. It was reported of this field that by 1934 the remaining ore deposits were too deep for open cut mining, and underground mining prevailed to the extent of 97 percent of the total output of the

[8] For discussion of the reasons for the fluctuation, see *ibid.*, Chap. 4.
[9] *Ibid.*, p. 218; *Minerals Yearbook*, 1940, p. 528.

field.[10] The other major iron mining area, that at Magnitogorsk, has been termed a "classic example" of open cut mining,[11] and it may be presumed that in 1937 its entire output, amounting to about 24 percent of total national production, was mined in this manner. The only other mines in which open cut mining appears to have been employed were those at Bakal and in the Kushvinsk-Nizhne Tagil group.[12] If the entire output of these groups is credited to open cut mining, the percentage for 1937 is increased to 30 percent of the national production.[13]

The output of merchantable iron ore in the United States in 1939 was 51,721,000 gross tons, or 52,594,000 metric tons.

THE LABOR FORCE

Table 24 contains the available statistics on the labor force in Soviet iron mining from 1928 to 1937. The several series for wage earners are not greatly divergent. The precise character of the series in column (5) is not known. However, the fact that for the years 1932 to 1935 it was fairly close to the "labor section" series permits us to use it with some confidence.[14]

The problem of wage earners engaged in operating mines (*po eksploatatsii*), which caused so much difficulty in the case of coal mining, does not appear to be a major one for iron mining. Even if this distinction were made in iron mining, the sources of the data in columns (3) and (4) of Table 24 would indicate that all wage earners were covered, which would presumably be true as well for the series in column (5), on the basis of relative magnitudes. In the United States, the operating labor force comprised 98.4 percent of the total labor force in 1939.[15]

It should be noted that the 1937 figure appearing in column (5) of Table 24 can be approximated by recourse to productivity data for individual mining areas (see Table 25).

[10] S. I. Shul'kin, "Proizvoditel'nost' truda v zhelezorudnoi promyshlennosti SSSR," in Akademiia Nauk, Institut Ekonomiki, *Proizvoditel'nost' truda v promyshlennosti SSSR*, p. 93.

[11] *Gornyi zhurnal*, 1936, No. 4, p. 6.

[12] *Ibid.*

[13] A somewhat more elaborate estimate yielded a figure of 32 percent for open cut mining in 1937. See Nicholas W. Rodin, *Productivity in Soviet Iron Mining*, p. 17.

[14] The sharp drop in wage earner employment shown for 1937 is supported by an estimate of 31.4 thousand wage earners as of July 1, 1936. *Zhenshchina v SSSR*, p. 62.

[15] U.S. Census, *Mineral Industries*, 1939, I, 324.

To the number of wage earners in 1937, 30.7 thousand, learners and junior service personnel must be added. Using the relative proportions of these groups on January 1, 1936,[16] the appropriate Soviet labor force for 1937 becomes 34.0 thousand.

TABLE 24

EMPLOYMENT IN SOVIET IRON ORE MINING, 1928–37

(In thousands of persons)

YEAR	(1) TOTAL EM- PLOYMENT JANUARY 1[a]	(2) WAGE EARNERS JANUARY 1 (LABOR SECTION)[b]	(3) AVERAGE ANNUAL NUMBER OF WAGE EARNERS (LABOR SECTION)[c]	(4) AVERAGE ANNUAL NUMBER OF WAGE EARNERS (INDUSTRY SECTION)	(5) AVERAGE ANNUAL NUMBER OF WAGE EARNERS[e]
1928	25.3	21.7	24.1	20.2[d]	21.6
1929	30.8	26.2	n.a.[f]	n.a.	22.9
1930	41.1	34.8	n.a.	n.a.	25.9
1931	42.9	34.0	n.a.	n.a.	31.6
1932	60.8	45.9	36.6	32.1[d]	34.2
1933	50.2	35.3	35.5	33.4[d]	35.8
1934	51.1	39.9	40.5	38.8[d]	41.7
1935	51.7	41.6	38.7	n.a.	41.1
1936	48.3	38.6	n.a.	n.a.	32.8
1937	n.a.	n.a.	n.a.	n.a.	30.7

[a] *Trud v SSSR*, 1936, p. 120.

[b] *Trud v SSSR*, 1936, p. 120, less the number of learners in *Sotsialisticheskoe stroitel'-stvo SSSR*, 1936, p. 516.

[c] *Trud v SSSR*, 1935, p. 62; *Trud v SSSR*, 1936, p. 121.

[d] *Sotsialisticheskoe stroitel'stvo SSSR*, 1936, p. 4.

[e] S. I. Shul'kin, "Proizvoditel'nost' truda v zhelezorudnoi promyshlennosti SSSR," in Akademiia Nauk, Institut Ekonomiki, *Proizvoditel'nost' truda v promyshlennosti SSSR*, p. 92.

[f] n.a. = information not available.

For reasons indicated in the chapter on "Coal Mining," the appropriate U.S. labor force is that reported for 1939 by the Bureau of Mines, i.e., 21,859.[17]

COMPARATIVE PRODUCTIVITY

The foregoing data on output and employment may be summarized as follows:

[16] *Trud v SSSR*, 1936, p. 122.
[17] *Minerals Yearbook*, 1940, p. 551. The Census figure for the same year is 20,137.

	RUSSIA, 1937	UNITED STATES, 1939
Output of iron ore (thousands of metric tons)	27,770	52,594
Number of wage earners	34,000	21,859
Annual output per wage earner (metric tons)	817	2,406
Russian productivity as a percentage of U.S. productivity	34	100

Separate estimates may be made for open cut and underground mining:

OPEN CUT MINING	RUSSIA, 1937	UNITED STATES, 1939
Output of iron ore (thousands of metric tons)	8,331[18]	33,266[19]
Number of wage earners	2,670[20]	5,800[21]
Average annual output per wage earner (metric tons)	3,120	5,734
Russian productivity as a percentage of U.S. productivity	54	100

UNDERGROUND MINING		
Output of iron ore (thousands of metric tons)	19,439[22]	19,328
Number of wage earners	31,330[22]	16,059
Average annual output per wage earner (metric tons)	620	1,204
Russian productivity as a percentage of U.S. productivity	51	100

The separate relative levels of Russian productivity in open pit and underground mining were considerably higher than the level for the entire industry. The reason for this, of course, was higher productivity in open cut mining combined with a larger proportion of this type of mining in the United States.

The only available Soviet comparison of Soviet-U.S. productivity in the industry is for 1937, when Soviet productivity was estimated at 26 percent of the U.S. level.[23] Actually, this figure reflects an error by the Russian statistician responsible for the estimate;[24] correction for this error would raise the Soviet figure to 32 percent of the U.S. level. Allowing for U.S. productivity changes from 1937 to 1939 and for differences in labor force concepts, this figure can be reconciled with the above estimate.

[18] Estimated on the basis of 30 percent of total output. See *supra,* p. 90.

[19] *Minerals Yearbook,* 1940, p. 528.

[20] Output per wage earner at Magnitogorsk was 3,460 tons in 1937. Shul'kin, *op. cit.,* p. 94. Assuming this to be representative of all open cut mining, the number of wage earners engaged in this branch of the industry in 1937 may be estimated at 2,410. Adding learners and junior service personnel, the figure of 2,670 is obtained.

[21] Estimated from the ratio of man-shifts worked on active days in open cut and underground mining. See U.S. Census, *Mineral Industries,* 1939, I, 320.

[22] Estimated as the residual between total and open cut mining.

TABLE 25

EMPLOYMENT OF WAGE EARNERS IN SOVIET IRON MINING,
BY FIELD, 1937

FIELD	OUTPUT (THOUSANDS OF TONS)	AVERAGE ANNUAL OUTPUT PER WAGE EARNER[f] (TONS)	ESTIMATED AVERAGE ANNUAL NUMBER OF WAGE EARNERS
Krivoi Rog	16,414[a]	971	16,900[h]
Magnitogorsk	6,665[b]	3,460	1,900
Other Ural mines	1,750[c]	341	5,100
Central region	1,361[d]	460	3,000
Other mines	1,580[e]	341[g]	4,600
Total	27,770		31,500

[a] *Gornyi zhurnal,* 1939, No. 12, p. 28.

[b] Estimated from Table 23.

[c] Estimated from Table 23. Includes Kushvinsk-Nizhne Tagil and Bakal mines.

[d] Estimated from Table 23. Includes Tula and Lipetsk mines.

[e] Residual figure.

[f] S. I. Shul'kin, "Proizvoditel'nost' truda v zhelezorudnoi promyshlennosti SSSR," in Akademiia Nauk, Institut Ekonomiki, *Proizvoditel'nost' truda v promyshlennosti SSSR,* p. 92.

[g] Assumed to be equal to productivity in the Ural mines.

[h] This figure is confirmed by a statement in Shul'kin, *op. cit.,* p. 98.

CHANGES IN SOVIET PRODUCTIVITY, 1928 TO 1937

The trend of labor productivity in Soviet iron mining from 1928 to 1937 is indicated in Table 26. Part of the increase may be attributed to the growing significance of open cut mining, but since even in 1937 this form of mining accounted for only 30 percent of the total product, the major portion of the productivity increase must be attributed to other factors.

Capital investment was undoubtedly a major element. The Ural mines, particularly those at Magnitogorsk, were accorded preference in this respect. For example, in 1933, when the Ural mines were contributing 28 percent of the total ore output, their share of the industry's

[23] Shul'kin, *op. cit.,* p. 98.

[24] It is stated in the Russian source that the U.S. wage earner figure for 1937 was not available and that therefore an estimate was made. The Russian statistician failed to recognize that the Bureau of Mines employment figure comprised only wage earners, not total employment, and he therefore reduced it by his own estimate of the number of administrative and clerical personnel.

TABLE 26

INDEXES OF LABOR PRODUCTIVITY IN SOVIET IRON MINING, 1928–37

(1928 = 100)

YEAR	OUTPUT PER WAGE EARNER (TONS)[a]	OUTPUT PER WAGE EARNER (RUBLES)[b]
1928	100.0	100.0
1929	123.0	114.7
1930	145.0	136.5
1931	118.0	123.7
1932	124.5	149.3
1933	142.2	166.8
1934	181.7	200.7
1935	232.1	253.9
1936	298.1	n.a.[c]
1937	318.6	n.a.

[a] S. I. Shul'kin, "Proizvoditel'nost' truda v zhelezorudnoi promyshlennosti SSSR," in Akademiia Nauk, Institut Ekonomiki, *Proizvoditel'nost' truda v promyshlennosti SSSR*, p. 92.

[b] *Trud v SSSR*, 1936, p. 120.

[c] n.a. = information not available.

investment total was 42 percent.[25] Partly in consequence of this policy, output per wage earner at Magnitogorsk rose by 327 percent from 1932 to 1937, compared with 87 percent at Krivoi Rog.[26]

PRODUCTIVITY TRENDS SINCE THE WAR

The Krivoi Rog mines were heavily damaged during the German occupation. It was reported that all superstructures were completely demolished and that the mouths of shafts were dynamited. Nevertheless, the assertion was made that as a consequence of greater mechanization effected in reconstruction, average productivity of mine face workers in October, 1948, exceeded the 1940 level by 3 percent.[27] In July, 1947, face work was said to be 10 percent more productive than in 1940, while

[25] *Gornyi zhurnal*, 1934, No. 1, p. 9.

[26] Shul'kin, *op. cit.*, p. 94. The fact that the mines at Krivoi Rog had been worked for many years while those at Magnitogorsk were just being developed must also be recalled in this connection.

[27] *Gornyi zhurnal*, 1949, No. 5, p. 3.

the 1940 productivity level for the entire labor force was exceeded by an unspecified amount, despite dilution of the labor force with young, untrained workers.[28]

No statistics have been released for other mining areas, so that it is difficult to judge postwar productivity trends for the industry as a whole. If it is assumed that Krivoi Rog actually attained the prewar productivity level by 1950, then it is quite likely that the prewar level of productivity was exceeded for the entire industry, with the qualification that the depletion of the easily available ores at Magnitogorsk, requiring more costly stripping investment, may have retarded the growth of productivity.

In the United States, the annual output per wage earner of merchantable ore rose by 24.7 percent from 1939 to 1950.[29] Therefore, even if one allows for a substantial productivity increase in the Russian industry from 1937 to 1939, say of the order of twice the increase from 1936 to 1937, i.e., of 14 percent,[30] output per worker in Russia would have had to rise about 25 percent from 1939 to 1950 merely to maintain the 1939 Soviet-U.S. productivity relationship.

[28] *Gornyi zhurnal,* 1950, No. 1, p. 6.

[29] U.S. Department of Labor, Bureau of Labor Statistics, *Productivity Trends in Selected Industries,* Bulletin No. 1046, p. 23.

[30] It might be argued that this is too small an allowance, in view of the greater percentage increases in earlier years. However, the share of the high productivity Magnitogorsk mines in total output changed very little from 1937 to 1939, whereas it was increasing substantially prior to 1937.

VII

CRUDE OIL AND NATURAL GAS[1]

THE PRODUCT

STATISTICS on the output of crude oil and natural gas in the Soviet Union are presented in Table 27.[2] The ratio of natural gas to crude oil output has been in the past, and probably remains, much lower than in the United States, which fact is attributed to Russian lack of pipe and pumping equipment for marketing the gas.[3] Since the marginal labor cost required to utilize the natural gas produced in conjunction with crude oil (casing-head gas) is low, the relative level of Soviet labor productivity is lower when measured in terms of the production of both crude oil and gas than in terms of crude oil alone.

Crude oil output in the United States in 1939 was 1,228 million barrels,[4] which may be expressed as 166 million metric tons at the rate of 7.4 barrels per metric ton.[5] The 1939 output of natural gas in the United States was 2,929,185 million cubic feet, of which 2,287,413 million cubic feet, or 78 percent, was marketed, and the balance was either used

[1] This chapter is confined to that part of the industry concerned with the drilling of wells and the extraction of crude oil and gas. It does not include the transportation, refining, or marketing of petroleum products.

[2] That portion of the petroleum industry with which we are concerned is customarily treated as a mining rather than a manufacturing industry, and consists in the production of crude oil, natural gas, and natural gasoline. Both in the Soviet Union and in the United States, employment data for the first two products are combined because of the difficulty of segregating labor inputs with respect to oil and gas produced jointly. However, the production of natural gasoline, which is extracted from natural gas, is treated as a separate mining industry in the United States but as a manufacturing industry in the Soviet Union. Since employment data are not available for the latter, the output data are here restricted to include only oil and gas.

[3] Demitri B. Shimkin, *Minerals—A Key to Soviet Power*, p. 203. One of the goals of the current five year plan is an 80 percent increase in the production of natural gas and natural gasoline by 1953 over that of 1950, compared with a less than proportional increase in crude oil production of 85 percent by 1955 as compared with 1950. See the New York *Times*, August 23, 1952, p. 6.

[4] U.S. Census, *Mineral Industries*, 1939, I, 136. The Bureau of Mines output figure for the same year was 1,265 million barrels.

[5] American Petroleum Institute, *Petroleum Facts and Figures*, 1947, p. 202.

TABLE 27

PRODUCTION OF CRUDE OIL AND NATURAL GAS IN THE
SOVIET UNION, 1928–52
(*In millions of metric tons*)

YEAR	CRUDE OIL[a]	NATURAL GAS[b]
1928	11.6[c]	0.3[c]
1929	13.7[c]	0.3[c]
1930	17.3[c]	0.4[c]
1931	22.4[d]	0.8[d]
1932	21.4[d]	0.9[d]
1933	21.4[d]	1.1[d]
1934	24.2[d]	1.4[d]
1935	25.1[d]	1.7[d]
1936	27.4[d]	1.8[d]
1937	28.4[e]	2.0[k]
1938	30.1[e]	2.1[f]
1939	n.a.[o]	n.a.
1940	31.0[g]	2.3[h]
1945	21.4[j]	n.a.
1946	22.6[j]	1.7[k]
1947	26.8[j]	2.1[k]
1948	30.5[j]	2.3[k]
1949	33.2[j]	2.4[k]
1950	37.8[l]	2.6[k]
1951	41.0[m]	n.a.
1952	47.0[n]	n.a.

[a] The U.S. Bureau of Mines currently converts Soviet crude oil from metric tons into barrels at the rate of 7.266 barrels per ton, compared with a rate of 7.274 barrels per metric ton for United States oil. See American Petroleum Institute, *Petroleum Facts and Figures,* 1950, p. 464. The 1939 U.S. rate was 7.4 barrels per metric ton.

[b] Russian natural gas output data are presented in Soviet statistics in oil tonnage equivalents, the conversion having been said to have been made at "approximately" 1,200 cubic meters per metric ton. See Heinrich Hassman, *Erdöl in der Sowjetunion,* p. 84. This is close to the 1,240 cubic meter conversion rate employed for U.S. natural gas (see *infra,* p. 98, *n* 8). Up to and including 1938, the natural gas tonnage data have been derived directly from Russian sources. For subsequent years, the tonnage figures have been converted at the U.S. rate of 1,240 cubic meters per metric ton.

[c] *Problemy ekonomiki,* 1937, Nos. 3–4, p. 154. These data are for the economic year October 1 to September 30.

[d] *Ibid.*

[e] *Neftianoe khoziaistvo,* 1939, No. 3, p. 8.

[f] Calculated by subtracting from the total of crude oil and natural gas production as given in *Sotsialisticheskoe stroitel'stvo SSSR,* 1939, p. 56, the crude oil output derived from another source. Hassman, *op. cit.,* p. 84, gives a figure of 1.67 million tons of natural gas for this year, but no source is cited.

[g] Gosudarstvennyi Nauchnyi Institut, *Bolshaia sovetskaia enksiklopediia,* 1948, p. 811.

---

[h] Hassman, *op. cit.,* p. 84. Demitri B. Shimkin, *Minerals—A Key to Soviet Power,* p. 198, cites a figure of 2 billion cubic meters for this year (the figure in the table converts to 2.9 billion cubic meters), but in the light of the gas produced in earlier years, his estimate appears low.

[j] Hassman, *op. cit.,* p. 173. Shimkin, *op. cit.,* p. 202, estimates somewhat lower figures for these years.

[k] Shimkin, *op. cit.,* pp. 198, 202.

[l] Report on fulfillment of the Fourth Five Year Plan in *Trud,* April 17, 1951, p. 1.

[m] New York *Times,* January 3, 1952, p. 53.

[n] *Ibid.,* August 10, 1953, p. 7.

[o] n.a. = information not available.

---

for repressuring or wasted. It is probable that Soviet natural gas production data include not only that portion utilized commercially (marketed) but also that portion used for repressuring oil wells. However, the amount used for the latter purpose does not appear to have been large,[6] and the error involved in equating to total Russian gas production the amount marketed in the United States is probably minor.[7] At a conversion rate of 1,240 cubic meters per metric ton (or 44,140 cubic feet per metric ton),[8] the 1939 U.S. marketed output of natural gas was 51.8 million metric tons.

In 1938, 73.5 percent of all Soviet oil was produced in Azerbaidjan, mainly at Baku, the Grozny and Maikop fields providing an additional 8.8 percent and 7.2 percent respectively.[9] It is estimated that Baku's share of the total declined to 56.5 percent by 1947, Grozny's was 8 percent, and Maikop was only barely coming into production after recon-

[6] Shimkin, *op. cit.,* p. 203.

[7] This assumes that the Russians did not include gas wasted in their production figures, a plausible hypothesis in view of the relatively small amount of production reported.

[8] To be quite literal, physical units of crude oil and natural gas cannot be equated, and any conversion ratio must be arbitrary. The use of heat value equivalents appears to be the most logical means of equation. For 1939, the U.S. Bureau of Mines assigned the following heat values to crude oil and natural gas: oil—6 million Btu per barrel; gas—1,075 Btu per cubic foot. See *Minerals Yearbook,* 1940, p. 789. In Works Progress Administration, *Technology, Employment and Output per Man in Petroleum and Natural-Gas Production* (hereinafter referred to as WPA, *Petroleum and Natural-Gas Production*), p. 331, the latter figure is reduced to 1,000 Btu per cubic foot to allow for the heat value of natural gas extracted. On this basis, the WPA gas to oil conversion ratio is 1,240 cubic meters per metric ton, which is close to what the Russians were using in their statistics (see Table 27, footnote *b*).

[9] *Neftianoe khoziaistvo,* 1939, Nos. 4–5, p. 15.

struction of war damage.[10] The so-called Second Baku, a large area in the eastern part of European Russia, had emerged by the latter year as a major producer.[11]

THE LABOR FORCE

Such statistics as are available concerning employment in Soviet oil production are presented in Table 28. It seems probable that the industry section statistics, in view of their magnitude, exclude employment in the

TABLE 28

EMPLOYMENT IN SOVIET CRUDE OIL PRODUCTION, 1928 TO 1938
(*In thousands of persons*)

YEAR	TOTAL EMPLOYMENT, JANUARY 1[a]	NUMBER OF WAGE EARNERS AND LEARNERS, JANUARY 1[a]	AVERAGE ANNUAL NUMBER OF WAGE EARNERS (LABOR SECTION DATA)	AVERAGE ANNUAL NUMBER OF WAGE EARNERS (INDUSTRY SECTION DATA)[g]
1928	43.4	35.6	31.9[b]	24.3
1929	38.8	32.6	n.a.	24.5
1930	38.6	32.3	n.a.	25.5
1931	49.5	41.5	39.7[c]	28.7
1932	54.0	44.1	42.3[d]	21.0
1933	60.3	46.8	39.2[e]	25.2
1934	57.3	46.9	47.7[e]	26.5
1935	62.6	50.2	43.3[d]	n.a.
1936	58.0	45.2	n.a.	n.a.
1937	n.a.[h]	n.a.	n.a.	n.a.
1938	n.a.	n.a.	43.3[f]	n.a.

[a] *Trud v SSSR*, 1936, p. 114.

[b] *Ibid.*, p. 115. This figure is net of an estimated 2 thousand learners.

[c] *Sotsialisticheskoe stroitel'stvo SSSR*, 1934, p. 325.

[d] *Trud v SSSR*, 1936, p. 115.

[e] *Ibid.*, 1935, p. 62.

[f] Output of oil and gas per wage earner in well drilling and production was 744 tons in 1938. See N. Nikolayevski, "Proizvoditel'nost' truda v neftiannoi promyshlennosti SSSR," in Akademiia Nauk, Institut Ekonomiki, *Proizvoditel'nost' truda v promyshlennosti SSSR*, p. 168. This figure applied to total output yields the 1938 labor force.

[g] *Sotsialisticheskoe stroitel'stvo SSSR*, 1935, p. 148; *ibid.*, 1936, p. 4.

[h] n.a. = information not available.

[10] Shimkin, *op. cit.*, pp. 201–2.

[11] Heinrich Hassman, *Erdöl in der Sowjetunion*, p. 108.

drilling of wells. No labor force data are obtainable for years subsequent to 1938.

The 1938 labor force can be subdivided into well drilling and oil producing employment on the basis of available productivity data, with the following results: drilling, 21.7 thousand wage earners; production, 21.6 thousand.[12] This ratio is not precisely consistent with similar data for the Baku fields, in which production employment was somewhat larger than employment in drilling,[13] but the difference may have been due to the relatively greater importance of drilling in the newer fields.

To employment of wage earners in 1938 must be added that of learners and junior service personnel. From 1933 to 1935 there was an average of 2.5 thousand learners per annum,[14] which figure may be used for 1938 in view of the relative stability of the labor force. On January 1, 1936, there were 2.4 thousand junior service personnel in the Soviet oil industry,[15] a figure which similarly can be used for 1938. Soviet oil employment in 1938 was thus 48.2 thousand for the purposes of the productivity comparison.

The average number of wage earners employed in U.S. oil production (excluding employees of contractors) was 105,505 in 1939, including inactive periods, whereas the average number of wage earners on active days was 112,678.[16] For reasons outlined in the chapter on the coal mining industry, the latter concept is the appropriate one for our purposes.[17] In contrast with coal mining, however, the magnitude of the difference between the two employment concepts is not great, reflecting the greater number of days worked per annum in the oil industry.

To the foregoing employment figure it is necessary to add the number

[12] The output of oil per wage earner in production alone was said to have been 1,484 tons in 1938. See *Neftianaia promyshlennosti SSSR*, 1940, No. 6, p. 26. A preliminary figure of 1,415 tons appears in *Sotsialisticheskoe stroitel'stvo SSSR*, 1939, p. 52. The figures in the text become 24.2 and 24.1 thousand, respectively, when learners and junior service personnel are added to the wage earners.

[13] In 1935 the average annual employment of production wage earners in Baku was 13 thousand and that of well drilling wage earners was 11 thousand. See N. Nikolayevski, "Proizvoditel'nost' truda v neftiannoi promyshlennosti SSSR", in Akademiia Nauk, Institut Ekonomiki, *Proizvoditel'nost' truda v promyshlennosti SSSR*, pp. 160–61.

[14] *Trud v SSSR*, 1936, p. 115.

[15] *Ibid.*, p. 114.

[16] U.S. Census, *Mineral Industries*, 1939, I, 136, 138.

[17] The Bureau of Mines collected no oil employment statistics for 1939. However, the Census "active day" concept is close to that of the Bureau of Mines.

of wage earners in the employ of contractors engaged in oil field development, of whom there were 43,308 (active day average) in 1939,[18] making total wage earner employment for 1939 some 156 thousand. Of these, 37.5 thousand were part-time workers "who worked substantially fewer hours per week than the number of hours in the full-time work week"; consequently, use of the total employment figure overstates labor input. However, it will be recalled that Russian employment statistics are similarly overstated by failure to adjust for part-time work, though there is no implication of an equality in the degree of overstatement, which cannot be determined for either country.

The number of U.S. wage earners in well development and production, respectively, can be estimated roughly from man-hour statistics as follows: well development, 61.5 thousand; producing, 94.5 thousand.[19] A relatively greater proportion of the U.S. labor force was engaged in production and a smaller proportion in development than was the case in Russia, reflecting in part, as we shall see, a comparative U.S. productivity advantage in well development (drilling).

COMPARATIVE PRODUCTIVITY

On the basis of the foregoing output and labor force data, the following productivity comparisons can be made:

	RUSSIA, 1938	UNITED STATES, 1939
Output of crude oil and natural gas (millions of metric tons)	32.2	217.8
Average number of wage earners (thousands)	48.2	156.0
Annual output of crude oil and natural gas per wage earner (metric tons)	688	1,396
Russian productivity as a percentage of U.S. productivity	47.9	100

[18] U.S. Census, *Mineral Industries,* 1939, I, 171.

[19] Estimated as follows: Of 190,674,000 man-hours worked by wage earners in development and producing in 1939, 151,308,000 man-hours were spent in production (operating and maintaining wells) and 31,919,000 man-hours in drilling and rig-building (excluding contract service employees). The number of man-hours worked by contract service employees, 66,479,000, can be assigned to development work, since contractors were engaged only in this branch of the industry. The resultant ratios are 60.6 percent of all wage earners assigned to production and 39.4 percent to development. Data are from the U.S. Census, *Mineral Industries,* 1939, Vol. I.

The paucity of data permits only a very rough approximation to man-hour productivity, as follows:

	RUSSIA, 1938	UNITED STATES, 1939
Number of man-hours worked by wage earners (millions)	85.4[20]	257.2[21]
Output of oil and gas per man-hour (metric tons)	0.377	0.847
Russian man-hour productivity as a percentage of U.S. productivity	44.5	100

In view of the approximate character of the man-day productivity estimate, the difference between man-year and man-hour productivity cannot be regarded as significant.

Estimates of productivity in well development and in production may be made separately, as follows:

	RUSSIA, 1937	UNITED STATES, 1939
Oil and gas wells drilled (thousands of meters)	1,907.8[22]	22,766[24]
Average number of wage earners engaged in drilling (thousands)	24.2[23] (1938)	61.5
Well drilling per wage earner (meters)	78.8	370
Russian productivity in drilling as a percentage of U.S. productivity	21.3	100

[20] Estimated as follows: The average number of days worked per wage earner in 1938 at Baku was 25.3. See Nikolayesvski, *op. cit.,* p. 161. Assuming that this was characteristic of the entire industry, and that there was a standard seven-hour working day, a total man-hours-worked figure is obtained. Among other things, this estimate does not allow for part-time work, since a wage earner appearing for work is counted as having contributed seven man-hours; nor, on the other hand, does it allow for overtime worked.

[21] U.S. Census, *Mineral Industries,* 1939, I, 138, 171. This is an approximation rather than an exact figure, since most reporting companies did not keep accurate time-worked records, but derived the man-day data by multiplying active day employment by the standard working day.

[22] Ia. A. Ioffe, *SSSR i kapitalisticheskie strany,* p. 206.

[23] In view of the stability of the labor force from 1935 to 1938, the error involved in using the 1938 labor force to match against 1937 output is probably negligible.

[24] U.S. Census, *Mineral Industries,* 1939, I, 136. This figure includes wells completed during 1939, though begun in the preceding year, but excludes wells not completed at the end of 1939.

	RUSSIA, 1938	UNITED STATES, 1939
Output of crude oil and natural gas (millions of metric tons)	32.2	217.8
Average number of wage earners in production (thousands)	24.1	94.5
Output of oil and gas per production wage earner (metric tons)	1,336	2,305
Russian productivity in production as a percentage of U.S. productivity	58.0	100

The foregoing estimates are merely approximate,[25] and are not for the same year. Nevertheless, it is abundantly clear from them that the United States enjoyed a larger comparative advantage in drilling than in production. A similar conclusion was reached by a Russian study, wherein Baku productivity in 1937 was compared with that for the entire U.S. industry in the same year, with the following results: Russian productivity as a percentage of that of the United States in drilling, 20 percent; as a percentage of U.S. production, 83 percent.[26]

CHANGES IN SOVIET PRODUCTIVITY, 1928 TO 1940

Indexes of Soviet oil productivity from 1928 to 1940 are shown in Table 29. The indexes in columns (1) and (2) pertain to the entire industry, while those in columns (3) and (4) are limited to the Baku fields. It would appear that from 1928 to 1938 Soviet oil productivity doubled. The value of output index (column 2) tended to outrun the physical output index (column 1), though in 1935, the last year for which both indexes were available, the difference was not great. The indexes for Baku are not conceptually akin to those for the entire industry;[27] nevertheless, in view of the overwhelming importance of Baku

[25] It will be noted that the average of the productivity estimates for production and drilling, even when weighted by employment, is lower than the combined productivity estimate derived above. However, since different output dimensions were employed in making these estimates, i.e., production of gas and oil well footage drilled, which are not necessarily correlated in any single year, such a difference does not call either of the estimates into question.

[26] N. Nikolayevski, "Proizvoditel'nost' truda v neftedobivayushchei promyshlennosti SSSR," *Neftianaia promyshlennosti SSSR*, 1940, No. 6, p. 26. The Baku fields were more productive than the average for the country; it may be estimated that the productivity comparison ratio falls to 74 percent for the entire USSR industry.

[27] The well drilling index for Baku is measured in meters drilled, rather than in oil output. The index of output of oil per wage earner for Baku excludes the labor force

TABLE 29

PRODUCTIVITY INDEXES IN SOVIET CRUDE OIL AND GAS
PRODUCTION, 1928–40
(1928 = 100)

YEAR	(1) OUTPUT OF OIL AND GAS PER WAGE EARNER IN DRILLING AND PRODUC- TION, USSR[a]	(2) VALUE OF OUT- PUT OF OIL AND GAS PER WAGE EARNER, USSR[b]	(3) METERS DRILLED PER WAGE EARNER AT BAKU[c]	(4) OUTPUT OF OIL PER WAGE EARNER IN PRODUCTION AT BAKU[c]
1928	100	100	100	100
1929	n.a.[d]	114	124	125
1930	n.a.	147	151	170
1931	157	164	146	221
1932	141	168	197	195
1933	154	176	215	250
1934	144	175	261	227
1935	166	178	336	291
1936	n.a.	n.a.	519	271
1937	n.a.	n.a.	n.a.	n.a.
1938	200	n.a.	n.a.	n.a.
1939	n.a.	n.a.	n.a.	n.a.
1940	n.a.	n.a.	481[e]	275[f]

[a] Calculated from Tables 27 and 28.

[b] *Trud v SSSR,* 1936, p. 114.

[c] *Problemy ekonomiki,* 1937, Nos. 3–4, p. 154.

[d] n.a. = information not available.

[e] Based on the average for the third quarter of 1940. See *Neftianaia promyshlennosti SSSR,* 1940, No. 6, p. 16.

[f] Based on the percentage increase in monthly output per wage earner from 1934 to 1940. See *ibid.*

at that time, it is difficult to reconcile the productivity growth shown in column (4) with that in columns (1) and (2). After 1935, however, the increase in Baku productivity leveled off.

The productivity levels of the major Soviet areas in 1938 are compared in Table 30. In terms of output per wage earner, Baku was the most productive, though output per well, reflecting the richness of the resource, was less than in the so-called Second Baku and Maikop. Low

engaged in well drilling, but a rough estimate indicates that the result would have been approximately the same had this group of wage earners been included.

TABLE 30

LABOR PRODUCTIVITY IN THE MAJOR SOVIET OIL AREAS, 1938

FIELD	ANNUAL OUTPUT OF OIL AND GAS PER WAGE EARNER (TONS)[a]	NUMBER OF WAGE EARNERS PER WELL[b]	AVERAGE OUTPUT PER DAY PER WELL (24 HOURS)
USSR	1,484	1.7	5.9
Baku	1,675	1.6	6.8
Second Baku	1,548	2.7	11.0
Maikop	1,157	2.6	7.9
Grozny	968	1.4	3.6
Emba	718	1.1	2.1

Source: *Neftianaia promyshlennosti SSSR*, 1940, No. 6, p. 26.
[a] Includes wage earners in production only, excluding drilling.
[b] Includes both active and inactive wells.

labor productivity in the latter field is attributed to insufficient development of machinery and other supporting industries,[28] while the poor record at Grozny is explained by the catastrophic decline in output from that area after 1932.[29]

FACTORS BEHIND THE DIFFERENCES IN PRODUCTIVITY

Resource conditions. During 1938–39 Soviet oil wells were far fewer in number than in the United States, but their average output was significantly greater. There were only 8,588 active wells in the Soviet Union in 1938, with a daily output per well (averaged over both active and inactive wells) of 5.9 metric tons.[30] The United States had 313,000 active wells on December 31, 1939, with a daily average output of 1.5 metric tons per well.[31] The greater daily output of the Russian wells can be attributed, among other things, to differences in the productive character of the fields in the two countries, in methods of exploitation, and in economic policy.[32]

[28] *Neftianaia promyshlennosti SSSR*, 1940, No. 6, p. 27.
[29] Grozny output fell from 7.7 million metric tons in 1932 to 2.4 million in 1940. Hassman, *op. cit.*, p. 92.
[30] *Neftianaia promyshlennosti SSSR*, 1940, No. 6, p. 26.
[31] U.S. Census, *Mineral Industries*, 1939, I, 139.
[32] Limitation of well output, either for conservation or in response to market demand, serves to reduce productivity, for labor cannot be reduced in proportion. Competitive drilling, by dissipating gas pressure too rapidly, may also reduce well output.

A study of the U.S. oil industry concluded that "although high average output per well is not strictly synonymous with high output per man, there is a close relation between the two factors."[33] In view of this fact, the margin of U.S. productivity superiority in oil production is surprising; it affords a good picture of the extent of U.S. technological superiority over that of the Soviet Union.[34]

Increased oil well depth carries with it greater difficulties in both drilling and production, particularly in the former.[35] In this respect, resource conditions in the two countries were not greatly dissimilar immediately before the war. The average depth of oil wells completed in the Soviet Union in 1939 was 1,026 meters,[36] compared with 975 meters in the United States.[37]

Technological and organizational factors. Any natural advantage possessed by the Russians was more than offset by U.S. superiority in the sphere of technology and industrial organization, as the following Russian statement indicates:

A comparison of data on labor productivity and the expenditure of labor per well attests to the backwardness of our industry compared with the American in the technical-productive sense. This backwardness is the result chiefly of insufficient mechanization in production and well drilling; excessive production time (for example, a great deal of idle time in drilling and production); the loss of oil and gas and less stable gas, and more rapid depreciation of the basic types of underground well equipment (pumps, rods, etc.). This is particularly true of the new and distant oil fields, where the construction of new industry is taking place and production is still not fully mastered.[38]

Soviet technological backwardness is illustrated by the following data, prepared by a Russian oil engineer (for 1938):[39]

	USSR	UNITED STATES
Average number of machine-months per well drilled	2.85	1.04
Average number of meters drilled per machine-month	336	920
Average number of wells drilled per drilling machine	4.2	11.5

[33] WPA, *Petroleum and Natural-Gas Production*, p. 46.

[34] It will be recalled that the failure of the Soviet industry to utilize much of the natural gas output was an important factor in low productivity.

[35] WPA, *Petroleum and Natural-Gas Production*, pp. 194–99.

[36] *Neftianaia promyshlennosti SSSR*, 1940, No. 2, p. 11.

[37] U.S. Census, *Mineral Industries*, 1939, I, 139.

[38] *Neftianaia promyshlennosti SSSR*, 1940, No. 6, pp. 32–33.

[39] *Industriia*, September 28, 1940, p. 2.

The data point to more effective and longer use of drilling equipment in the United States, though the margin of superiority was not as great as that indicated by the labor productivity figures shown above. United States technical superiority was apparently greatest in the construction of towers and in the installation and dismounting of equipment, as the following data indicate:[40]

	8 WELLS IN BAKU, OCTOBER, 1937	27 WELLS IN TEXAS, 1936
Average depth (meters)	2,224	2,170
Drilling (meters per machine-month)	580	3,000
Average days per well drilled	115.0	21.41
Preparatory work (construction and installation of equipment)	37.8	1.95
Demounting of equipment	9.1	1.24
Drilling	68.1	18.22

[40] *Neftianoe khoziaistvo,* 1937, No. 7, p. 5.

VIII

IRON AND STEEL

THE SCOPE OF THE BASIC IRON AND STEEL INDUSTRY[1]

THE basic iron and steel industry may be divided into three major sectors: the production of pig iron, the production of steel ingots, and the rolling of steel. Because of limitations in the employment data, this chapter will compare for the Soviet Union and the United States only (*a*) the output of pig iron per wage earner employed in blast furnace operation and (*b*) the output of steel ingots and hot-rolled steel per wage earner employed in steel works and rolling mills.

Differences in industrial classification between the Soviet Union and the United States make it necessary to define carefully the boundary of the industry:

Foundries. American iron and steel foundries not integral parts of steel works and rolling mills were treated by the 1939 Census of Manufactures as separate industries (gray iron and semisteel castings, malleable iron castings, steel castings). Direct steel castings produced in conjunction with rolling mills amounted to 152 thousand tons in 1939, compared with 548 thousand tons produced in the steel castings industry.[2] Comparable data are not available for other types of castings.[3]

In 1934, some 1.7 million tons of iron castings and 240 thousand tons

---

[1] This term is used synonymously with the following 1939 U.S. Census industry classifications: Blast Furnace Products, Steel Works and Rolling Mills.

[2] This and the U.S. data cited subsequently in this section are from the U.S. *Census of Manufactures,* 1939, Vol. II, Part II.

[3] It would seem, however, that very little, if any, cast iron production was attributed to the iron and steel industry. It is noted of gray iron and semisteel castings, for example, that they "are made to a considerable extent in establishments classified in other industries, that incidentally operate foundry departments for production of gray iron castings for their own consumption in the manufacture of such products as motor vehicles, stoves, furnaces, plumbing fixtures, machinery, etc." U.S. *Census of Manufactures,* 1939, II, p. 196. Some 62 percent of all gray iron and semisteel castings produced in 1939 were attributed to the castings industry, the balance to other, presumably noniron and steel group industries. A similar statement was made regarding malleable iron castings, and there it is indicated that 73 percent of all the malleable iron castings produced in 1939 were classified in the malleable castings industry, 18 percent in noniron and steel industries, and only 9 percent in other industries within the group—

of steel castings were produced in the Soviet metalworking and machinery industry.[4] In the same year, 2.9 million tons of foundry pig iron were produced, out of which, in addition to the iron castings, 470,000 tons of cast iron pipe were manufactured. The balance of about 500,000 tons of iron castings was produced either in foundry departments of iron and steel mills or, more likely, in other industries, such as railroad repair shops.

It thus appears that both in the United States and the Soviet Union, the great bulk of foundry products were separated from basic iron and steel (in the United States, from the census classifications "Blast Furnace Products" and "Steel Works and Rolling Mills"), both as to product and labor force. They may therefore be disregarded for the purpose at hand.

Cast iron pipe. The sole exception to the foregoing generalization appears to be cast iron pipe, which was classified as a separate industry by the 1939 U.S. Census, but which appeared as a part of basic iron and steel in the Soviet Union, though its tonnage was shown separately.[5] The best way of handling this item appears to be to disregard the output for both countries but to put the labor force on a comparable basis by adding to employment in U.S. basic iron and steel the 16.5 thousand wage earners who were engaged in the manufacture of cast iron pipe in 1939. The item is too small, relative to iron and steel production in general, to cause any distortion in productivity through omission of the output data, even if it were true that comparative productivity for this industry was significantly at variance with comparative productivity in iron and steel generally.

Steel pipe. Finished steel pipe was not included in the total of ordinary rolled steel in the Soviet Union; detailed lists of ordinary rolled products include, instead, skelp and pipe billets.[6] However, the plans do include the output of finished pipe among the products of the iron and steel industry,[7] and there is little doubt that the labor force engaged in the manufacture of this product is part of the iron and steel industry

---

iron and steel and their products. See *ibid.*, p. 201. The foregoing percentages are based on gross value-of-product data.

[4] *Sotsialisticheskoe stroitel'stvo SSSR*, 1936, pp. 171–72.

[5] *Ibid.*, p. 135.

[6] *Sotsialisticheskoe stroitel'stvo SSSR*, 1936, p. 135.

[7] For example, *1941 Plan*, p. 25.

labor force. The 1939 U.S. Census carried steel pipe manufacture in a
separate industry and included semifinished rather than finished pipe
in the total of hot-rolled steel. As in the case of cast iron pipe, the appropriate procedure is to add the number of U.S. wage earners engaged
in the production of steel pipe, 8.4 thousand, to that of steel works and
rolling mills.

Fabricated structural steel. The fabrication of structural steel and
ornamental metalwork was classified partly with rolling mills and
partly as a separate industry by the 1939 U.S. Census, depending on
where the work was actually performed. In that year, 2.9 million long
tons of structural shapes were turned out by rolling mills, of which 1.5
million long tons were subjected to further fabrication in the Fabricated
Structural Steel and Ornamental Metal Works Industry.

Soviet statistics provide little guidance to the classification of comparable products. There is no direct evidence on the classification of
the numerous miscellaneous products that constituted part of the U.S.
fabricating industry: steel grating, fire escapes, iron fences and grills,
ornamental iron and steel. Under the circumstances, it is simply assumed
that the division of the output of these products and the labor force in
the two countries, between basic iron and steel and other industries, is
similar.

Bolts, nuts, etc. The manufacture of bolts, nuts, washers, and rivets
was included by the 1939 U.S. Census either with rolling mill products
or in a separate industry, depending on whether such items were manufactured in departments of rolling mills or in separate establishments.
However, the output of these items was separated from the total of
rolled steel, although presumably the wage earners employed in the
bolt and nut departments of rolling mills were not thus segregated.
Soviet practice appears to have been to classify such items under metalworking rather than iron and steel.[8] Therefore, that portion of the U.S.
labor force engaged in the production of these commodities in rolling
mills should be removed from the basic iron and steel labor force; on
the basis of relative values of product in rolling mills and in the bolts,
nuts, etc., industry, the number of such wage earners was 3 thousand.

Wire and wire products. The comparative industrial classification of
these products is exceedingly complicated. The 1939 U.S. Census classi-

[8] *Ibid.,* pp. 54, 55.

fied wire with steel works and rolling mills when it was manufactured in departments of rolling mills, and in an industry named "Wire Drawn from Purchased Rods" when it was manufactured independently, the latter industry embracing also a portion of the manufacture of non-ferrous metal wire. In addition, wire products were classified into two separate industries: "Nails, spikes not made in wire mills or rolling mills," and "Wirework not elsewhere classified," the latter including fencing, screening, netting, concrete reinforcing wire, grillwork, and kitchen goods. While precision is not possible, the data indicate that a substantial portion of wire and wire products was produced by steel rolling mills, though the majority of such items appear to have been produced independently.[9]

Under the Soviet classification scheme, the production of wire and wire products appeared partly in basic iron and steel and partly in metal-working. From the *1941 Plan* data, for example, it is possible to identify 138 thousand tons of steel wire included in iron and steel (p. 21) and 177 thousand tons of wire (trade, telegraph, electric) included in metal-working (p. 54). However, since the planned manufacture of steel wire rods was 775 thousand tons (p. 19), it is not possible to indicate with any precision how the bulk of the bare wire was classified. In the case of wire products, such as nails, screens, reinforcing wire, and kitchen-ware, their exclusive listing under metalworking indicates a greater possibility of their preponderant classification in that industry.[10] In general, one might hazard the guess that a greater proportion of bare wire was classified, both as to product and labor force, with basic iron and steel in the Soviet Union than in the United States, but that the reverse was true of wire products. It is not possible, however, to adjust for the differ-

[9] Of 357.4 million dollars worth of bare wire produced in 1939, 21 percent is attributed to wiredrawing departments of steel works and rolling mills. However, an additional 14 percent is attributed to nonferrous rolling mills, and since a portion of the wire manufactured in the independent establishments was also nonferrous, the proportion of iron and steel wire produced in conjunction with rolling mills is substantially over the indicated 21 percent. In the case of wire products, 22 percent by value is attributed to steel rolling mills, 12 percent to nonferrous rolling mills, and the balance to other industries, suggesting again that the role of the steel rolling mill in this industry was substantial though not preponderant. However, these figures must be considered as being suggestive only, because they are based on gross value data and also because of great differences in unit values between ferrous and nonferrous metal wire and products. See U.S. *Census of Manufactures*, 1939, II, p. 214.

[10] See *1941 Plan*, pp. 54–55; and *Sotsialisticheskoe stroitel'stvo SSSR*, 1936, p. 170.

ences, and it must be recognized that the possibility of error exists on this account.

Iron and steel forgings. These products were classified by the 1939 U.S. Census according to the place of manufacture: with rolling mills, if manufactured in forging departments of rolling mills; in a separate industry, "Iron and Steel Forgings," if independently produced; and in the motor vehicle, railway car, machinery, etc., industries, if manufactured and consumed in the latter industries. It would appear that most forgings were produced by steel works and rolling mills.[11]

In the Soviet Union, to judge by available statistics, forgings, principally railroad axles and wheels, were classified primarily as iron and steel products,[12] although undoubtedly some forgings were produced within the machinery industry. Under the circumstances, the best procedure is to omit the U.S. iron and steel forgings industry, since no physical output statistics were collected for it in 1939; and further to make the assumption that in both countries the bulk of the forgings and the attached labor force was classified as part of the basic iron and steel industry.

Cold-rolled steel. Cold-rolling of sheets, strips, and bars generally represents a further processing of steel that has already been rolled hot. The 1939 U.S. Census classified cold-rolled steel as part of the output of steel works and rolling mills, except for a relatively small amount produced in separate establishments, which was carried as a separate industry employing 5.6 thousand wage earners. However, the output of cold-rolled steel in the former industry was shown separately from that of hot-rolled steel.

Cold-rolled steel was either carried among quality steel products or handled separately in the Soviet Union,[13] and the labor force engaged in its manufacture was presumably included in that of the iron and steel industry generally.

[11] The production of iron and steel forgings by steel works and rolling mills amounted to 446.8 thousand net tons in 1939. The output of forging billets in the same year was 600.6 thousand tons. See American Iron and Steel Institute, *Annual Statistical Report,* 1939, pp. 22, 37. If one makes allowance for wastage, roughly three-quarters of total forgings may be attributed to steel works and rolling mills.

[12] *Sotsialisticheskoe stroitel'stvo SSSR,* 1936, p. 135.

[13] Compare *1941 Plan,* p. 24, with Alexander Gerschenkron and Nancy Nimitz, *A Dollar Index of Soviet Iron and Steel Output,* p. 11.

Since the productivity comparison will run solely in terms of hot-rolled ordinary (nonquality) steel, the only adjustment necessary is to add to the labor force for steel works and rolling mills the 5.6 thousand U.S. wage earners engaged in the manufacture of cold-rolled steel in independent enterprises.

Summary. The foregoing adjustments entail adding to the U.S. labor force in steel works and rolling mills some 27.5 thousand wage earners. It must be emphasized that gaps in our knowledge regarding the classification of some of the product groups, as well as others which may not be apparent, render this adjustment of a very approximate character, despite the deceiving precision of the decimal point. It seems likely, however, that the adjustment is at least in the right direction, owing to the U.S. Census practice of fragmenting iron and steel manufacture by industry, as distinct from the Soviet practice of including a wide variety of products within a single iron and steel industry.

THE PRODUCT

The output of pig iron, steel, and rolled steel in the Soviet Union from 1928 to 1951 is shown in Table 31. Tables 32 and 33 show, respectively, the composition of pig iron and steel output for the Soviet Union (first quarter, 1937) and the United States (1939).

Considering pig iron first, one notes that the principal difference in composition of product for the periods indicated lay in the greater proportion of Russian pig iron destined for use in the foundry rather than for conversion into steel. Russian statisticians habitually assigned a weight of 115 to casting iron, with conversion iron equal to 100,[14] but although it would appear that a higher grade of iron is required for casting than for conversion, I have not been able to find any U.S. labor input weights which would serve to substantiate the Russian weight. Under the circumstances, no adjustment will be made in pig iron tonnage for this quality difference.[15] Both countries produced about the

[14] For example, S. G. Strumilin, *Chernaia metallurgiia v Rossii i v SSSR,* p. 302.

[15] Gerschenkron and Nimitz, *op. cit.,* assign a price of $20.75 per metric ton to Soviet conversion iron and of $21.25 per metric ton to ordinary and hematite foundry iron. Malleable foundry iron, which carries a substantial premium over conversion iron, constituted an insignificant proportion of total pig iron production. Thus, on this basis, failure to weight for casting iron involves only a slight error.

TABLE 31

PRODUCTION OF IRON, STEEL, AND ROLLED STEEL IN THE
SOVIET UNION, 1928–51

(In millions of metric tons)

YEAR	PIG IRON	STEEL	ROLLED STEEL[a]
1928	3.3	4.3	3.4
1929	4.0	4.9	3.9
1930	5.0	5.8	4.5
1931	4.9	5.6	4.2
1932	6.2	5.9	4.3
1933	7.1	6.9	4.9
1934	10.5	9.7	6.7
1935	12.6	12.6	9.0
1936	14.4	16.4	11.9[b]
1937	14.5	17.7	12.4[b]
1938	14.6	18.0	13.3[c]
1939	n.a.[d]	n.a.	n.a.
1940	15.0	18.3	13.4[c]
1945	9.2	11.2	8.5[c]
1946	10.2	12.2	9.6[c]
1947	11.7	13.3	11.0[c]
1948	14.3	17.0	n.a.
1949	n.a.	n.a.	n.a.
1950	19.4	27.3	21.3[c]
1951	22.1	31.3	n.a.

Sources: 1928–37: *Sotsialisticheskoe stroitel'stvo SSSR*, 1936, pp. 134–45; Ia. A. Ioffe, *SSSR i kapitalisticheskie strany*, pp. 158–60. Data for 1927 to 1929 are for the economic rather than for the calendar year.

1938: *Teoriia i praktika metallurgii*, 1939, No. 13, p. 8.

1940–48: Abram Bergson and others, "Postwar Economic Reconstruction and Development in the USSR," *Annals of the American Academy of Political and Social Science*, May, 1949, p. 56. The 1940 rolled steel figure is from Alexander Baykov, *The Soviet Economic System*, p. 291. The rolled steel data for 1945 to 1947 are from Abram Bergson and Lynn Turgeon, *Prices of Ordinary Rolled Steel in the Soviet Union*, p. 2.

1950: Estimated from statistics on fulfillment of the Fourth Five Year Plan. *Trud*, April 17, 1951, p. 1.

1951: New York *Times*, January 3, 1952, p. 53.

[a] This includes semifinished steel marketed as such, but not semifinished steel consumed within the same plant. *Sotsialisticheskoe stroitel'stvo SSSR*, 1936, p. 135, note to Table 71.

[b] These differ from the data given in the source, which include pipe and forgings from ingots. The correction factor is taken from Alexander Gerschenkron and Nancy Nimitz, *A Dollar Index of Soviet Iron and Steel Output*, p. 148.

[c] These figures may include pipe and forgings from ingots.

[d] n.a. = information not available.

TABLE 32

COMPOSITION OF PIG IRON AND FERROALLOY PRODUCTION IN THE USSR (FIRST QUARTER, 1937) AND THE UNITED STATES (1939)

	PERCENTAGE OF TOTAL OUTPUT	
	USSR	United States
Total pig iron and ferroalloy	100.0	100.0
Conversion iron	77.3	88.0
Foundry, malleable iron	20.3	9.5
Ferromanganese and spiegeleisen	2.0	1.3
Ferrosilicon and other ferroalloys	0.4	1.2

Sources: USSR: *Sovetskaia metallurgiia*, 1937, No. 5, p. 68.
United States: American Iron and Steel Institute, *Annual Statistical Report, 1939*, p. 6.

same proportions of ferroalloys, and any quality difference in this group could not significantly affect the total pig iron tonnage.

As for steel, it is evident from Table 33 that there was greater reliance in the United States on the open hearth furnace, the Russians producing a greater proportion of Bessemer, electric, and crucible steel. In general, Bessemer steel can be produced more cheaply than open hearth steel, provided that the price of steel scrap is not too low; but there does not

TABLE 33

COMPOSITION OF STEEL PRODUCTION IN THE USSR (FIRST QUARTER, 1937) AND THE UNITED STATES (1939)

	PERCENTAGE OF TOTAL OUTPUT	
	USSR	United States
Total ingot and casting steel	100.0	100.0
Open hearth	86.3	91.7
Bessemer	7.3	6.3
Thomas	1.9	
Electric and crucible	4.5	2.0

Sources: USSR: *Sovetskaia metallurgiia*, 1937, No. 5, p. 68.
United States: American Iron and Steel Institute, *Annual Statistical Report, 1939*, p. 14.

appear to be any invariant labor input relationship between the two types of steel as such.[16] Electric furnace steel is generally superior to Bessemer or open hearth because of the possibility of closely regulating its production,[17] but its share in total steel production was not sufficiently great to warrant any effort at securing appropriate weights.

The comparison of rolled steel output in the two countries is a far more complicated matter, owing to the great diversity of forms into which steel ingots are rolled. There must first be noted the sharp distinction made in Russian statistics between ordinary and quality rolled steel, a distinction with no counterpart in U.S. statistics. The Russians included within quality steel about 20 percent of total rolled steel in 1937; this figure rose to more than half the rolled steel during the war years, but declined again to 20 percent (*Plan* data) in 1950.[18] The production of alloy and stainless steel bars, which were classified as quality steels by the Russians, constituted about 5 percent of total hot-rolled steel output in the United States in 1939,[19] but additional amounts of what would have been classified as quality steel in the USSR were merged with other steels. Because of the form in which the Russian rolled steel data are available, as well as the character of the weights that will be employed, it is necessary in the following analysis to compare the composition of "ordinary" rolled steel production in the Soviet Union with total rolled steel, less alloy and stainless steel bars, produced in the United States. However, there is no reason to expect a serious bias in the distribution of the quality steel (Russian definition) remaining within the U.S. product category among the various types of rolled steel products, although some bias undoubtedly exists.[20] An even more

[16] See H. M. Boylston, *Iron and Steel*, p. 235; J. M. Camp and C. B. Francis, *The Making, Shaping and Treating of Steel*, pp. 355–56, 380.

[17] Douglas A. Fisher, *Steel Making in America*, p. 58.

[18] Abram Bergson and Lynn Turgeon, *Prices of Ordinary Rolled Steel in the Soviet Union*, p. 2.

[19] American Iron and Steel Institute, *op. cit.*, 1939, pp. 21, 38.

[20] Russian quality steel production appears to have been widely distributed among bar steel, sheets, wire, skelp, forgings, and castings. See Abram Bergson and Lynn Turgeon, *Prices of Quality Rolled Steel in the Soviet Union, 1928–1950*, pp. 26–29. However, it is unlikely that quality steels appeared among rails, structural shapes, and concrete reinforcing bars, and on this account these U.S. rolled steel categories were understated in relative importance, and the remaining categories were overstated. The most significant discrepancy is in the steel rails group, since the relative importance of this group in total output varied sharply in the two countries.

serious problem, which can only be noted, is the possibility of a significant difference in the ratios of quality to total rolled steel output for the Soviet Union and the United States during the years under comparison.[21]

The problem of quality steel aside, the international comparison of ordinary rolled steel output is beset with the difficulty of matching statistical categories and securing an adequate system of weighting the diverse elements that make up this product group. The first step taken was to classify hot-rolled steel products into eleven major categories, as shown in Table 34.[22] Then three sets of weights were applied: estimates of value added per ton, gross value per ton, and unit labor requirements. The weights are shown in Table 35. The value added estimates were made by the U.S. National Research Project in 1939 and were based on U.S. Census data during the years 1921 to 1935. The unit labor requirements data were computed by the National Research Project on the basis of a study made by the Bureau of Labor Statistics for an unspecified period.[23] The gross value data were computed from the 1939 Census of Manufactures.[24]

The application of these weights yielded the following results: ton for ton, the value of the U.S. rolled steel output exceeded that of the Russian rolled steel output for the years in question by 29 percent, using value added weights; by 66 percent, using unit labor requirement weights; and by 7 percent, using gross value weights.

These variations are attributable, of course, to internal differences in

[21] It may be noted, however, that a Soviet authority fixed the U.S. percentage of quality steel, according to the Russian definition, at about 25 percent in 1939. See S. M. Veingarten, *Ekonomika i planirovanie chernoi metallurgii,* p. 236. This would compare with about 20 percent for the USSR in 1937.

[22] Excluded were semifinished rolled products—billets, blooms, and slabs—from which finished products are rolled, and cold rolled steel. Apart from forgings, most steel ingots are processed into one of the semifinished forms, depending on the intended end use. Sheet and strip designed for such products as automobile bodies, where greater strength and more beautiful finish are desired, are then further processed by cold-rolling. For a classification of rolled steel by major type, see Camp and Francis, *op. cit.,* pp. 668–70.

[23] *Monthly Labor Review,* May, 1935, pp. 1158–59.

[24] Strictly speaking, these data are admixtures of gross values, value added, and, in some cases, purely arbitrary values assigned by manufacturers to goods transferred within the enterprise. Goods "produced for sale" were presumably valued at market prices, but for those produced for interplant transfer, value "is usually based on market price or on the cost of manufacture, but sometimes it is purely arbitrary."

Table 34

THE COMPOSITION OF FINISHED HOT-ROLLED STEEL IN THE SOVIET UNION AND THE UNITED STATES[a]

	USSR, 1938		UNITED STATES, 1939	
	Thousands of metric tons	*Percentage of total*	*Thousands of metric tons*	*Percentage of total*
1. Bar steel[b]	3,143	38.0	4,956	14.9
2. Sheet steel [c]	526	6.4	9,606	28.8
3. Plates	1,147[d]	13.9	3,016[e]	9.1
4. Black plate	92	1.1	3,017	9.1
5. Rails (including mine and streetcar)	1,107	13.4	1,194	3.6
6. Structural shapes				
a. Light	191	2.3	486	1.5
b. Heavy	337	4.1	2,485	7.5
7. Wire rod	536	6.5	3,268	9.8
8. Strip and skelp[f]	427	5.2	2,826	8.5
9. Pierced billets, rounds, blanks	317	3.8	2,195	6.6
10. Axle blanks	170	2.1	77	0.2
11. Car and locomotive wheels	265[g]	3.2	145	0.4
Totals:	8,258	100.0	33,271[h]	100.0

Sources: USSR: L. P. Shul'kin, *Potreblenie chernykh metallov v SSSR,* pp. 31 ff
United States: U.S. Department of Commerce, Bureau of the Census, *Census of Manufactures,* II, Part II, 187.

[a] The classification of hot-rolled steel into eleven categories must necessarily be arbitrary, in view of the tremendous diversity of products involved. The principal aim has been to secure comparability of product between the two countries. A comparative analysis for 1935 appearing in *Sovyetskaya Metallurgia,* 1937, No. 2, p. 12, was useful in indicating what categories of their products the Russians considered to be the equivalent of U.S. product groups. A recent work by Alexander Gerschenkron and Nancy Nimitz, *A Dollar Index of Soviet Iron and Steel Output,* was also most helpful in respect to classification.

[b] This group includes a great variety of shapes—square, round, half round, oval, hexagonal, octagonal, flat—used primarily in the production of machinery. Concrete reinforcing bars are not shown separately in the Soviet statistics and are therefore added to merchant bars on the U.S. side. What are called "reinforcement bars" in the Russian statistics appear to be used for the manufacture of railroad tie plates and joints; and since rail joints and fastenings are added to the U.S. merchant bar classification, they are added to bar steel on the Russian side. See Gerschenkron and Nimitz, *op. cit.,* pp. 180–81, 250, 251. Alloy and stainless steel merchant bars are deducted from the U.S. merchant bar total, since these are classified as quality rather than ordinary rolled steel in the USSR. A comparatively small amount of Russian "forging blanks" is included in this category, however.

[c] The term "sheet steel" is employed generically in the Soviet Union and covers plates, sheets, strips, and black plate. The items listed here include only "thin sheets" (*listovoe tonkoe zhelezo*), up to 3 millimeters in thickness (see *Sotsialisticheskoe stroitel'stvo SSSR,* 1936, p. 135), corrugated steel for roofing, and pickled steel.

NOTES TO TABLE 34 (*Continued*)

d Obtained as the residual of sheets (*list*) and thin sheets.

e Armor plate and ordnance are excluded from this figure, since they are treated as quality steel in the Soviet data.

f The Russian figure is the sum of strip (*shtripsy listovye*) and skelp (*shtripsy sortovye*). See Gerschenkron and Nimitz, *op. cit.,* pp. 182–83, for information on the correct interpretation of these Russian terms. The figure for the United States is the sum of skelp and "other strips" for sale. U.S. output of bands, flats, and scrolls is omitted as probably falling within the Soviet quality steel classification.

g Includes wheels, wheel centers, and rims.

h This total does not equal that for finished hot-rolled steel given in the source by virtue of omission of the following items, which are presumed to have been the equivalent of Russian "quality" steel: alloy steel; stainless steel; bands, flats, and scrolls; armor plate and ordnance; sheet piling; miscellaneous.

the systems of weights employed. For example, sheets and black plate figured much more prominently in the U.S. than in the Soviet product mix, reflecting the greater importance of the consumption goods industries in the United States as consumers of steel. The unit labor requirements weighting system assigned to sheet steel 3.8 times as much labor input per ton as to bar steel (which bulked large in the Soviet product mix and was used chiefly in machinery manufacture), whereas the ratio of the weights in terms of value added was 1 to 1.9, and in terms of gross value, 1 to 1.4.

For the problem at hand, i.e., ensuring that a ton of finished metal represents about the same labor input in the two countries, unit labor requirement weights are clearly the most appropriate. However, there is considerable doubt concerning the adequacy of the particular weights shown in Table 35. The National Research Project study commented as follows on them: "These figures, which refer to 55–60 percent of capacity utilization, may not be typical since utilization varies widely, not only from product to product at any given time but also from year to year."[25] The underlying study on which they were based covers an unspecified period, and it is difficult to determine to what extent they are representative.

The Census gross value weights, on the other hand, are deficient not only by virtue of lack of correspondence between gross value and labor inputs, but also because they are based on only a portion of total out-

[25] Works Progress Administration, National Research Project, *Production, Employment and Productivity in 59 Manufacturing Industries,* Part II, p. 96, 10n.

TABLE 35

ALTERNATIVE WEIGHTS FOR ROLLED STEEL PRODUCTS, BASED ON UNITED STATES DATA

	(1) VALUE ADDED (DOLLARS PER GROSS TON)	(2) LABOR REQUIRE- MENTS (MAN- HOURS PER GROSS TON)	(3) GROSS VALUE (DOLLARS PER TON)[1]
1. Bar steel	$20.50[a]	4.89[a]	$34[a]
2. Sheet steel	39.23	18.50	48
3. Plates	12.03	1.93	46
4. Black plate	50.31[b]	18.50[g]	54
5. Rails	8.84[c]	4.52[h]	41
6. Structural shapes			
a. Light	13.86	2.27[j]	50
b. Heavy	8.94	2.27[j]	46
7. Wire rod	10.49	4.39	47
8. Strip and skelp	7.29[d]	2.87[k]	38[d]
9. Pierced billets, rounds, blanks	7.29[e]	2.87	39
10. Axle blanks	20.50[f]	4.89[f]	34[f]
11. Car and locomotive wheels	67.48	20.83	92

Sources: Column (1): Works Progress Administration, National Research Project, *Production, Employment and Productivity in 59 Manufacturing Industries,* Part III, pp. 66–67.

Column (2): *Ibid.,* Part II, p. 96.

Column (3): U.S. Department of Commerce, Bureau of the Census, *Census of Manufactures,* II, Part II, 187.

[a] Weighted average of data for bar steel and concrete reinforcing bars.

[b] Separate weights were not available for black plate. This weight was estimated on the basis of the relationship of the Census gross unit values of black plate made for sale to sheets made for sale.

[c] Represents value added for new rails only.

[d] Represents value added and gross value for skelp only. Data for strip separately were not available.

[e] Separate weights were not available for pierced billets, rounds, and blanks. The weight for skelp was assigned to this item on the basis of close correspondence between the gross unit values for the two items.

[f] Separate weights were not available for axle blanks. The weight given for steel bars were assigned to this item.

[g] This item was assigned the same man-hour weight as that given for sheet steel generally.

[h] Includes standard rails and fastenings.

[j] Separate unit labor requirement weights were not available for light and heavy structural shapes.

[k] Labor weights were available only for finished pipe and tubing. This figure was

estimated on the basis of the ratio of value added per ton of skelp to value added per ton of finished pipe and tube.

[1] The price weight assigned is the weighted average of the price given for goods produced for sale and for interplant transfer.

put—that produced for sale and interplant transfer—excluding production for use within the same plant, to which no value was assigned.

The value added weights are the most satisfactory in terms of their empirical basis, but they are not without certain drawbacks, the principal one of which may be their obsolescence by 1939.[26] It is also important to note that all three weighting systems are derived from U.S. data, and that quite conceivably a set of Russian-derived weights would yield dissimilar results.

All things considered, the National Research Project value added weights, notwithstanding their deficiencies, appear to be the best that are available for comparing the value of U.S. rolled steel production in 1939 with Soviet rolled steel production in 1938. On this assumption, a comparison of productivity in terms of unadjusted physical product would tend to result in understatement of comparative U.S. productivity. However, the understatement is not of the order of the full 29 percent by which the unit value of U.S. rolled steel exceeded that of the Soviet Union, for under the procedure employed in measuring productivity in steel manufacture and rolling, steel ingot tonnage is added to that of rolled steel to secure the numerator of the productivity ratio, and, as already indicated, there seemed to be little difference in unit value between U.S. and Soviet steel ingots during the period in question. The actual productivity bias would be somewhat less than half that indicated by comparing rolled steel tonnages alone. Since the data are so inadequate, it seems wise not to attempt any precise adjustment for this factor, but instead merely to note that an error factor is involved.

[26] For example, it has been suggested that, as a consequence of the growth of continuous rolling since the 1921 to 1935 period on which the value added weights are based, a weight of $20 per ton of sheets might be more appropriate than the $39 value assigned in Table 35 for 1939 production. See *Company Testimony before the Presidential Fact-finding Board, Steel Industry Case,* August, 1949, I, 399–400. A study conducted by the Carnegie-Illinois Steel Company revealed that the production of tin plate required 34.8 man-hours per ton in an old style hot mill and 12.4 man-hours in

On the basis of the foregoing considerations, the output of steel ingots and hot-rolled steel for the two countries may be summarized as follows:

	THOUSANDS OF METRIC TONS	
	USSR, 1937	United States, 1939
Steel ingots	11,700	47,807
Finished hot-rolled steel products and forgings	11,542[27]	36,289

Semifinished rolled products—billets, blooms, and slabs—are omitted from consideration, since a clear-cut grouping of such products was not available for the Soviet Union. The inclusion of such products would do little more than add to the tonnage of each country a roughly equivalent proportion of steel ingot output, the magnitude of which would lie between steel ingot and finished rolled steel tonnages.

THE LABOR FORCE

The Russian steel labor force statistics available directly from Soviet published sources are presented in Table 36. The labor and industry section statistics diverged significantly only in 1936 for the years for which both sets were available. The labor section figure for 1937 was derived by making the assumption that the trend in the labor series data followed that in the industry series data from 1936 to 1937.

The labor force data in Table 37 were calculated by comparing output statistics with productivity statistics. It is at once evident that the productivity statistics, which were widely quoted in the Soviet literature, were calculated on the basis of figures pertaining to a restricted portion of the employed wage earners, probably those whom the Russians term

---

a new continuous mill. See R. Conrad Cooper, *Productivity in the Steel Producing Subsidiaries of United States Steel,* p. 13.

[27] Derived as follows:

		THOUSANDS OF METRIC TONS
	Total rolled steel output, 1937	12,377
Less:	Semifinished rolled steel	1,085
		11,292
Add:	Forgings made directly from ingots	250
		11,542

Source: Gerschenkron and Nimitz, *op. cit.,* pp. 19–21.

TABLE 36

THE LABOR FORCE IN SOVIET IRON AND STEEL MANUFACTURE,
1928 to 1937
(*In thousands of persons*)

YEAR	TOTAL EMPLOY-MENT, JANUARY 1 (LABOR SECTION)[a]	WAGE EARNERS, JANUARY 1 (LABOR SECTION)[b]	AVERAGE ANNUAL NUMBER OF WAGE EARNERS (LABOR SECTION)	AVERAGE ANNUAL NUMBER OF WAGE EARNERS (INDUSTRY SECTION)[j]
1928	205.3	167.8	185.3[c]	180.5
1929	228.5	189.6	n.a.[d]	188.9
1930	245.7	201.0	n.a.	202.1
1931	301.0	230.3	n.a.	219.2
1932	361.3	254.1	253.1[e]	259.4
1933	362.5	261.6	281.5[f]	287.2
1934	373.6	300.1	306.1[f]	310.5
1935	386.2	318.1	315.5[e]	n.a.
1936	384.1	318.5	310.7[g]	331.0[k]
1937	n.a.	n.a.	309.0[h]	329.5[l]

[a] *Trud v SSSR,* 1936, p. 142.

[b] 1929–33: *Sotsialisticheskoe stroitel'stvo SSSR,* 1934, pp. 326, 327; 1928, 1934–36: *Trud v SSSR,* 1936, p. 142, less the number of learners from *Sotsialisticheskoe stroitel'stvo SSSR,* 1936, p. 516.

[c] *Trud v SSSR,* 1936, p. 143, less the average of the numbers of learners at the beginning and end of 1928 from *Sotsialisticheskoe stroitel'stvo SSSR,* 1936, p. 516.

[d] n.a. = information not available.

[e] *Trud v SSSR,* 1936, p. 143.

[f] *Trud v SSSR,* 1935, p. 62.

[g] This is the number of wage earners as of July 1, 1936. See *Zhenshchina v SSSR,* 1937, p. 62. Monthly labor force data for the Metallurgical Trust, which in 1936 produced virtually all the nation's pig iron and 83 percent of the steel, indicate that the average of the numbers of wage earners in June and July, 1936, centered on July 1, was almost precisely equal to the average of the twelve monthly figures for 1936. See issues of *Sovetskaya metallurgiia* for 1936 and 1937. Therefore, the July 1 figure may be taken as representative for the year.

[h] Based on the assumption that the trend in the labor section data was the same as that in the industry section data from 1936 to 1937.

[j] *Socialist Construction in the USSR,* 1936, p. 152.

[k] S. M. Veingarten, *Ekonomika i planirovanie chernoi metallurgii,* p. 85. This figure is attributed in the source to *Sovetskaya metallurgiia,* 1937, No. 3. However, the figure does not appear in that journal; the only labor force data that do appear there are for the Metal Trust, and exclude the so-called small metallurgy (*malaia metallurgiia*). Veingarten apparently had access to additional information through which he could secure the total employment figure.

[l] This figure was derived by a comparison of total fixed capital and fixed capital per wage earner. Sources: *Sotsialisticheskoe stroitel'stvo SSSR,* 1939, p. 37; L. M. Kantor, *Osnovnye fondy promyshlennosti i ikh ispol'zovanie,* p. 25; and an unpublished manuscript by Norman Kaplan. This figure finds support in a statement in *Planovoe khoziaistvo,* 1939, No. 2, p. 45, where it is indicated that "about" 300 thousand wage earners were employed in iron and steel manufacture in 1937.

Table 37

WAGE EARNERS IN SOVIET IRON AND STEEL MANUFACTURE, CALCULATED FROM PRODUCTIVITY STATISTICS

	PIG IRON			STEEL INGOTS			ROLLED STEEL		
YEAR	Output per wage earner (metric tons)[a]	Production for the year (millions of metric tons)[b]	Number of wage earners employed in blast furnaces (thousands)	Output per wage earner (metric tons)[c]	Production for the year (millions of metric tons)[b]	Number of wage earners employed in steel mills (thousands)	Output per wage earner (metric tons)[d]	Production for the year (millions of metric tons)[b]	Number of wage earners employed in rolling mills (thousands)
1932	253	6.2	24.5	179	5.9	33.0	80	4.3	53.8
1933	265	7.1	26.8	187	6.9	36.9	80	4.9	61.3
1934	370	10.5	28.4	233	9.7	41.6	120	6.7	55.8
1935	483	12.6	26.1	273	12.6	46.2	145	9.0	62.1
1936	640	14.4	22.5	338	16.4	48.5	157	11.9	75.8
1937	756	14.5	19.2	484	17.7	36.6	163	12.4	76.1

[a] The data from 1932 to 1935 are from *Planovoe khoziaistvo*, 1936, No. 11, p. 41. The remaining data are from A. A. Arakelian, "Proizvoditel'nost' truda v chernoi metallurgii SSSR," in Akademiia Nauk, Institut Ekonomiki, *Proizvoditel'nost' truda v promyshlennosti SSSR*, p. 50. Arakelian converted all pig iron into conversion iron equivalents, apparently using the following weights, derived from S. G. Strumilin, *Chernaia metallurgiia v Rossii i v SSSR*, p. 302:

Conversion iron	100
Foundry iron	115
Ferromanganese and spiegeleisen	200
Ferrosilicate	250

For the years in which the productivity data are available, both in kind and reduced to conversion iron equivalents, the former exceeded the latter by about 6 percent. This factor was applied to the data for 1936 to secure the figure shown in the table. Arakelian's 1937 figure is actually in kind, though it is labeled "tons of conversion iron." Cf. Ia. A. Ioffe, *SSSR i kapitalisticheskie strany*, p. 78, and *Teoriia i praktika metallurgii*, 1939, No. 12, p. 12.

[b] Data are from Table 31.

[c] The basic data are from Arakelian, *op. cit.*, p. 73. However, they are limited to the production of open hearth steel. Bessemer productivity was higher; e.g., it is indicated that in 1936 output per wage earner of Bessemer steel was 374 percent of the open hearth level. See Ioffe, *op. cit.*, p. 78. Therefore, the open hearth data have been adjusted to reflect total steel productivity, assuming the constancy of the 1936 ratio between open hearth and Bessemer productivity. The proportion of Bessemer to total steel produced (including electric and crucible steel, for which no productivity data were available) was: 1932—10.3 percent; 1933—10.5 percent; 1934—8.8 percent;

Notes to Table 37 (*Continued*)

1935—7.9 percent; 1936—7.3 percent; 1937 (first quarter)—7.7 percent. Data are from *Sotsialisticheskoe stroitel'stvo SSSR*, 1936, p. 134; *Sovetskaya metallurgiia*, 1936, No. 2, p. 65; *ibid.*, 1937, No. 3, p. 63; *ibid.*, 1937, No. 5, p. 68.

[d] Arakelian, *op. cit.*, p. 76.

"basic production" labor.[28] This assertion is supported by the equivalence of the ratio of the production workers, as thus calculated, to the total number of wage earners as shown in Table 38, with similar ratios emanating from other sources.[29]

[28] The wage earners employed in iron and steel mills were customarily subdivided into three major groups: (*a*) basic production, engaged immediately in the manufacture of the metal; (*b*) subsidiary production, engaged in the procurement of materials, e.g., sand for castings; (*c*) auxiliary service, including maintenance, power supply, and in-plant transport. See S. M. Levin, *Tekhnicheskoe normirovanie v chernoi metallurgii*, p. 391. It is not clear whether the data in Table 37 include or exclude category (*b*), but there is little doubt that they exclude category (*c*). This is confirmed by the following statistics: At the end of 1932, with a total labor force fixed at 246.9 thousand, the following percentage breakdown, by department, was given.

	PERCENTAGE OF TOTAL WAGE EARNERS
Blast furnace departments	9.9
Open hearth and other steel departments	11.0
Rolling mills	20.2
Total	41.1
Foundries	3.7
Forging departments	1.9
Mechanical departments	7.7
Boiler construction	2.3
Power stations	7.5
Transportation	9.7
Other auxiliary services	26.1
Total	100.0

Source: Strumilin, *op. cit.*, p. 315.

Using the first three departments only, the estimated number of wage earners at the end of 1932 would be: blast furnaces, 24.4 thousand; steel mills, 27.2 thousand; and rolling mills, 49.9 thousand. The corresponding figures for 1932 from Table 37 are: blast furnaces, 24.5 thousand; steel mills, 33.0 thousand; rolling mills, 53.8 thousand. While the correspondence is not exact, partly because a different global labor force figure was used in the two sources, it is sufficiently close to warrant the assumption that only the first three departments in the foregoing table were included in the calculation of the productivity data in Table 37. Quite clearly, inclusion of the remaining so-called auxiliary departments would have produced a wide divergence in the resulting productivity data.

[29] For example, A. A. Arakelian, "Proizvoditel'nost' truda v chernoi metallurgiia

TABLE 38

ESTIMATED NUMBER OF DIRECT PRODUCTION WAGE EARNERS
IN SOVIET IRON AND STEEL MANUFACTURE
(*In thousands of persons*)

YEAR	AVERAGE ANNUAL NUMBER OF WAGE EARNERS	ESTIMATED NUMBER OF DIRECT PRODUCTION WAGE EARNERS	RATIO OF DIRECT PRODUCTION TO TOTAL WAGE EARNERS (PERCENT)
1932	253.1	111.3	44.0
1933	281.5	125.0	44.4
1934	306.1	125.8	41.1
1935	315.5	134.4	42.6
1936	310.7	146.8	47.2
1937	309.0	131.9	42.7

Sources: Tables 36 and 37.

It will be noted from Table 38 that there was a fall in the ratio of production to total wage earners from 1936 to 1937. There are several possible explanations for this: there may have been a real decline in the proportion of production to total wage earners; the 1936 total may be inaccurate; or the production worker concept may have changed. In view of the instability of the ratio in previous years and of the fact that the ratio for 1937 falls within a range which has a basis in previous experience, the 1937 figure of 309 thousand wage earners may be accepted as being not inconsistent with the size of the "productive" labor force for that year.

The determination of a separate labor force figure for blast furnaces involves some special problems. The principal one is that, both in the Soviet Union and the United States, most blast furnaces are closely integrated with steel mills, and it is difficult to apportion any but direct production labor between them.[30] It is doubtful whether the 1939 U.S.

SSSR," in Akademiia Nauk, Institut Ekonomiki, *Proizvoditel'nost' truda v promyshlennosti SSSR*, p. 82, indicates that in 1939 "more than half" of the total number of wage earners were employed in auxiliary departments. In 1937, from 50 percent to 60 percent of the total number of iron and steel wage earners were said to be in auxiliary departments. See *Plan*, 1937, No. 10, p. 10.

[30] L. Rostas, *Comparative Productivity in British and American Industry*, p. 97, observes that the validity of his British-U.S. productivity comparison in steel "really

Census of Manufactures succeeded in allocating to the blast furnace industry all the labor, direct and indirect, associated with the manufacture of pig iron.[31] The Soviet statistical authorities apparently made no effort to secure a precise segregation of all blast furnace labor, for the only labor force data available for this industry relate to production labor, excluding maintenance men, power station operators, in-plant transport workers, and other general services.[32] The only possible procedure is to act upon the assumption that for each country the census labor force attributed to blast furnaces represents a comparable proportion of the total number of wage earners employed in this branch of the industry.[33]

To summarize: the number of wage earners employed in Soviet

---

depends on the extent to which the integrated firms succeeded in supplying separate reliable data on this sector," but does not pursue the inquiry.

[31] A sample study of the manning of U.S. blast furnaces in 1950 indicated that the average was 37.5 wage earners engaged in direct production; 57.5 wage earners engaged in indirect production; and 40 wage earners engaged in maintenance. See Anglo-American Council on Productivity, *Iron and Steel*, p. 34. There were 228 active coke blast furnaces in the United States in 1939. See *Annual Statistical Report of the American Iron and Steel Institute, 1939*, p. 4. Without any allowance for increased productivity from 1939 to 1950, this would mean 21.7 thousand production wage earners (direct and indirect) in 1939, compared with the reported figure of 19.5 thousand. Moreover, if maintenance men were included, there would be an additional 9 thousand men; nor does this include 4.3 thousand wage earners engaged in sintering and ore preparation.

[32] This is clear from *supra*, p. 125, *n* 28. However, attempts were made to secure full labor accounting for costing purposes, as the following data for the southern steel trust indicate:

LABOR COST PER TON, IN RUBLES, 1934

	Pig iron	Open hearth steel	Ordinary steel bars
Production wage earners	3.02	5.93	10.09
Auxiliary and service	1.29	3.29	2.99
Overhead, social insurance, etc.	1.93	4.17	5.24
Non-wage earners	0.73	2.00	1.65
Vacation pay, etc.	0.02	0.04	0.38
Total	6.99	15.43	20.35

Source: *Sovetskaya metallurgiia*, 1936, No. 1, p. 5.

[33] For what it is worth, it should be noted that the various Soviet comparisons of Soviet-U.S. blast furnace productivity were based on the same procedure. See *Sovetskaia metallurgiia*, 1937, No. 2, p. 3; Arakelian, *op. cit.*, p. 79; and Ia. A. Ioffe, *SSSR i kapitalisticheskie strany*, p. 78. However, there is no evidence that the coverage of the respective census labor force groups was examined in any of these comparisons.

blast furnaces in 1937 was 19.2 thousand; the number in steel works and rolling mills, 289.8 thousand (i.e., 309 thousand less 19.2 thousand). Trainees and junior service personnel must be added. Using the ratio of these two groups to wage earners that prevailed on January 1, 1936,[34] one obtains the following labor force figures: blast furnaces, 21.0 thousand; steel works and rolling mills, 316.8 thousand.

The comparable figures for the United States for the year 1939 are: blast furnaces, 19.5 thousand wage earners; steel works and rolling mills, 396.4 thousand.[35]

COMPARATIVE PRODUCTIVITY

The foregoing data may now be brought together as follows:

	USSR, 1937	UNITED STATES, 1939
Output of pig iron (millions of metric tons)	14.5	32.0
Average number of wage earners employed in blast furnaces (thousands)	21.0	19.5
Output per wage earner (metric tons)	690	1,641
Comparative productivity (U.S. = 100)	42	100

	USSR, 1937	UNITED STATES, 1939
Output of steel ingots and hot-rolled steel (millions of metric tons)	29.2	84.1
Average number of wage earners in steel works and rolling mills (thousands)	316.8	396.4
Output of steel and rolled steel per wage earner (tons)	92	212
Comparative productivity (U.S. = 100)	43	100

The evidence regarding the course of Soviet labor productivity during the prewar years subsequent to 1937 is conflicting. Data for ten iron-producing enterprises, which in 1936 produced 62 percent of the nation's pig iron, indicate a 25 percent productivity increase from 1937 to 1939. Similarly, data for eight steel manufacturing enterprises, which produced 36 percent of all Soviet steel in 1936, indicate a 34 percent productivity rise from 1937 to 1939.[36] On the other hand, some productivity data based on value of output per wage earner indicate at best a 4 per-

[34] *Trud v SSSR,* 1936, p. 144.

[35] U.S. *Census of Manufactures,* 1939, II, Part II, 180, 186, adjusted in accordance with the conclusions reached in the first section of this chapter.

[36] The statistics for individual enterprises were from Arakelian, *op. cit.,* pp. 72, 75, and I. P. Bardin and N. P. Bannyi, *Chernaia metallurgiia v novoi piatiletke,* p. 166. Enterprise weights for 1936 employed in securing the averages were from *Sovetskaia*

cent productivity increase from 1937 to 1938; no comparable figure is available for 1939, but a rough estimate for 1940 would point to little productivity advance from 1938 to 1940 (see Table 39). Moreover, the performance of the steel industry during the years 1938 and 1939 was described as "unsatisfactory,"[37] which hardly seems consistent with the productivity gain derived from the individual enterprise data. The most plausible hypothesis is that Soviet iron and steel productivity in 1939, while above the 1937 level, was still less than half the level prevailing in the United States in 1939.

The foregoing results may be compared with the results obtained by Soviet economists:

1. One of the most widely quoted comparisons in the Soviet literature is a ratio of 47 percent (756 versus 1,620 tons) as expressive of the ratio of Soviet to U.S. output of pig iron per wage earner in 1937.[38] Similar comparisons are available for earlier years.[39]

2. Some comparative manning data for blast furnaces were given as follows:

a. The number of wage earners required to man a nonmechanized blast furnace in the United States in 1929 was put at 102; and for a mechanized furnace, at 75 to 85. Comparable Soviet furnaces were said to require from 300 to 400 and from 200 to 240 wage earners, respectively.[40]

b. A large blast furnace at Magnitogorsk was manned by 150 wage earners; blast furnaces at Kuznetsk and Makeyevka, by 195 wage earners. A furnace of similar size in the United States was said to require 95 men.[41]

---

metallurgiia, 1937, No. 3, pp. 60–61. The reader is cautioned that the enterprise productivity data on which these figures are based were obviously calculated by the use of a more restricted labor force concept even than that employed for the entire industry as shown in Table 37, for the absolute output per wage earner magnitudes for the individual facilities cannot be reconciled with the global figure.

[37] Stal', 1947, No. 11, p. 968.

[38] Ioffe, op. cit., p. 78. The U.S. figure was obtained from the Census of Manufactures by dividing pig iron production by the number of wage earners manning blast furnaces, without adjustment. Measured in this way, U.S. productivity increased by only 2 percent from 1937 to 1939.

[39] For example, see Arakelian, op. cit., p. 79; I. G. Gorelik, Metodika planirovania chernoi metallurgiia, p. 78.

[40] Sovetskaya metallurgiia, 1937, No. 2, p. 3.

[41] Problemy ekonomiki, 1940, Nos. 11–12, p. 102.

c. In comparison with 75 to 85 wage earners per American mechanized blast furnace, the following manning figures were given for individual Soviet furnaces in 1937: Nos. 7 and 8 at Dzherzhinsk, 192; Nos. 1 and 2 at the Voroshilov plant, 180; Nos. 1 and 2 at Azovstal', 204; and Nos. 1 and 2 at Krivoi Rog, 224.[42]

3. The following comparative data are available for steel works and rolling mills:

a. For a U.S. plant "near Pittsburgh" versus a new Soviet plant:[43]

	U.S. PLANT, 1935–36			SOVIET PLANT, 1940		
	Output (millions of tons)	Number of wage earners	Total personnel	Output (millions of tons)	Number of wage earners	Total Personnel
All departments	..	5,234	5,979	..	11,580	13,508
Blast furnaces	1.5	376	448	1.5	498	560
Open hearth furnaces	2.5	1,495	1,694	1.7	1,474	1,636
Rolling mills	1.7	2,058	2,354	1.2	2,692	2,944

These figures imply much higher comparative productivity ratios for the Soviet Union than those derived above.

b. In 1936 the open hearth department of the Inland Steel Company employed 260 men to operate 7 furnaces, whereas the Makeyevka plant, with 6 furnaces, employed 1,070 wage earners.[44]

c. The 150-ton open hearth furnaces at Magnitorgorsk and Makeyevka required 100 wage earners; those at Kuznetsk, 95 wage earners. The average U.S. furnace of similar size was manned by 32 wage earners (circa 1937).[45]

d. The number of wage earners manning an open hearth furnace in the United States (1935) was 35, which, it was claimed, corresponded to 60 to 70 wage earners under Soviet organization, where repair and other services were performed by the plant labor force rather than by utilization of outside staff. Comparable figures for Kuznetsk and Magnitogorsk were 128 wage earners; and for the southern steel trust, 165 wage earners.[46]

[42] A. Shevchenko, *Stakhanovski rukh i osvoyennya tekhniki v chernoi metallurgii,* p. 91.

[43] *Problemy ekonomiki,* 1940, Nos. 11–12, p. 102.

[44] *Planovoe khoziaistvo,* 1936, Nos. 9–10, p. 30.

[45] Arakelian, *op. cit.,* p. 81.

[46] *Planovoe khoziaistvo,* 1936, Nos. 9–10, p. 30.

The foregoing Soviet data must be interpreted with caution. In many cases their purpose was exhortatory, and it can be surmised that extreme examples were chosen. Differences in industrial organization affect the comparability of manning tables. Moreover, manning is typically subject to sharp variation from plant to plant.[47] However, in general the data tend to support a 40 percent to 50 percent USSR-U.S. productivity ratio in iron and steel for prewar years.

TRENDS IN SOVIET PRODUCTIVITY, 1928 TO 1940

Available data do not permit a breakdown of the Soviet iron and steel labor force among iron, steel, and rolled steel back to 1928. As an index of productivity change, therefore, we will employ the ratio of steel ingot production to the number of wage earners in the entire industry. Undoubtedly this will result in an understatement of the productivity increase in view of the trend toward more labor-consuming rolled steel products, particularly quality rolled steel. However, the preparation of an index of production which would take such changes into account would require an indigenous set of labor input weights, the determination of which would involve virtually a separate monograph.

There are shown in Table 39 two indexes of labor productivity, the first based on physical output per wage earner, the second, the official Soviet index, calculated in terms of value of output per wage earner. For the period up to 1937 as a whole, the value index outran the physical index by a considerable margin, not unexpected in view of the increase in the production of quality steel during the index period.

The index figures for 1938 to 1940 must be regarded with caution. As already noted, substantial productivity claims were made for individual enterprises for the years 1938 and 1939, though the performances of the industry for those years were described as unsatisfactory.[48]

From 1928 to 1937, there was an indicated productivity increase to 247 (1928 = 100) when measured in physical output per wage earner. The coming into production of new facilities in the early thirties was

[47] Anglo-American Council on Productivity, *Iron and Steel,* pp. 34–37. See also Veingarten, *op. cit.,* p. 403, where it is indicated that in 1935 there was a range from 92 wage earners per open hearth furnace at Dzherzhinsk to 246 at the Ordzhonokidze plant.

[48] See *supra,* p. 129.

TABLE 39

INDEXES OF LABOR PRODUCTIVITY IN THE SOVIET IRON AND STEEL INDUSTRY, 1928–40

(1928 = 100)

YEAR	ANNUAL OUTPUT OF STEEL PER WAGE EARNER[a]	VALUE OF ANNUAL OUTPUT OF STEEL PRODUCTS PER WAGE EARNER
1928	100.0	100.0[b]
1929	111.8	115.1[b]
1930	123.7	128.7[b]
1931	110.1	122.4[b]
1932	100.5	133.7[b]
1933	105.6	141.3[b]
1934	136.6	179.2[b]
1935	172.1	219.2[b]
1936	227.5	279.9[c]
1937	246.8[g]	302.6[d,g]
1938	n.a.[h]	302.9—315.2[e]
1939	n.a.	n.a.
1940	n.a.	319.6[f]

[a] Data are from Tables 31 and 36. For the years 1929 to 1931, inclusive, industry section data rather than labor section employment data are used, due to the unavailability of the latter. For the early years, however, the two series run closely parallel.

[b] Trud v SSSR, 1936, p. 142. Use of the industry section labor force data and value of output in Sotsialisticheskoe stroitel'stvo SSSR, 1936, p. 7, yields the following index figures, also based on 1928: 1932—126.7; 1933—135.6; and 1934—173.8.

[c] Planovoe khoziaistvo, 1939, No. 3, p. 151. The series from which this figure is derived differs slightly from those published in the official statistical yearbooks. An alternative figure of 253.5 is found in S. M. Veingarten, Ekonomika i planirovanie chernoi metallurgii, p. 86, calculated from industry section labor force data and consistent with the alternative figures for 1932–34 given in note b, supra.

[d] E. L. Granovskii and B. L. Markus, Ekonomika sotsialisticheskoi promyshlennosti, p. 460. The series as given in Table 39 is consistent with the claims that labor productivity in the iron and steel industry rose by 35.8 percent during the First Five Year Plan and by 126.3 percent during the Second Five Year Plan. See Stal', 1947, No. 11, p. 1042.

[e] Sotsialisticheskoe stroitel'stvo SSSR, 1939, p. 38. The figures are given in the source as percentage increases in productivity based on 1929 and 1933. The application of these percentages to the index numbers for the earlier years yields the alternate data shown in the table.

[f] The 1941 Plan, p. 516, called for an output of 14,938 rubles per wage earner in enterprises under the jurisdiction of the Commissariat of Ferrous Metallurgy, which in turn was 110.2 percent of the expected output in 1940. In 1936, average annual output per wage earner for the Metal Trust, which was later transformed into the Commissariat of Ferrous Metallurgy, was 11,868 rubles. Sovetskaia metallurgiia, 1937, No. 3, p. 58. The index figure was obtained by comparing these two magnitudes.

[g] On the basis of a production index calculated by pricing Soviet iron and steel com-

NOTES TO TABLE 39 (*Continued*)

modities in 1939 dollars, the 1937 index of output per wage earner may be calculated at 282.7, based on the economic year 1927/28. Alexander Gerschenkron and Nancy Nimitz, *A Dollar Index of Soviet Iron and Steel Output,* p. 52.
[h] n.a. = information not available.

probably responsible in a large measure for this increase. For example, Magnitogorsk experienced a productivity increase of 450 percent in pig iron production from 1932 to 1938.

FACTORS AFFECTING PRODUCTIVITY

Technological. There appears to be a positive relationship between the size of a blast furnace or an open hearth furnace and the labor productivity associated with it.[49] During the thirties the emphasis in Russia was upon the enlargement of furnaces. The average area of a Russian blast furnace increased from 290 cubic meters on October 1, 1928, to 468 cubic meters on January 1, 1938; the comparable figures for open hearth furnaces were 21.8 and 27.0 cubic meters.[50] Of 38 blast furnaces constructed during the first three five year plans, 29 had a capacity exceeding 800 cubic meters, the capacity of the largest being 1,300 cubic meters.[51] By comparison, two new furnaces of the Edgar Thomson works of the U.S. Steel Company, brought into production in 1945, had capacities of 1,460 cubic meters each.[52] However, the older Soviet furnaces resulted in a lower average for the Soviet industry than for the U.S. industry as a whole.

The average heat of U.S. open hearth furnaces constructed during the decade from 1930 to 1940 was 170 net tons; from 1940 to 1950 it was 220 net tons.[53] The "standard" size during the thirties was said to run about 120 tons.[54] The average furnace built in Russia during the thirties

[49] William T. Hogan, *Productivity in the Blast-Furnace and Open-Hearth Segments of the Steel Industry,* p. 127. The U.S. Steel Company reported that a 20-foot blast furnace with an area of 314 square feet will produce 705 tons of iron a day, and that a 27-foot furnace with an area of 573 square feet will produce 1,283 tons a day, with exactly the same crew. See R. Conrad Cooper, *op. cit.,* p. 14.

[50] Veingarten, *op. cit.,* p. 334.

[51] Bardin and Bannyi, *op. cit.,* p. 76.

[52] Hogan, *op. cit.,* p. 44.

[53] *Ibid.,* p. 92.

[54] Boylston, *op. cit.,* p. 240.

exceeded 165 tons, and it was asserted that in 1940 the large furnace played a relatively more important role in the USSR than in the United States.[55]

In rolling, the principal U.S. advantage lay in the greater advancement of the technique of continuous hot-rolling. In 1938 there were in operation in the United States 28 continuous hot strip mills, with a rated capacity of 12.5 million tons out of a total rated capacity for the same year of 16.2 million tons of sheet and strip.[56] In the Soviet Union, it appears that continuous hot strip mills were to be found in 1940 only at Zaporozhstal, Makeyevka, and Magnitogorsk.[57]

It is difficult to compare differences in the mechanization of furnaces. According to Russian statistics, 49 percent of all Russian blast furnaces were "completely mechanized" in 1939, 35.6 per cent were "partly mechanized," and the rest were nonmechanized.[58] Comparable U.S. statistics are not available, except for the fact that by 1950 the hand-charged furnaces had been completely eliminated.[59]

The influence of the various technological factors upon Russian productivity is evident from Table 40, where the level of productivity in 1938 is shown for various enterprises, classified according to their modernity. There was, in general, a direct relationship between the modernity of plants, either because of recency of construction or reconstruction, and their productivity.

Organization. Among the organizational factors that have been cited as contributory to comparatively low Soviet productivity are poor organization of repair,[60] excessive Soviet employment in in-plant transport,[61] and excessive specialization and insufficient general training of Soviet workers.[62] The following comparison of the structure of the labor force in a U.S. Steel Company plant and a Soviet plant of com-

[55] Bardin and Bannyi, *op. cit.,* p. 88.

[56] Camp and Francis, *op. cit.,* p. 1209; American Iron and Steel Institute, *Annual Statistical Report,* 1939, p. 43.

[57] Bardin and Bannyi, *op. cit.,* p. 111.

[58] *Ibid.,* p. 127. Part mechanization consisted in mechanization of stocking and charging. Nonmechanization meant vertical hoisting of the charge and hand charging.

[59] Anglo-American Council on Productivity, *Iron and Steel,* p. 35.

[60] "Each metallurgical plant tries to concentrate within itself all the necessary repairmen. In addition, each department tries to maintain its own repair staff." Veingarten, *op. cit.,* p. 404.

[61] *Problemy ekonomiki,* 1940, Nos. 11–12, p. 102.

[62] *Planovoe khoziaistvo,* 1936, Nos. 9–10, p. 30.

TABLE 40

LABOR PRODUCTIVITY IN SOVIET IRON AND STEEL ENTERPRISES,
CLASSIFIED ACCORDING TO MODERNITY, 1938

	OUTPUT OF PIG IRON PER WAGE EARNER (METRIC TONS)	OUTPUT OF STEEL PER WAGE EARNER (METRIC TONS)	OUTPUT OF ROLLED STEEL PER WAGE EARNER (METRIC TONS)
New Plants			
Magnitogorsk	2,523	928	480
Kuznetsk	1,835	813	436
Krivoi Rog	1,605	n.a.[a]	n.a.
Azovstal'	1,611	610	n.a.
Completely Reconstructed			
Dzherzhinsk	707	485	270
Kirov	2,024	530	362
Voikov	1,251	n.a.	407
Voroshilov	1,049	311	194
Partially Reconstructed			
Petrovsk	677	380	266
Ordzhonokidze	626	388	219
Nonreconstructed			
Frunze	538	345	112
Almaznyansk	420	n.a.	n.a.

Source: A. A. Arakelian, "Proizvoditel'nost' truda v chernoi metallurgiia SSSR", in Akademiia Nauk, Institut Ekonomiki, *Proizvoditel'nost' truda v promyshlennosti SSSR,* pp. 55, 68, 72, 75.

[a] n.a. = information not available.

parable size (probably Magnitogorsk) brings out some of these differences:[63]

DEPARTMENT	U.S. STEEL COMPANY PLANT, 1935–36 (PERCENTAGE OF TOTAL LABOR FORCE)	SOVIET PLANT, 1940 (PERCENTAGE OF TOTAL LABOR FORCE)
Basic iron and steel	73.1	38.0
Repair	5.0	11.3
Power	3.6	6.2
Laboratory and technical control	1.7	4.8
Technical safety	0.2	0.6
Transportation	12.7	30.9
Health	1.5	3.2
Engineering	0.5	1.2
Managerial	1.7	3.8
Total	100.0	100.0

[63] *Problemy ekonomiki,* 1940, Nos. 11–12, p. 102.

PRODUCTIVITY TRENDS SINCE 1940

Although it has been claimed by the Russians that their iron and steel labor productivity rose by 31 percent in the unoccupied portion of the country from 1940 to 1944,[64] it was admitted that in 1946, for the entire country, the output of iron and steel per wage earner, measured in constant rubles, was below the 1940 level; in the formerly occupied portions of southern Russia, productivity was only slightly more than 50 percent of 1940.[65] By 1950, however, iron and steel labor productivity was put at 133 percent of the 1940 level,[66] this new level having purportedly been attained in 1948.[67] Reported productivity increases in 1951 and 1952 would put the index for the latter year at 157, based on 1940.[68] During the first half of 1948, productivity in the eastern, nonoccupied facilities was given as 117.3 percent of 1940,[69] and in the southern mills at 86.1 percent of 1940.[70] The output of steel per wage earner in June, 1948, was stated to be 115 percent of 1940 performance at Kuznetsk and 124 percent at Magnitogorsk.[71]

This is virtually all the information available with respect to postwar productivity in this industry. Since the percentage changes are in most cases based on the value indexes of production, an upward bias may have been imparted to the productivity data through pricing methods employed in constructing the index. A productivity increase of some magnitude in the iron and steel facilities of unoccupied Russia, from 1940 to 1950, cannot be ruled out. Even assuming, however, that productivity in the iron and steel mills of the Urals and Siberia stood, say, at 150 percent of the 1940 level by 1950 (compared with 117 percent in January-June, 1948), labor productivity in the central and southern mills, most of which were damaged or destroyed, would have had to be in the vicinity of 120 percent of 1940 in 1950 to yield the average level claimed for the latter year, given the geographic distribution of indus-

[64] *Stal'*, 1947, No. 11, p. 1042.
[65] *Ibid.*, No. 4, p. 291.
[66] *Planovoe khoziaistvo*, 1952, No. 1, p. 29.
[67] *Voprosy ekonomiki*, 1951, No. 8, p. 47.
[68] *Trud*, January 29, 1952, p. 1; *ibid.*, January 23, 1953, p. 1.
[69] *Ibid.*, 1948, No. 6, p. 79.
[70] *Professional'nye soiuzy*, 1949, No. 3, p. 9.
[71] *Stal'*, 1948, No. 9.

try.[72] In support of this proposition there is the assertion that the reconstructed facilities were enlarged and modernized, with a consequent gain in productivity.[73] However, it is at least questionable that the productivity of the war-damaged portion of the industry could have risen to this height from the 86 percent of the 1940 level reported for 1948.[74]

No official index of U.S. steel productivity is available since 1939. The best unofficial estimate places the 1950 level at 34.2 percent above that prevailing in 1939, though the drastic changes in the product mix between 1939 and 1950 dictate the acceptance of any such estimate only with considerable caution.[75] It is of some interest to note, however, that the general magnitude of the productivity increase is very close to that claimed for the Soviet steel industry during the same period.

[72] The distribution of iron and steel production in the Soviet Union may be estimated as follows:

| | PERCENTAGE OF TOTAL OUTPUT | | | |
| | Pig iron | | Steel | |
	1939	1950	1939	1950
South and central	73.3	57	71.3	54
Urals	16.4	34	18.6	34
Siberia	10.3	9	10.1	12
Total	100.0	100	100.0	100

The 1939 data are from Bardin and Bannyi, *op. cit.*, p. 27. The percentages for 1950 were estimated by means of data contained in the results of the Fourth Five Year Plan. See *Trud,* April 17, 1951, p. 1.

[73] For example, open hearth furnaces with heat capacities of 300 to 350 tons were constructed at Makeyevka and Azovstal'. See *Stal'*, 1947, No. 3, p. 195. A reconstructed blast furnace at the Stalin Works in the Donbas was said to be manned by 113 wage earners, as compared with 338 before reconstruction. See *Stal'*, 1947, No. 7, p. 579.

[74] M. Gardner Clark has argued that the 1950 productivity level claimed by the Russians was not "impossible, or even improbable, of attainment." His assertion is based on the fact that in late 1948, 1949, and 1950 some of the largest and most modern of the southern furnaces first came into production. See Abram Bergson (ed.), *Soviet Economic Growth*, p. 224.

[75] Wage Stabilization Board, *Productivity, Statement of Jules Backman*, p. 45.

IX

MACHINERY

THE procedure employed for the measurement of productivity in the other industries covered in this volume is not appropriate for the machinery manufacturing industries. Variation in product between countries, as well as heterogeneity of the product within each country's industry, renders comparisons in kind of dubious validity. Such international productivity comparisons as have been made have been based on census value of output per wage earner, the currency conversion problem being taken care of either by using some official or actual rate of exchange,[1] or by developing a special rate of exchange appropriate to machinery products,[2] after expressing the productivity of each country in local values.

The procedure followed in this section involves the use of a dollar index of Soviet machinery products constructed in the following manner:

An attempt was made to obtain Soviet data on quantities of output for as many items and for as many years as possible within the machinery group. . . .Thereafter, the maximum number of American prices of the year 1939 was determined for the individual items of Soviet machinery output. The multiplication of such prices by the quantities of output yielded the dollar values of equipment.[3]

Where the Machinery Index coverage of a Soviet machinery group is sufficiently complete, the gross value of Soviet output per wage earner, expressed in 1939 dollars, may be compared with Census value of product per wage earner in the United States for corresponding product

---

[1] L. Rostas, in his *Comparative Productivity in British and American Industry,* employs the official rate of exchange prevailing in the years with which he is concerned.

[2] A dollar-ruble conversion rate appropriate to machinery manufacturing was developed by S. Yugenburg in *Planovoe khoziaistvo,* 1937, No. 3, p. 39. For a critique of the results, see Alexander Gerschenkron, *A Dollar Index of Soviet Machinery Output, 1927–28 to 1937,* pp. 59–67 (hereinafter referred to as the *Machinery Index*).

[3] *Ibid.,* p. 13.

groups. In this way the use of an official exchange rate, which would be particularly hazardous in the case of the ruble-dollar ratio, is avoided.

It should be emphasized, however, that this procedure differs fundamentally from that employed elsewhere in this volume. Once a departure is made from a comparison of productivity measured in homogeneous physical units, index number problems cannot be avoided. In this case, the use of U.S. gross value weights for valuing Soviet output results in the adoption of U.S. technological and economic relationships as norms. The resultant aggregates would equal those secured by the use of Soviet value weights for both countries, or of indigenous weights for each country, only upon the assumptions (*a*) that the labor input structures of the two countries were proportional, i.e., that there was a fundamental likeness in technology and economic scarcity relationships, and (*b*) that the U.S. gross value weights reflected relative U.S. labor inputs. An appraisal of these assumptions would involve us in another volume. Suffice it to note that the alternative procedure mentioned above, that of valuing the output of each country in local currency and converting one of the currencies into the other, involves assumptions which are at least as stringent.

There are also some practical drawbacks in the procedure followed. For the years after 1935, the Machinery Index is based to a large extent on estimates rather than on actual Soviet physical output data, decreasing its reliability.[4] Moreover, the Machinery Index is not complete for many of the U.S. Census machinery groups, either because individual items had no U.S. counterpart or could not be priced in dollars for other reasons. It has been necessary to fill in the gaps by imputing rough, sometimes arbitrary prices to items of machinery not included in the Index in order to secure comparable industry groups for the two countries. Finally, discrepancies in industrial classification rendered it necessary to undertake adjustment in some cases, usually on the basis of insufficient data.

THE INDUSTRIES COVERED

The branches of machinery production for which comparison can be made are: (*a*) locomotives and railroad cars; (*b*) tractors; (*c*) agricul-

---

[4] See *ibid.*, p. 18.

tural machinery; (*d*) construction machinery; and (*e*) automobiles. The importance of these branches relative to the machinery industry as a whole, in terms of wage earner employment, is shown in Table 41 for both Russia and the United States. While the coverage would appear

TABLE 41

WAGE EARNER EMPLOYMENT IN FIVE BRANCHES OF THE AMERICAN AND RUSSIAN MACHINERY INDUSTRIES

BRANCH	UNITED STATES[a]		RUSSIA[b]	
	Number of Wage Earners, 1939	*Percentage of Total Machinery Wage Earners*	*Number of Wage Earners, January 1, 1936*	*Percentage of Total Machinery Wage Earners*
Locomotives and cars	30,993	2.3	107,200	9.3
Tractors	31,275	2.3	44,700	3.9
Automobiles	397,537	29.8	41,900	3.6
Agricultural machinery	27,806	2.1	75,700	6.6
Construction machinery	17,259	1.3	19,000	1.7
Total	504,870	37.8	288,500	25.1
All machinery, including electrical	1,335,507[c]	100.0	1,152,300[c]	100.0

[a] U.S. Department of Commerce, Bureau of the Census, *Census of Manufactures,* 1940, II, Part II, 361 ff.

[b] *Trud v SSSR,* 1936, p. 65.

[c] The absolute totals for all machinery are not conceptually identical for the two countries and therefore do not constitute an index of the relative size of the two industries.

more complete for the United States than for Russia, the reverse is true if the automobile industry, which bulks so large in the United States, is abstracted. In fact, four of the five groups are major industries in Russia, whereas they are of lesser importance in the United States.

Some gauge of the representativeness of these groups can be secured, for the United States, by comparing value added per wage earner in the five groups shown in Table 41 with the same measure for the entire Census machinery industry. In 1939, value added per wage earner in the five groups equaled $3,345, compared with $3,565 for the industry as a whole.[5] The difference of about 6 percent is not sufficiently large to impugn the representativeness of the sample. For Russia, gross value of output per wage earner in 1934 was 10,773 1926/27 rubles in the five groups against 9,525 rubles for machinery as a whole.[6] However, the gross value figures, which are used in the absence of value added data, are less reliable for the purpose at hand.

All of the five machinery groups were important and expanding industries in Russia during the late thirties. In the United States, on the other hand, there had been a considerable shrinkage in production during the thirties, and by 1939 the output levels of the previous decade were just being recovered. Fabricant has found a rapid rate of productivity growth in new, expanding industries but no clear relationship between productivity and output in the more mature phases of an industry's existence.[7] Declining output may well be correlated with increasing productivity, under certain circumstances; e.g., from 1937 to 1939, value added by U.S. agricultural machinery production fell by 24 percent, yet output per wage earner increased by 20 percent.

The method employed by the Machinery Index of computing gross value of output for industry groups entails some adjustments in matching Russian and American industry groups. The Machinery Index simply prices the individual items of machinery at 1939 dollar levels, multiplies price by quantity, and aggregates to secure the industry total. In the U.S. Census of Manufactures, the gross value product of an industry is normally represented by the following component elements:

Machinery products (classified)

Parts manufactured

Miscellaneous products not specified

Receipts for contract and repair work

Other products (not classified in the industry)

In effect, the method employed in computing the Machinery Index produces a figure comparable only to the first of the U.S. components, machinery products (classified). Presumably some of the additional U.S. components have their counterpart in the Russian industry; and

[5] U.S. *Census of Manufactures*, 1939, Vol. II.

[6] *Sotsialisticheskoe stroitel'stvo*, 1936, p. 8. This figure excludes repair facilities.

[7] Solomon Fabricant, *Employment in Manufacturing, 1899–1939*, Chap. 4.

the Russian labor force figures are global, relating to the totality of products manufactured in the industry.

In general, the procedure followed has been simply to assume that the product of each Russian industry group other than machinery products (classified) bears the same relation to the total product of the group as in the corresponding U.S. industry group. In specified cases, however, more refined adjustments have been made where a blanket assumption of proportionality would have led to obvious error.

PRODUCTIVITY TRENDS IN MACHINERY MANUFACTURING AS A WHOLE

The available statistics on employment in the Soviet machinery industry from 1928 to 1938 are shown in Table 42. The first two columns include the production of such metalware as electric lamps, armatures, instruments, cable, screens, chains, etc.; the third is limited to employment in the production of machinery proper.[8] The differences in magnitude between the first two series are presumably due to the different coverage of the industry and labor section statistics.[9]

The first of the series, that relating to the number of wage earners in machinery and metalworking of the industry section type, was employed in the computation of two indexes of labor productivity, which in Table 43 are compared with official productivity figures released by the Soviet authorities. The use of the third series, that limited to wage earners in machinery construction, would have produced a somewhat lower rate of growth; e.g., the index figure for 1934 would have stood at 206.7, compared with the 220.0 shown in the table. However, this series had the serious disadvantage of terminating in 1934. Use of the employment series compiled according to the labor section concept, while it would have produced wide variation from the computed index for individual years, would have shown a rate of productivity growth approximating that in the computed index for the period 1928 to 1934 (226.3 compared with 220.0).

If one turns to the data in Table 43,[10] it is evident that the series

[8] The Soviet categories of machine production (*mashinostroenie*) and manufacture of metalware (*metallicheskie izdeliia*) have no precise analogue in U.S. Census classification practice.

[9] See *supra*, pp. 38ff.

[10] It should be noted that these figures are limited to the Soviet census classification

culled from published productivity figures and that computed on the basis of the official productivity index are in substantial agreement, despite deviations for particular years. They indicate that in 1938 Soviet

TABLE 42

EMPLOYMENT OF WAGE EARNERS IN THE SOVIET MACHINERY AND METALWORKING INDUSTRY, 1928–38

(*In thousands of persons*)

YEAR	AVERAGE ANNUAL NUMBER IN MACHINE CONSTRUCTION AND METALWORKING (INDUSTRY SECTION)[a]	NUMBER OF WAGE EARNERS AND LEARNERS IN MACHINE CONSTRUCTION AND METALWORKING, JANUARY 1[c] (LABOR SECTION)	AVERAGE ANNUAL NUMBER OF WAGE EARNERS IN MACHINE CONSTRUCTION, INCLUDING REPAIR SHOPS (INDUSTRY SECTION)
1928	599.7	454.2	479.9[d]
1929	708.0	503.3	543.3[a]
1930	998.2	640.4	771.2[a]
1931	1,440.9	1,152.6	1,192.9[a]
1932	1,811.3	1,485.3	1,485.8[d]
1933	1,761.4	1,401.0	1,487.6[d]
1934	1,896.9	1,397.2	1,615.0[d]
1935	n.a.[g]	1,631.8	n.a.
1936	n.a.	1,901.0[e]	n.a.
1937	2,570.4[b]	n.a.	n.a.
1938	2,674.3[f]	n.a.	n.a.

[a] *Socialist Construction in the USSR*, 1936, p. 65.

[b] Based on data relating to total fixed capital and fixed capital per wage earner. The sources are: *Sotsialisticheskoe stroitel'stvo*, 1939, p. 37; L. M. Kantor, *Osnovnye fondy promyshlennosti i ikh ispol'zovanie*, p. 25; and an unpublished manuscript by Norman Kaplan.

[c] *Trud v SSSR*, 1936, p. 150.

[d] *Sotsialisticheskoe stroitel'stvo*, 1936, p. 8. For 1932 and 1933, the following figures appear in an otherwise identical series in *Sotsialisticheskoe stroitel'stvo*, 1935, p. 33: 1932—1,429.6; 1933—1,484.9.

[e] A figure of 1,904.1 can be derived for July 1, 1936, from *Zhenshchina v SSSR*, 1937, pp. 62, 65.

[f] Estimated from *Sotsialisticheskoe stroitel'stvo*, 1939, pp. 36, 38.

[g] n.a. = information not available.

"large-scale industry." However, "small-scale industry" was of relatively little importance in this sector of the economy. In machinery manufacture, wage earner employment in small-scale industry was only 0.7 percent of that in large-scale industry in 1933. The figure was somewhat higher for metalware manufacture (3.3 percent). Only in the case of repair shops was the contribution of small-scale industry significant. See *Sotsialisticheskoe stroitel'stvo*, 1935, pp. 7–8.

TABLE 43

INDEXES OF PRODUCTIVITY IN SOVIET MACHINERY
MANUFACTURING, 1928–38
(1928 = 100)

YEAR	INDEX AS STATED IN VARIOUS OFFICIAL SOURCES	COMPUTED FROM OFFICIAL PRODUCTION INDEX[d]	COMPUTED FROM GERSCHENKRON MACHINERY INDEX[f]
1928	100.0[a]	100.0[g]	100[g]
1929	117.6[a]	112.6[g]	120.3[g]
1930	124.9[a]	124.3[g]	126.7[g]
1931	139.5[a]	157.6	109.4
1932	157.4[a]	153.2	87.4
1933	190.1[a]	186.9	101.4
1934	221.1[a]	220.0	114.1
1935	252.1[b]	n.a.[h]	n.a.
1936	313.5[b]	n.a.	n.a.
1937	330.4[b]	344.0	122.4
1938	373.0[c]	364.3[e]	n.a.

[a] *Trud v SSSR*, 1936, p. 150.

[b] K. I. Klimenko, "Proizvoditel'nost' truda v mashinostroitelnoi i metalloobrabatyvai-ushchei promyshlennosti," in Akademiia Nauk, Institut Ekonomiki, *Proizvoditel'nost' truda v promyshlennosti SSSR*, p. 216.

[c] *Sotsialisticheskoe stroitel'stvo*, 1939, p. 38.

[d] This index was computed from the official Soviet index of machinery production, as compiled in the Machinery Index, p. 28. However, see *ibid.*, Appendix VIII, for an analysis of the inconsistencies in the various Soviet sources. The labor force used is that shown in the first column of Table 42, relating to the number of wage earners employed in machinery construction and metalworking.

[e] The output data for this figure were secured by applying to the production index shown in *Machinery Index*, p. 28, the percentage increase in output shown for machinery products in *Sotsialisticheskoe stroitel'stvo*, 1939, p. 36.

[f] Computed from the Gerschenkron index of Soviet machinery production, *Machinery Index*, p. 25, and the first labor force series in Table 32.

[g] The production data for these years related to the fiscal rather than the calendar years. No attempt has been made to adjust for this; it was merely assumed that data covering the fiscal year October 1–September 30 related to the following calendar year.

[h] n.a. = information not available.

machinery output per wage earner stood at between 364 percent and 373 percent of the 1928 level, accepting the official Soviet index of machinery production at face value. On the other hand, the index of labor productivity based on the Gerschenkron Machinery Index presents a radically different picture. That index, terminating in 1937, shows only a very moderate rise in productivity up to that point.

Which of the indexes should be accepted as a better approximation of the trend in Soviet machinery labor productivity is a question not susceptible of easy answer. Professor Gerschenkron has said of his own production index: "It provides . . . a very inadequate idea of the effort which the expansion of their machinery output has cost the Russians. Its coverage is incomplete, and there is a suspicion that the implied rate of growth is somewhat lower than the one that would have emerged from a fuller coverage. . . . With all its deficiencies, the index should still provide a possible basis for gauging the development of a crucial branch of Russia's industrial economy."[11] Yet the increase in labor productivity yielded by the Gerschenkron Index is so much less than that estimated for almost every other industry considered in this study, including industries in which capital investment was held to a minimum, that the appropriateness of this Index for the purpose in hand may well be subject to question. We will return to this matter after having examined productivity trends in the component branches of the industry.

No firm estimate of relative Soviet–U.S. productivity in machinery production as a whole is possible in the absence of a conversion factor by which to translate adequately the gross value of Soviet machinery output in rubles into dollars; the Machinery Index is limited in its coverage and does not yield the requisite global dollar value.[12] Soviet estimates of relative productivity range from 41.4 percent to 48.9 percent for the years USSR 1936–U.S. 1929; there is also an estimate of 55.7 percent for the years USSR 1936–U.S. 1934.[13] The figure most frequently quoted in Russian economic literature is that of 41.4 percent cited immediately above.[14] There are no summary figures for U.S. machinery

[11] *Machinery Index,* p. 58.

[12] Professor Hodgman has calculated very roughly, on the basis of the *Machinery Index,* that "*total output* of the Soviet machinery industry at 1939 dollar prices in 1937 may have been about 34 percent of the *total output* of the American machinery industry in 1939." Donald R. Hodgman, "Soviet Machinery Output," *The American Slavic and East European Review,* February, 1953, p. 63. On this basis, Soviet productivity in 1937 may be estimated as having been between 23 percent and 27 percent of the 1939 U.S. level, depending on the assumptions that are made with regard to comparative classification of particular component industries.

[13] K. I. Klimenko, "Proizvoditel'nost' truda v mashinostroitelnoi i metalloobrabatyvaiushchei promyshlennosti," in Akademiia Nauk, Institut Ekonomiki, *Proizvoditel'nost' truda v promyshlennosti SSSR,* p. 179.

[14] This estimate is to be found in Ia. A. Ioffe, *SSSR i kapitalisticheskie strany,* p. 79. There is no indication in the source of the method of computation.

manufacturing productivity between 1929 and 1939. Therefore, an appraisal of the relative productivity standing of the Soviet and U.S. machinery manufacturing industries in the late thirties is best deferred until some of the component machinery industries are examined.

THE MANUFACTURE OF RAILROAD LOCOMOTIVES AND CARS

The production of railroad equipment has long been one of Russia's major machinery industries. In 1913, 664 steam locomotives (including industrial) were produced;[15] the reported number produced in 1938 was 1,626.[16] By comparison, 1939 production in the United States was 400 railroad and 430 mining and industrial locomotives.

Statistics for the United States.[17] For purposes of comparison with the Soviet industry, two U.S. Census industry groups must be combined: locomotives, and cars and car equipment. The relevant production data are as follows:

GROSS VALUE OF LOCOMOTIVE PRODUCTION, UNITED STATES, 1939

(In thousands of dollars)

Locomotives and parts made in the locomotive industry	$38,766
Less: Estimated value of parts made in the locomotive industry	7,366[18]
	$31,400
Add: Locomotives made in the railroad car industry[19]	4,388
Gross value of locomotives	$35,788[20]

---

[15] *Sotsialisticheskoe stroitel'stvo,* 1936, p. 163.

[16] P. E. Garbutt, *The Russian Railways,* p. 45.

[17] All U.S. data in the following sections have been taken from the U.S. *Census of Manufactures,* 1939, Vol. II, Part II. No specific references will be made.

[18] For the rationale of this deduction, see *supra,* p. 141.

[19] The gross value of locomotives made in the car industry and in railroad repair shops was $8,777,000. Only the portion of locomotives made in the car industry should be included here. It is assumed arbitrarily to be one half of the total.

[20] Several items of equipment are included in these totals which are not included in the *Machinery Index* and which presumably were not produced in quantity in Russia at the time, e.g., trackless trolleys. They are not deducted from the U.S. data on the assumption that they had no Russian counterpart. The U.S. data also included $1,782,000 worth of electric railroad and self-propelled cars, but there appears to be a corresponding item in the Russian "passenger car" category.

GROSS VALUE OF RAILROAD CAR PRODUCTION, UNITED STATES, 1939

(In thousands of dollars)

Cars and car equipment made in the
    car industry $110,414

Less: Estimated value of parts made in
    the car industry   29,812[21]

                                 $ 80,602

Add: Cars made in the locomotive in-
    dustry   12,274

Gross value of cars $ 92,876[22]

Gross value of cars and locomotives   128,664

In determining the size of the labor force to apply to these data, it is necessary to take into account certain differences in product composition between the Russian and American industries.[23] Among other things, the U.S. locomotive industry produced in 1939 power shovels, drag lines and cranes, and castings for sale outside the industry, while the car industry produced structural steel and air conditioning units, presumably because of excess capacity. It seems reasonable to assume that Russian facilities were devoted exclusively to manufacture of the principal products and that there was no substantial production of secondary products. Therefore the following adjustments should be made, on the basis of relative value of product:

LOCOMOTIVES

    Wage earners, 1939   6,470

    Less: Number attributable
        to "other" products (11 percent)   710   5,760

CARS

    Wage earners, 1939   24,523

    Less: Number attributable
        to "other" products (6 percent)   1,470   23,053

    Adjusted number of wage earners   28,813

[21] See *supra*, p. 141.

[22] See *supra*, p. 146, *n* 20.

[23] There was in the U.S. car industry a substantial value item for contract and repair work, and the question arises as to whether the labor force should be reduced accordingly. Although Russian labor force statistics include a separate category for railroad repair shops, it is likely that the machinery plants also performed repair work. To prevent understatement of Russian productivity, no adjustment is made in the U.S. labor force for this item.

TABLE 44

PRODUCTION AND EMPLOYMENT IN SOVIET LOCOMOTIVE AND
RAILROAD CAR MANUFACTURING, 1928–36

YEAR	GROSS VALUE OF LOCOMOTIVES AND CARS (MILLIONS OF 1926/27 RUBLES)	GROSS VALUE OF LOCOMOTIVES AND CARS[d] (MILLIONS OF 1939 DOLLARS)	NUMBER OF WAGE EARNERS (THOUSANDS) (INDUSTRY SECTION)
1928	n.a.[a]	73.8	45.5[e]
1929	n.a.	87.0	63.4[e]
1930	n.a.	118.9	83.0[e]
1931	n.a.	165.2	103.4[f]
1932	545[b]	169.9	96.4[b,g]
1933	589[b]	187.7	90.7[b]
1934	759[b]	239.7	99.4[b,h]
1935	n.a.	305.6	n.a.
1936	1,365[c]	228.0	135.0[e,h]

[a] n.a. = information not available.

[b] *Sotsialisticheskoe stroitel'stvo*, 1936, p. 10.

[c] K. I. Klimenko, "Proizvoditel'nost' truda v mashinostroitelnoi i metalloobrab-atyvaiushchei promyshlennosti SSSR," in Akademiia Nauk, Institut Ekonomiki, *Proizvoditel'nost' truda v promyshlennosti SSSR*, p. 184.

[d] *Machinery Index*, p. 71.

[e] These figures are from *Sotsialisticheskoe stroitel'stvo SSSR*, 1934, p. 324. They were given as of the first of each year; the data in the table were estimated for each year by averaging the numbers at the beginning and at the end of the year.

[f] *Sotsialisticheskoe stroitel'stvo SSSR*, 1934, p. 325.

[g] See *ibid.;* a figure of 96.9 thousand appears on p. 325 as a continuation of the series for the years 1928 to 1931. Thus we may surmise that the latter data are industry section type statistics.

[h] The number of wage earners on July 1, 1934, according to a labor section source, was 84.4 thousand; on January 1, 1936, 107.2 thousand. See *Trud v SSSR*, 1935, p. 74; *ibid.*, 1936, p. 65.

Statistics for Russia. Table 44 contains Russian production and employment data for the years 1928 to 1936. Information is lacking for subsequent years.

The Machinery Index carries a gross value figure of $103,375,000 for locomotive production alone in 1936. Several items known to have been produced in 1935, and probably also in subsequent years, were omitted from the Index because of the difficulty of finding appropriate 1939 U.S. prices. These were tank locomotives, narrow gauge locomotives, self-propelled track inspection cars, standard gasoline switching locomotives, and narrow gauge switching locomotives. Of these, only the first two were in quantity production, to judge by the 1935 output data (output data for subsequent years are not available). Prices are imputed to those items as follows:

	OUTPUT, 1935	IMPUTED PRICE	GROSS VALUE
Tank locomotives	109	$80,000[24]	$8,720,000
Narrow gauge locomotives	161	6,200[25]	998,000
			$9,718,000

The total of $9,718,000 for these two items equaled 7 percent of the Index value of locomotive output in 1935. Assuming that this ratio remained constant during the following year, the adjusted value of locomotive output is (in thousands of 1939 dollars):

	1936
Machinery Index value of locomotives	$103,375
Add: Adjustment for tank and narrow gauge locomotives	7,236
	$110,611

The Machinery Index estimates as the gross value of Russian railroad cars and equipment in 1936 the total of $124,612,000. The following items could not be priced, and therefore were not included in the Index:

	OUTPUT, 1935	OUTPUT, 1936	IMPUTED PRICE	1936 VALUE (THOUSANDS OF DOLLARS)
Tank cars, 4-axle	3,839	2,096	$4,500[26]	$9,432
Tank cars, 2-axle	2,807	898	3,600[27]	3,234
Self-dumping cars, 4-axle	33	n.a.[28]		
Self-dumping gondolas, factory use	16	n.a.		
Slag ladle cars	31	n.a.		
Pig iron ladle cars	25	n.a.		
				$12,666

Only the first two items shown were significant quantitatively. The addition of their imputed values to the Machinery Index total increases

[24] Average *Machinery Index* price for freight locomotives.
[25] *Machinery Index* price for mining locomotives.
[26] *Machinery Index* price for 4-axle refrigerator car.
[27] *Machinery Index* price for 2-axle refrigerator car.
[28] n.a. = information not available.

the 1936 output to $137,278,000. The adjusted combined gross value of locomotives and cars becomes $247,889,000.

The choice of an appropriate labor force figure is complicated by the existence of a substantial difference between the industry and labor section series (see Table 44, note h). The only conceptual difference between the two series which appears to provide a possible explanation of the variance is inclusion in the industry section data of wage earners employed in the repair of locomotives and rolling stock outside the manufacturing establishments.[29] We will adhere to the previous practice in this volume of employing labor section data, where available. The appropriate figure for 1936 is 116.8 thousand (including learners and junior service personnel).[30]

Comparative productivity. The foregoing data may now be summarized as follows:

	RUSSIA, 1936	UNITED STATES, 1939
Gross value of output (millions of 1939 dollars)	$247.9	$128.7
Wage earners (thousands)	116.8	28.8
Output per wage earner (1939 dollars)	$2,122	$4,469
Russian productivity as a percentage of U.S. productivity	47	100

These results may be compared with a Soviet attempt to compare productivity based on unit labor requirements for specified types of equipment, as shown in Table 45. The data for locomotives purport to demonstrate that man-hour requirements at the Russian Voroshilovgrad plant in 1936 for the production of an FD (133-ton) locomotive were about twice as great as the estimated requirements to build a similar locomotive at the Baldwin works in the United States, but not substantially greater than the average U.S. requirements. The Voroshilovgrad plant was one of the two principal locomotive plants built during the planning period and was presumably one of the most efficient. It is therefore appropriate to compare it with the largest U.S. plant, that of the Baldwin Locomotive Company, rather than with the U.S. industry in general.

The comparison of freight car productivity in Table 45 indicates that the relatively efficient Red Profintern plant required about 50 percent

[29] See *supra,* p. 39.
[30] This figure is actually that given for January 1, 1936.

more man-hours to build a freight car than the Pressed Steel Car Company in the United States, for the years shown. However, the relatively greater production of large goods cars in the United States renders this comparison of somewhat dubious validity.

TABLE 45

COMPARISONS OF PRODUCTIVITY IN LOCOMOTIVE AND
RAILROAD CAR PRODUCTION DERIVED
FROM RUSSIAN SOURCES

LOCOMOTIVES	1923	1929
All U.S. Locomotive Plants		
Thousands of man-hours per locomotive	17.1	23.5
Adjusted to Russian type FD locomotive	13.8	17.5
Baldwin Locomotive Company, United States		
Thousands of man-hours per locomotive	. . .	14.3
Adjusted to Russian type FD locomotive	. . .	10.7
Voroshilovgrad Plant, USSR (1936)		
Thousands of man-hours per FD locomotive	21.6	
FREIGHT CARS		
All U.S. Freight Car Industry		
Number of cars per wage earner	4.1	3.53
Man-hours per car	620	723
Pressed Steel Company, United States		
Man-hours per car (years of highest output)	530	
Red Profintern Plant, USSR		
Man-hours per 50-ton freight car, 1936	774–851	

Source: K. I. Klimenko, "Proizvoditel'nost' truda v mashinostroitelnoi i metal-loobrabatyvaiushchei promyshlennosti," in Akademiia Nauk, Institut Ekonomiki, *Proizvoditel'nost' truda v promyshlennosti SSSR,* pp. 197, 204.

Another comparison, based on a specially estimated ruble-dollar conversion ratio, yielded the conclusion that Russian railroad equipment output per wage earner in 1936 equaled 31 percent of the 1929 U.S. level.[31] Had the author used labor section rather than industry section statistics in his comparison, the relative level of Russian productivity would have been 36 percent. There was a substantial decline in U.S.

[31] Klimenko, *op. cit.,* p. 240.

productivity in this industry between 1929 and 1939,[32] which serves
further to explain the difference between the estimate above and the
Russian estimate.

Soviet productivity trends, as measured by the official Soviet index
and the Machinery Index, are shown in Table 46 for the years 1928

TABLE 46

INDEXES OF PRODUCTIVITY IN SOVIET LOCOMOTIVE AND
RAILROAD CAR MANUFACTURE, 1928–37
(1932 = 100)

YEAR	BASED ON OFFICIAL SOVIET PRODUCTION INDEX	BASED ON THE MACHINERY INDEX
1928		92.1
1929		77.9
1930		81.3
1931		90.7
1932	100.0	100.0
1933	114.9	117.4
1934	135.1	136.9
1935	n.a.[a]	n.a.
1936	178.8	95.8
1937	200.0[b]	

Source: Table 44.
[a] n.a. = information not available.
[b] *Planovoe khozi'aistvo*, 1937, Nos. 11–12, p. 61.

to 1937. Noteworthy is the extreme divergence in the two indexes after
1934; this was occasioned entirely by the behavior of the respective production indexes, since identical labor force figures were employed. For
prewar years subsequent to 1936 there is only one indication of a productivity increase from 1936 to 1937 (see Table 46, note *a*).

Of the two major locomotive plants constructed during the thirties,
that at Kolomna was converted during the war to the production of
armaments, while the Voroshilovgrad plant was heavily damaged.
However, a new locomotive works was built at Krasnoyarsk, and part of
the evacuated machinery from Voroshilovgrad was used, as was part of

---

[32] According to Fabricant, wage earner employment per unit of output was 46 percent higher in railroad car production and 99 percent higher in locomotive production
in 1939 than in 1929. See Fabricant, *op. cit.*, p. 326.

the personnel. In 1947, labor productivity in the locomotive and railroad car industry as a whole was said to be below the 1940 level, although individual plants were more productive.[33] An unspecified railroad car plant, said to have achieved a "very high" level of productivity in 1948, required 580 man-hours to construct a gondola car in 1948, compared with 860 man-hours in 1940. For the plant as a whole, output per wage earner in 1948 was 123.2 percent of the 1940 level.[34] The Fourth Five Year Plan imposed upon this industry the obligation of doubling its productivity,[35] the highest goal set for any branch of the machinery industry. There is no information regarding the productivity level actually achieved in 1950.

THE MANUFACTURE OF TRACTORS

Statistics for the United States. The gross value of 1939 U.S. tractor production was $156,958,000. Associated with this output were 31,275 wage earners. There was a substantial output of parts and attachments, but since a separate Russian labor force figure relating to tractor parts production is available, it is not necessary to adjust the U.S. tractor labor force. The U.S. tractor industry produced, in addition to tractors, such "other" products as road building and agricultural machinery, with a 1939 gross value of $51 million. It is not unlikely that Soviet tractor plants had similar secondary products, though their relative magnitude was probably smaller. Failure to include the secondary items with U.S. tractor output probably resulted in an understatement of U.S. productivity.

Statistics for Russia. Data on output and employment in the Russian tractor industry for the years 1928 to 1936 are shown in Table 47. It will be noted that in 1928 there was virtually no tractor industry and that not until 1931 did output assume significant proportions. The productivity experience of the industry prior to this year is thus of little relevance.

[33] Unit labor requirements per finished car platform in a plant in the Urals were 20 percent less in 1947 than in 1940. At Kolomna, output per wage earner in 1947 exceeded the 1940 level by 31 percent. See Sh. Turetskii, *Vnutripromyshlennoe nakoplenie v SSSR,* p. 170.

[34] *Narodnoe khoziaistvo SSSR,* Moscow, 1950, p. 172.

[35] *Voprosy ekonomiki,* 1948, No. 6, p. 33.

To judge by published statistics, the Machinery Index appears to have omitted but one product of the industry: traction engines, wheel type. The output of this item in 1935 was only 1,000 units, however, and its omission is not a serious matter.

TABLE 47

PRODUCTION AND EMPLOYMENT IN SOVIET TRACTOR
PRODUCTION, 1928–36

YEAR	GROSS VALUE OF TRACTORS (MILLIONS OF 1926/27 RUBLES)	GROSS VALUE OF TRACTORS (MILLIONS OF 1939 DOLLARS)[e]	NUMBER OF WAGE EARNERS IN THOUSANDS (INDUSTRY SECTION)
1928	n.a.	1.362	n.a.
1929	n.a.	3.367	n.a.
1930	15[a]	8.877	n.a.
1931	119[a]	41.814	n.a.
1932	279[b]	62.160	28.2[f]
1933	469[b]	97.222	36.9[f]
1934	676[b]	137.905	42.3[f,g]
1935	n.a.[c]	177.060	n.a.
1936	1,040[d]	195.310	42.3[d,g]

[a] The figures for 1930 and 1931 are from *Sotsialisticheskoe stroitel'stvo*, 1935, p. 15. The following figures are presented in *Sotsialisticheskoe stroitel'stvo*, 1934, p. 30: 1928—7.0; 1929—21.8; 1930—63; 1931—196. The figures in the later source are accepted as more likely to be consonant with data for subsequent years. However, it is clear that the industry was very small in 1928.

[b] *Sotsialisticheskoe stroitel'stvo*, 1936, p. 9.

[c] n.a. = information not available.

[d] K. I. Klimenko, "Proizvoditel'nost' truda v mashinostroitelnoi i metalloobrabaty-vaiushchei promyshlennosti," in Akademiia Nauk, Institut Ekonomiki, *Proizvoditel'nost' truda v promyshlennosti SSSR*, p. 204.

[e] *Machinery Index*, p. 71. Data for 1928–30 are for fiscal rather than calendar years.

[f] *Sotsialisticheskoe stroitel'stvo*, 1936, p. 9. The industry section statistics for prior years show only aggregate figures for automobile and tractor production. See *Sotsialisticheskoe stroitel'stvo*, 1934, p. 324. These figures exclude wage earners engaged in the manufacture of spare parts for tractors.

[g] According to a labor section source, the number of wage earners in tractor manufacture (excluding spare parts) on July 1, 1934, was 39.4 thousand; on January 1, 1936, it was 44.7 thousand. See *Trud v SSSR*, 1935, p. 74; *ibid.*, 1936, p. 65.

The number of wage earners engaged in tractor production in 1936 was 42.3 thousand, according to an industry section source (Table 47).

However, the labor section figure for January 1, 1936, 44.7 thousand, is so close that the former figure may be accepted as average employment for the year. With the inclusion of learners and junior service personnel,[36] the appropriate figure for our purposes is 46.9 thousand. In addition, there were employed on January 1, 1936, some 20.8 thousand wage earners, learners, and junior service personnel engaged in the manufacture of spare tractor parts (labor section data), who should be included by virtue of the fact that such wage earners were included in the U.S. tractor labor force.[37] Total Soviet employment, comparable to the U.S. Census figure, was thus 67.7 thousand.

Comparative productivity. The foregoing data may be summarized as follows:

	RUSSIA, 1936	UNITED STATES, 1939
Gross value of output (millions of 1939 dollars)	$195.3	$157.0
Wage earners (thousands)	67.7	31.3
Output per wage earner (1939 dollars)	$2,885	$5,016
Russian productivity as a percentage of U.S. productivity	58	100

A Soviet source places Russian tractor productivity in 1936 at 76 percent of the U.S. level in 1929.[38] The same source contains comparative data for a number of machinery groups, and only for electrical machinery was the relative Soviet level estimated as being higher than that for tractor manufacture.

Indexes of labor productivity in Soviet tractor production for the years 1932 to 1937 are presented in Table 48. The disparity between the productivity gains as measured by the official production index and by the Machinery Index is much smaller than in the case of railroad equipment; both record a substantial increase in productivity between 1932 and 1936. Also included in Table 48 are unit labor requirements for two particular tractors from 1932 to 1937, indicating a very substantial

[36] On the basis of the relative employment of wage earners, learners, and junior service personnel on January 1, 1936. See *Trud v SSSR,* 1936, p. 65.

[37] For 1934, the ratio of wage earners manufacturing spare parts to those producing tractors was 41.8 percent (industry section data). The same ratio for January 1, 1936, was 40.3 percent (labor section data). Using the January 1, 1936, labor section figure to represent employment in spare parts manufacture would thus appear to involve only a small potential error.

[38] Klimenko, *op. cit.,* p. 204.

TABLE 48

INDEXES OF PRODUCTIVITY IN SOVIET TRACTOR
MANUFACTURE, 1932–37
(1932 = 100)

YEAR	BASED ON THE OFFI-CIAL SOVIET PRODUCTION INDEX	BASED ON THE MACHIN-ERY INDEX	MAN-HOUR LABOR RE-QUIREMENTS FOR MODEL STZ	KhTZ
1932	100.0	100.0	100.0	100.0
1933	128.4	119.6	177.8	215.6
1934	161.7	147.9	211.6	278.0
1935	n.a.[a]	n.a.	235.0	308.0
1936	248.5	209.5	311.9	420.1
1937	n.a.	n.a.	311.9	420.1

Source: Table 47, and K. I. Klimenko, "Proizvoditel'nost' truda v mashinestroitelnoi i metalloobrabatyvaiushchei promyshlennosti," in Akademiia Nauk, Institut Ekonomiki, *Proizvoditel'nost' truda v promyshlennosti SSSR,* p. 213.

[a] n.a. = information not available.

decline in labor inputs per unit during the period, particularly during the first few years of production.[39]

Productivity data for years subsequent to 1936 are scanty indeed. At the beginning of 1947, unit labor requirements for an STZ tractor produced at the Stalingrad Tractor Plant were reported to be twice as great as in 1940; for a tractor produced at the Altai Agricultural Machine Plant, two and one-half times as great; for cultivator tractors at the Krasni Aksai plant, two times; while for the entire industry, labor productivity was below the 1940 level.[40] No further information was released.

AGRICULTURAL MACHINERY

Statistics for the United States. The gross value of agricultural machinery produced in the United States in 1939 was $118,882,000.

[39] Model STZ was first put into production in 1930; from 1930 to 1931, man-hour unit requirements fell from 1,023 to 386. Model KhTZ was put into production in 1932, and in one year man-hour requirements fell from 442 to 205. Thereafter, the decline was more gradual: to 105 for both models by 1937. See *ibid.,* p. 213.

[40] *Planovoe khoziaistvo,* 1947, No. 1, p. 48. The Altai tractor plant was constructed during the war, while the Krasni Aksai plant was reconstructed after the war. See *Planovoe khoziaistvo,* 1950, No. 1, p. 45.

Attachments and parts valued at an additional $31,696,000 presumably had their counterpart in the Soviet industry and thus need not be included. "Other" products, such as engines, road building machinery, and castings, valued at $11,964,000, were probably not proportionately represented in the Russian industry, but there is no basis for making an adjustment.

Average 1939 wage earner employment in the industry was 27,806.

Statistics for Russia. Available statistics on production and employment for the years 1928 to 1936 are presented in Table 49.

The Machinery Index includes twenty-seven items of agricultural machinery, but omits the ten items listed in Table 50 because of the lack of appropriate prices. To round out the product value of the industry, rough prices have been imputed to these items. The quantities produced during the last year for which output data are available were assumed to apply to the year 1936. The result of this calculation is to add $11,901,000 to the Machinery Index output total, yielding a 1936 estimate for the entire industry of $167,673,000.

Average wage earner employment in the industry during 1936 was 71.8 thousand (industry section source). Employment on January 1, 1936, according to a labor section source, was 75.7 thousand. Since the difference is not great, the average annual employment figure will be used; together with learners and junior service personnel (on the basis of employment of these groups as of January 1, 1936), the appropriate total is 78.9 thousand.

Comparative productivity. The foregoing data may be summarized as follows:

	RUSSIA, 1936	UNITED STATES, 1939
Gross value of output (millions of 1939 dollars)	$167.7	$118.9
Wage earners (thousands)	78.9	27.8
Output per wage earner (1939 dollars)	$2,125	$4,277
Russian productivity as a percentage of U.S. productivity	50	100

A Soviet estimate puts Russian labor productivity in this industry in 1936 at 41.8 percent of the U.S. level in 1929.[41] It has been estimated that output per wage earner in the U.S. agricultural implements indus-

[41] Klimenko, *op. cit.*, p. 204.

TABLE 49

PRODUCTION AND EMPLOYMENT IN THE SOVIET
AGRICULTURAL MACHINERY INDUSTRY, 1928–36

YEAR	GROSS VALUE OF PRODUCT (MILLIONS OF 1926/27 RUBLES)	GROSS VALUE OF PRODUCT (MILLIONS OF 1939 DOLLARS)[e]	NUMBER OF WAGE EARNERS (THOUSANDS) (INDUSTRY SECTION)
1928	139[a]	76.5	40.5[f]
1929	196[a]	118.7	53.8[f]
1930	352[a]	171.0	83.7[f]
1931	431[a]	122.5	106.6[f]
1932	384[b]	86.8	73.0[g]
1933	398[b]	75.8	61.4[g]
1934	373[b]	76.8	56.3[g,j]
1935	n.a.[c]	100.9	n.a.
1936	779[d]	155.8	71.8[h,j]

[a] *Sotsialisticheskoe stroitel'stvo*, 1935, p. 15. Identical figures appear in *Sotsialis-ticheskoe stroitel'stvo*, 1934, p. 30.

[b] *Sotsialisticheskoe stroitel'stvo*, 1936, p. 9. For 1933, the earlier issues of *Sotsialis-ticheskoe stroitel'stvo* show an identical figure, but for 1932 they carry the figure of 430 million rubles, rather than the 384 million rubles shown in the table.

[c] n.a. = information not available.

[d] K. I. Klimenko, "Proizvoditel'nost' truda v mashinostroitelnoi i metalloobra-batyvaiushchei promyshlennosti," in Akademiia Nauk, Institut Ekonomiki, *Proizvoditel'-nost' truda v promyshlennosti SSSR*, p. 192. This figure is consistent with the figure of 384 million rubles for 1932.

[e] *Machinery Index*, p. 71. Data for 1928–30 are for the fiscal year.

[f] *Sotsialisticheskoe stroitel'stvo*, 1934, p. 325. The figures appear in the source as of the first of each year (up to and including 1930); the data in the table were estimated by averaging the number employed at the beginning and at the end of each year. For the years 1928 and 1929, the data include a small number of wage earners engaged in the production of tractors.

[g] *Sotsialisticheskoe stroitel'stvo*, 1936, p. 9. The 1934 edition of *Sotsialisticheskoe stroitel'stvo* puts wage earner employment in 1932 at 86.9 thousand rather than 73.0 thousand as shown in this source. Thus a sharp drop in employment for 1931 to 1932 is recorded in the former source, although not as severe as that shown in the table.

[h] Klimenko, *op. cit.*, p. 192.

[j] The number of wage earners on July 1, 1934, according to a labor section source, was 66.7 thousand; on January 1, 1936, it was 75.7 thousand. See *Trud v SSSR*, 1935, p. 74; *ibid.*, 1936, p. 65.

TABLE 50

ITEMS OF AGRICULTURAL EQUIPMENT NOT INCLUDED IN THE MACHINERY INDEX

	UNIT OUTPUT		ASSIGNED PRICE	GROSS VALUE (THOUSANDS OF 1939 DOLLARS)
Gang plows, tractor drawn	2,627	(1935)	$ 76[a]	$ 200
Interplowing cultivators	15,806	(1935)	82[b]	1,296
Combined plows and drills, tractor drawn	289	(1934)	. . .[c]	. . .
Flax planters	2,400	(1936)	77[d]	185
Reapers, self-raking	37,068	(1935)	81[e]	3,003
Cotton harvesters, pneumatic	75	(1935)	. . .[c]	. . .
Fiax pulling machines	3,300	(1936)	100[f]	330
Grain threshers, horse drawn	6,501	(1935)	983[g]	6,390
Grain grading machines	2,861	(1935)	131[h]	375
Potato grading machines	1,490	(1934)	82[j]	122
Total				$11,901

[a] Average price of moldboard plows, tractor drawn, United States, 1939, from U.S. Department of Commerce, Bureau of the Census, *Manufacture and Sale of Farm Equipment and Related Products,* 1940.

[b] Average of prices assigned by the *Machinery Index* to Cultivators for All-around Plowing, Horse Drawn, and Cultivators for All-around Plowing, Tractor Drawn.

[c] . . . = not significant.

[d] Price assigned by the *Machinery Index* to Universal Planters.

[e] Price assigned by the *Machinery Index* to Reapers, Nonraking.

[f] Average price of Pea and Bean Harvesters, 1939. See note *a* for source.

[g] Price assigned by the *Machinery Index* to Grain Threshers, Tractor Drawn.

[h] Average price of Grain Cleaners and Graders, 1939. See note *a* for source.

[j] Average price of Potato Sorters and Graders, 1939. See note *a* for source.

try rose by 17.8 percent from 1929 to 1939,[42] increasing the disparity between the two estimates.

Indexes of the trend in Soviet labor productivity, based on the Soviet production indexes and the Machinery Index, are shown in Table 51. Over the period from 1932 to 1936 as a whole, both indexes show a sizeable productivity gain. However, for the period prior to 1932 the indexes display a completely different behavior. The Soviet-based index shows a steady rise in productivity (apart from a small drop in 1931),

[42] U.S. Department of Labor, Bureau of Labor Statistics, *Productivity and Unit Labor Cost,* p. 2.

TABLE 51

INDEXES OF LABOR PRODUCTIVITY IN THE SOVIET
AGRICULTURAL MACHINERY INDUSTRY, 1928–36
(1932 = 100)

YEAR	BASED ON THE OFFICIAL SOVIET PRODUC- TION INDEX	BASED ON THE MACHINERY INDEX
1928	65.2	158.9
1929	69.3	185.5
1930	79.9	171.8
1931	76.9	96.6
1932	100.0	100.0
1933	123.2	103.9
1934	126.0	114.7
1935	n.a.[a]	n.a.
1936	206.3	182.5

Source: Table 49.
[a] n.a. = information not available.

with a threefold rise from 1928 to 1936. The Machinery Index-based index, on the other hand, shows a very substantial decline in productivity for 1929 to 1932, and for the period from 1928 to 1936 shows a net increase of only 15 percent.[43]

Unit labor requirements for some individual pieces of agricultural equipment from 1931 to 1936 are shown in Table 52. They indicate that very rapid productivity gains were achieved in the first years following introduction of new equipment models, and it is clear that the weight assigned to such new equipment, if related to value added, would be quite different if taken as of the first year of production, or, say, the fifth year; and that if the new products were of sufficient importance in relation to total output, the resultant indexes of production would similarly vary widely.

[43] The explanation for this difference must be sought in the same factors that caused a difference in the productivity trends as shown by the respective indexes for the entire industry. See *supra,* p. 145. The fact that the production indexes behaved so differently from 1928 to 1932, when the industry was expanding rapidly and new products, with initially high costs, were being introduced, suggests that the use of U.S. 1939 price weights understated (or, conversely, that the use of current Soviet price weights overstated) the increase in "real" output of agricultural implements.

TABLE 52

LABOR REQUIREMENTS FOR THE PRODUCTION OF
AGRICULTURAL MACHINERY IN RUSSIA, 1931–36,
IN NORM-HOURS REQUIRED AT THE END OF THE
SPECIFIED PERIOD FOR BASIC PRODUCTIVE WORK

| | YEAR | | | | |
ITEM	1931	1932	1933	1935	1936
Rostselmash 20-foot combine	. . .	644	561	461	310
Kommunar combine	767	544	450	324.9	245.8
Drill plow, 24-series, Krasnaya zvezda factory	136.4	100.0	75.6	. . .	. . .
Rostselmash drill plow	. . .	. . .	. . .	61.2	46.6

Source: K. I. Klimenko, "Proizvoditel'nost' truda v mashinostroitelnoi i metalloobra-batyvaiushchei promyshlennosti," in Akademiia Nauk, Institut Ekonomiki, *Proizvoditel'-nost' truda v promyshlennosti SSSR*, p. 192.

The 1946 productivity of labor in the Soviet agricultural machinery industry was stated to have been significantly below the 1940 level.[44] Subsequent developments cannot be ascertained.

HEAVY CONSTRUCTION MACHINERY

Statistics for the United States. The U.S. Census construction machinery classification is somewhat broader than the Russian, including cranes, derricks, and hoists and winches, which are carried separately in Russian statistics. On the assumption of equal productivity between the latter items and other construction machinery, no adjustment is necessary.

The gross value of U.S. construction machinery and parts produced in 1939 amounted to $113,875,000. "Other products" in the additional amount of $18,368,000, including metalworking machinery, fabricated steel, trucks, and wheelbarrows, are omitted on the assumption that there were some secondary products produced in the Soviet industry not reflected in the Machinery Index. However, it is necessary to deduct the value of parts and attachments produced in the U.S. industry, $9,753,000, thus reducing the gross value of the machinery proper to $104,122,000. Average U.S. wage earner employment in 1939 was 17,259.

[44] *Voprosy ekonomiki,* 1951, No. 8, p. 47.

Statistics for Russia. Production and employment data for the Soviet construction machinery industry from 1932 to 1936 are presented in Table 53. The gross value of $19.5 million for 1936 carried for this industry by the Machinery Index[45] excludes only one item of consequence: "rooters," or stubbing machines, of which 1,267 were produced in 1935. The 1950 U.S. price of a large stubbing machine, suitable for use behind a truck and probably of greater size than the Russian machines produced in 1936, was $800.[46] If one uses the wholesale metal price index as a deflator, a 1939 price of $400 may be assigned to this

---

TABLE 53

PRODUCTION AND EMPLOYMENT IN THE SOVIET
CONSTRUCTION MACHINERY INDUSTRY, 1932–36

YEAR	GROSS VALUE OF PRODUCT (MILLIONS OF 1926/27 RUBLES)	GROSS VALUE OF PRODUCT (MILLIONS OF 1939 DOLLARS)[b]	NUMBER OF WAGE EARNERS (THOUSANDS) (INDUSTRY SECTION)
1932	49[a]	12.2	9.4[a]
1933	73[a]	11.7	13.8[a]
1934	97[a]	12.3	15.4[a]
1935	n.a.[c]	15.3	n.a.
1936	n.a.	19.5	19.0[d]

[a] *Sotsialisticheskoe stroitel'stvo,* 1936, p. 9.

[b] *Machinery Index,* p. 86.

[c] n.a. = information not available.

[d] This is an industry section figure as of January 1, 1936, from *Trud v SSSR,* p. 65. The consistency of this figure with those for the earlier years is questionable, since the labor section wage earner figure as of July 1, 1934, was only 12.6 thousand, compared with the 15.4 thousand shown in the table as an average for 1934. No industry section figure is available for 1936. The possible lack of consistency renders productivity trends computed through the employment of this series of dubious validity, though it does not affect the appropriateness of the 1936 data for purposes of measuring comparative productivity.

---

[45] The *Machinery Index* (p. 70) shows a total of $32.6 million dollars for "road building equipment and cranes" for 1936. However, Soviet statistical sources carry these items in two separate industries: "equipment for construction and road work" and "hoisting-transport equipment." See *Sotsialisticheskoe stroitel'stvo,* 1936, p. 166. Only the machinery items included within the first-named industry are taken into account here, since the labor force is similarly broken down as between the two industries. The value totals were obtained from summing individual items in *Machinery Index,* p. 86.

[46] This information was obtained by consultation with several U.S. machinery dealers.

item, adding $507,000 to the value previously given (on the assumption that 1936 output was equal to that of 1935) and rendering the total $20 million.

The appropriate labor force figure for 1936, including learners and junior service personnel, was 21.5 thousand.[47]

Comparative productivity. The foregoing data may be summarized as follows:

	RUSSIA, 1939	UNITED STATES, 1939
Gross value of output (millions of 1939 dollars)	$20.0	$104.1
Wage earners (thousands)	21.5	17.3
Output per wage earner (1939 dollars)	$930	$6,017
Russian productivity as a percentage of U.S. productivity	15	100

The estimated comparative level of productivity shown above is far lower than that computed for any other branch of the machinery industry. The fact that, in terms of gross value of output, the Russian construction machinery industry was less than a fourth as large as that of the United States, whereas in railroad equipment, tractor, and agricultural machinery, Russian prewar production appeared to be absolutely greater than that of the United States, may help to account for the discrepancy. However, the magnitude of the divergence between the comparative productivity level of this industry and that of the remaining machinery industries studied is striking indeed; nor are there any Soviet estimates with which the results obtained here can be compared.

From Table 53 it can be ascertained that, on the basis of the Machinery Index, 1936 labor productivity in the Soviet construction machinery industry stood at 79 percent of the 1932 level. The official Soviet production index, available only through 1934, yielded a productivity increase of 20 percent between 1932 and 1934. Between 1932 and 1934 the official Soviet production index for the entire machinery industry yielded a productivity rise of 44 percent (Table 43), so that even as measured by the official statistics, labor productivity in the production of heavy construction and road-building machinery lagged during this period.

[47] The January 1, 1936, labor section figure is assumed to represent average employment in 1936.

The following index purports to represent the postwar trend in labor productivity at the Molotov plant in Dnepropetrovsk, one of the leading producers of heavy construction machinery[48] (1940 = 100):

YEAR	LABOR PRODUCTIVITY
1940	100.0
1947	120.7
1948	135.0
1949	146.6
1950	166.3

This plant is located in war-occupied territory and was presumably damaged during the occupation. Moreover, the index is based on value of output and is apparently affected by price changes, for it is indicated in the same source that the output of metal construction per wage earner rose by only 25 percent from 1940 to 1950. For the industry as a whole, no postwar productivity information is available.

Output per man-hour in the production of construction machinery in the United States is estimated to have declined by about 2 percent from 1939 to 1950.[49] Therefore it is not improbable that, taking into account possible Soviet productivity gains from 1936 to 1939, Soviet productivity in 1950 was substantially higher, relative to the U.S. level in the same year, than the prewar relationship estimated above.

AUTOMOBILE MANUFACTURING

Comparing productivity in the automobile industries of Russia and the United States, the last of the machinery-producing industries to be considered, involves some special problems arising out of the great difference in the size and structure of the industries in the two countries. The prewar Soviet automobile industry was insignificant in size compared with that of the United States;[50] it emphasized the production of trucks rather than passenger cars; and production of bodies, parts, and accessories was more closely tied to final assembly than in

[48] The data are from *Trud,* March 24, 1951, p. 2.

[49] U.S. Department of Labor, Bureau of Labor Statistics, *Trends in Man-hours Expended per Unit: Selected Types of Construction and Mining Machinery,* p. 3.

[50] In 1939, the U.S. automobile industry produced 2,824,000 passenger cars and 440,000 commercial vehicles. The Soviet industry produced in 1938 only 27,000 passenger cars and 184,000 commercial vehicles.

the United States. However, the Soviet industry was advanced in technique relative to other branches of machinery production, having been built virtually from scratch during the First Five Year Plan[51] and incorporating the latest methods in U.S. automobile manufacture. The latter circumstance enabled the Soviet automobile industry to overcome, to some extent, its disadvantage in scale as compared with the U.S. industry.

In order to reduce these problems to manageable proportions, it seemed desirable to restrict the comparison of productivity to that portion of the automobile industry engaged in the production of complete automobiles, omitting the production of bodies, parts, and accessories as well as of secondary products. A comparison for the entire industry would require much finer labor force and production data than are available, to take into account such things as the relatively greater development of parts manufacture in the United States.

Statistics for the United States. The value of complete motor vehicles produced in the United States in 1939 was $2,143,898,000. A portion of this was produced in other Census industries, however, to an amount which may be estimated roughly at $19 million,[52] leaving as the gross value of complete vehicles produced in the automobile industry the amount of $2,124,898,000.[53]

Employment of wage earners in the automobile industry in 1939 was 397,537. However, this included both the manufacture of bodies and parts and of completed vehicles, for the 1939 Census merged the two

[51] The first large automobile plants came into operation in 1930 and 1931—the Stalin Plant in Moscow and the Molotov Plant in Gorky.

[52] The gross value of vehicles, parts, and accessories made in other industries was $31,650,000. This is divided in the ratio of value of complete motor vehicles to total value of vehicles, parts, and accessories produced in the automobile industry.

[53] This figure excludes $160 million worth of passenger and commercial chassis carried by the Census under complete vehicle production. According to the 1939 U.S. *Census of Manufactures,* II, Part II, p. 524, there was an inflation in the U.S. gross value data arising from duplication in reporting. Since the Machinery Index valued passenger cars at a unit price derived from the Census data, any inflation in the U.S. data was imputed equally to the Soviet product. The unit value for Russian trucks employed by the Machinery Index for 1939, $1,198, is considerably above the unit value that may be derived from the Census data and presumably reflects differences in the composition of the product between the two countries. It is possible that duplication of values in the U.S. data may have resulted in relative overstatement of U.S. truck production, but the amount of such overstatement cannot be estimated.

sectors of the industry, previously separated. In 1935, wage earners engaged in the production of complete vehicles constituted 38 percent of the combined complete vehicle-body and parts labor force, and in 1937, 41 percent.[54] If an average of roughly 40 percent is extrapolated for 1939, wage earner employment for that year may be estimated at 159,000.

Statistics for Russia. Production and employment statistics for Soviet automobile manufacturing are presented in Table 54, from which it is apparent that prior to 1931 the industry was a very small-scale one. Separate labor force data are not available prior to 1932.

The Machinery Index contains the following value data for Soviet automobile production for 1936 and 1937:

	1936	1937
Passenger automobiles	$ 2,351,000	$ 11,593,000
Trucks	159,274,000	217,653,000
Fire engines	4,778,000	4,778,000
Total	$166,403,000	$234,024,000

These data purport to include all finished motor vehicles produced in those years.

Wage earner employment for the GAZ, ZIS, and Ya AZ plants, which in 1936 and 1937 appear to have been the sole producers of finished vehicles,[55] is shown in Table 54 for these years.[56] In addition, there were in 1937 some twenty-three plants producing parts and accessories only, employing 25,000 persons.[57] However, since the productivity comparison is confined to the plants manufacturing complete vehicles, this group of employees need not be taken into consideration.

In the source of the data for 1936 and 1937, it is stated that about 30 percent of the total output of the complete vehicles plants consisted of parts and supplies.[58] If one assumes that there was no corresponding

[54] Fabricant, *op. cit.,* p. 207.

[55] See D. B. Shimkin, "The Automobile Industry That's Behind the Iron Curtain," *Automotive Industries,* February 15, 1948, p. 34.

[56] It is not clear from the source whether the separate assembly plants attached to these combines were included. The magnitude of the figures would indicate either that the assembly plants were covered or that employment in the latter was relatively small.

[57] I am indebted to D. B. Shimkin for this information. His source is *Avtotraktornoe Delo,* 1938, No. 2, p. 6.

[58] Klimenko, *op. cit.,* p. 200.

TABLE 54

PRODUCTION AND EMPLOYMENT IN THE SOVIET AUTOMOBILE
INDUSTRY (COMPLETED VEHICLES AND PARTS), 1928–37

YEAR	GROSS VALUE OF PRODUCT (MILLIONS OF 1926/27 RUBLES)	GROSS VALUE OF PRODUCT (MILLIONS OF 1939 DOLLARS)[e]	NUMBER OF WAGE EARNERS (THOUSANDS) (INDUSTRY SECTION)
1928	23[a]	605	n.a.
1929	42[a]	1,395	n.a.
1930	92[a]	4,737	n.a.
1931	180[a]	10,047	n.a.
1932	336[b]	40,839	31.2[f]
1933	566[b]	65,050	36.4[f]
1934	810[b]	82,192	38.8[f,h]
1935	n.a.[c]	109,853	n.a.
1936	1,422[d]	166,403	56.2[g,h]
1937	1,830[d]	234,024	67.1[g]

[a] *Sotsialisticheskoe stroitel'stvo*, 1935, p. 15.

[b] *Sotsialisticheskoe stroitel'stvo*, 1936, p. 10.

[c] n.a. = information not available.

[d] K. I. Klimenko, "Proizvoditel'nost' truda v mashinostroitelnoi i metalloobrabaty-vaiushchei promyshlennosti," in Akademiia Nauk, Institut Ekonomiki, *Proizvoditel'nost' truda v promyshlennosti SSSR*, p. 199. This source, which also presents labor force data, is annotated to the effect that the data cover only the three major automobile plants: the Stalin Plant at Moscow; the GAZ plant at Gorky; and the Ya AZ plant at Yaroslavl. It is not clear whether the limitation applies to the production as well as to the labor force data; if it does, the data for 1936 and 1937 are understated by comparison with earlier years.

[e] *Machinery Index*, p. 71. Data for 1928–30 are for the corresponding fiscal years.

[f] *Sotsialisticheskoe stroitel'stvo*, 1936, p. 10.

[g] Klimenko, *op. cit.*, p. 199. These data cover only three plants (see note *c, supra*) and are presumably inconsistent with the data for earlier years.

[h] The labor section figure for July 1, 1934, 38.1 thousand (*Trud v SSSR*, 1935, p. 76) is almost identical with the industry section average for 1934. However, the labor section figure for January 1, 1936, 41.9 thousand (*Trud v SSSR*, 1936, p. 65), is considerably below the industry section figure of 56.2 thousand shown in the table. Part of the difference may have been due to the fact that employment in the industry was expanding rapidly during 1936, as evidenced by the increase of 12 thousand in employment from 1936 to 1937.

production in U.S. plants producing completed vehicles, the Russian labor force engaged in turning out parts within the complete vehicle plants should be subtracted. The U.S. data indicate higher productivity (measured by value of product) in the manufacture of complete automobiles than of parts; in 1939, the 40 percent of the labor force engaged in the production of complete vehicles turned out about 60 percent of the combined products. If this ratio is applied to the Russian data, it may be estimated that wage earners producing complete vehicles numbered 26.4 thousand in 1936 and 31.5 thousand in 1937.[59] These figures should be increased to 29.3 thousand and 35.0 thousand, respectively, to allow for learners and junior service personnel.[60]

Comparative productivity. The foregoing data may be summarized as follows:

	RUSSIA		UNITED STATES
	1936	1937	1939
Gross value of output (millions of 1939 dollars)	$ 166.4	$ 234.0	$ 2,124.9
Wage earners (thousands)	29.3	35.0	159.0
Output per wage earner (1939 dollars)	$5,679	$6,686	$13,364
Russian productivity as a percentage of U.S. productivity	42	50	100

In a Soviet source, Russian automobile labor productivity in 1936 was estimated at 39.4 percent of the U.S. level in 1929.[61] Since U.S. output per wage earner declined by an estimated 10 percent from 1929 to 1939,[62] this estimate comes very close to our own estimate.

Productivity trends in the Soviet automobile industry from 1932 to

[59] It is assumed here that the relative productivity of complete vehicle and automobile parts employees indicated for the United States prevailed in Russia as well. There would appear to be some warrant for this assumption, in that whereas the Russians imitated U.S. methods in conveyor lines for assembly, all indications point to a less well-developed technology in the production of parts and accessories. This would apply particularly to the small parts-producing plants, but in all probability also to the large plants producing both parts and complete vehicles.

It must be emphasized that alternative assumptions would yield considerably different productivity results. For example, if an assumption of equal productivity between parts and complete vehicle production were made, Soviet productivity would fall (for 1937) to about 34 percent of the U.S. level.

[60] On the basis of the ratio of these groups to wage earners as of January 1, 1936. See *Trud v SSSR,* 1936, p. 65. The use of industry section data for 1936 and 1937, in the face of a lower labor section figure (see Table 54, note *h*) appears to be justified by the specific character of the industry section figures in this case, as well as by the possibility that much of the difference between the two figures may have been due to the different time period covered (January 1 versus average for the years). The close correspondence between the labor and industry section data for 1934 supports the latter hypothesis.

[61] Klimenko, *op. cit.,* p. 204.

[62] U.S. Department of Labor, Bureau of Labor Statistics, *Productivity and Unit Labor Cost in Selected Manufacturing Industries.*

1937 are shown in Table 55. As noted above, both the value of product and labor force data for 1936 and 1937 may cover only a portion of the industry (this is not true of the value data abstracted from the Machinery Index, however). In consequence, the index based on the Machinery

TABLE 55

INDEXES OF LABOR PRODUCTIVITY IN SOVIET AUTOMOBILE MANUFACTURING, 1932–37
(1932 = 100)

YEAR	BASED ON OFFICIAL SOVIET PRODUCTION INDEX	BASED ON THE MACHIN- ERY INDEX
1932	100.0	100.0
1933	144.4	136.5
1934	193.9	161.8
1935	n.a.[a]	n.a.
1936	234.9	226.2
1937	253.2	266.5

Source: Table 54.
[a] n.a. = information not available.

Index may be overstated for these years, compared with the index based on Soviet value of output data. Nevertheless, there is little doubt that the automobile industry achieved a very substantial improvement in labor productivity from 1932 to 1937, which was to be anticipated in view of its newness and its initial access to advanced technology.

Table 56 shows the course of labor productivity in the production of a truck in the Molotov Plant at Gorky, based on norm-hour unit requirements. These data, which show very large initial productivity gains, followed by a leveling off during the late thirties and a decline during the war, are not inconsistent with the data in Table 55. Unit labor requirements for models in continuous production were likely to decline more rapidly than labor requirements for a composite of production in which new models, with an initially low productivity, were being introduced.[63]

In view of the conversion of part of the Soviet automobile industry to

[63] For an analysis of the automobile models produced by the Soviet industry, see D. B. Shimkin, "The Automobile Industry That's Behind the Iron Curtain," *Automotive Industries,* February 15, 1948, p. 37.

military production in the late thirties, it is doubtful whether there was
any substantial productivity gain from 1938 to 1940.[64] For postwar years,
it is claimed that 1950 labor productivity in the Molotov Plant at Gorky
exceeded the 1940 level by 32 percent;[65] and that 1949 labor productivity

TABLE 56

INDEX OF LABOR PRODUCTIVITY IN PRODUCTION OF A GAZ-AA
TRUCK AT THE MOLOTOV PLANT IN GORKY, 1933–45
(1933 = 100)

YEAR	INDEX	YEAR	INDEX
1933	100	1940	350
1934	204	1941	343
1935	221	1942	241
1936	296	1943	205
1937	328	1944	187
1938	330	1945	195
1939	366		

Source: *Avtomobil'naia Promishlennost'*, 1946, No. 1, p. 4.

in the Stalin Plant at Moscow exceeded the 1940 level by 36 percent.[66]
If these figures are accorded credence, there is little doubt that productivity for the entire automobile industry was substantially higher in
1950 than in 1940 (or in 1937). Reliable statistics on U.S. automobile
productivity since 1939 are lacking.

It has been suggested[67] that, despite differences in the composition
of automobile output in the United States and Russia, a more valid comparison of productivity can be obtained simply by measuring relative
output per wage earner in physical automotive units. The argument is
that little, if any, additional labor is involved in producing trucks than
is required for producing passenger cars, despite the considerably higher
average unit gross value of the former. (It will be recalled that unit
gross value of product constituted our weighting system.)

Unfortunately, data are lacking with which to test the hypothesis
of equal unit labor requirements for trucks and passenger cars. A very

[64] The gain from 1936 to 1937 is shown in Table 55 to have been substantial.
[65] *Voprosy ekonomiki*, 1952, No. 1, p. 24.
[66] *Trud*, November 20, 1949, p. 1.
[67] By Alan Sweezy, of the California Institute of Technology, in a letter to the author.

rough calculation based on the 1929 U.S. Census of Manufactures seems to indicate that the production of trucks might well require more labor than the production of passenger automobiles, though not in the two to one ratio assigned by our gross value weights.[68] The underlying data are not sufficiently precise, however, to permit of any firm conclusion on this point.

Comparison on the basis of physical output per wage earner for the entire industry, including the manufacture of bodies and parts, yields the following data: the Russians produced approximately 200,000 motor vehicles in 1937, with an estimated total labor force of some 112,000.[69] Of these, perhaps 86,000 were wage earners (on the basis of earlier ratios of wage earners to the total labor force), so that the output per wage earner was 2.3 vehicles. The U.S. automobile industry employed 397,500 wage earners in 1939 and produced 3,269,000 vehicles, or 8.2 vehicles per wage earner. On this basis, Soviet productivity in 1937 was only 28 percent of the U.S. 1939 level.

The difference between this figure and our estimate of 50 percent as derived above is largely accounted for by the difference in the weights employed. However, limitation of our comparison to the complete motor vehicle industry, exclusive of bodies and parts, probably served

---

[68] The calculation was made as follows:

1. Total value of passenger cars produced in the motor vehicle (complete assembly) industry	$2,767,339,000
2. Less the value of passenger bodies and parts produced in the bodies and parts industry	1,250,634,000
3. Value added by the motor vehicle industry for passenger cars	$1,516,705,000
4. Value added per passenger car produced	$348
5. Total value of commercial vehicles, excluding busses	277,352,017
6. Less value of commercial bodies and parts produced in the bodies and parts industry	101,489,959
7. Value added by the motor vehicle (complete assembly) industry for commercial vehicles	175,862,058
8. Value added per commercial vehicle produced	$449

Source: U.S. Department of Commerce, Bureau of the Census, *Manufactures: 1929,* Washington, 1933, pp. 1225, 1230.

Note: Data on value of bodies were directly available. The total value of parts was allocated to passenger and commercial vehicles on the basis of the relative value of bodies shown for the two types of vehicles. The reader will note the assumption of correspondence between relative value added and relative unit labor requirements.

[69] Shimkin, *op. cit.,* p. 34.

to raise relative Soviet productivity, since the assembly operation there appears to have been more efficient, in relation to the production of bodies and parts, than was the case in the United States. The answer to the question as to which of the two estimates is nearer to reality must wait upon the availability of labor requirement weights for various types of motor vehicles.

SUMMARY

Soviet labor productivity in 1936 as a percentage of U.S. 1939 productivity for five branches of machinery manufacturing may be summarized as follows:

	PERCENTAGE
Railroad locomotives and cars	47
Tractors	58
Agricultural machinery	50
Heavy construction machinery	15
Automobiles (complete vehicles only)	42

Weighted by U.S. employment in 1939, these figures average 43.5 percent; whereas using 1936 Soviet employment, the average is 47.5 percent. The difference is attributable to the relatively great variance in automobile employment in the two countries; if the automobile industry is eliminated, U.S. and Soviet employment weights yield results that are closer together (46 percent and 48 percent).

It will be recalled that Soviet estimates of Russian-U.S. productivity for all machinery manufacturing ranged from 41.8 percent to 48.9 percent, using the year 1936 for Russia and 1929 for the United States. There are no estimates of changes in U.S. machinery productivity (entire industry) from 1929 to 1939. For individual machinery groups, Fabricant estimated, alternatively, an increase of 4 percent and a decrease of 7 percent in employment per unit of automobile output; an increase of 46 percent for railroad cars; an increase of 99 percent for locomotives; and an increase of 22 percent for total transportation machinery.[70] The Bureau of Labor Statistics, on the other hand, estimated that output per man-hour in automobile manufacture increased by 18.8 percent

[70] Fabricant, *op. cit.*, pp. 325–28.

from 1929 to 1939; and in agricultural implements manufacture, by 53.2 percent.[71] These figures, together with an increase of 32.4 percent in output per man-hour in all manufacturing,[72] suggest that U.S. machine manufacturing productivity may have increased from 1929 to 1939 and that the Soviet estimates quoted above should be scaled down, if anything, in converting to a 1939 U.S. productivity base.

Whether it may be concluded that the Russian machinery industry in 1937 was from 40 to 50 percent as efficient, in terms of unit labor inputs, as the U.S. machinery industry in 1939 depends on the degree to which the samples of machinery industries for which estimates were made can be deemed representative. Representativeness in terms of magnitude of employment was discussed above. Obviously, the omission of such important machinery groups as industrial machinery, household and other consumer machinery (in which Soviet productivity was undoubtedly far below the U.S. level), machine tools, electrical machinery, and armaments makes it necessary to use the present estimates with great caution. Their major, and perhaps sole, virtue is that they constitute the only alternative to a frank admission that there are no adequate statistics in the area of comparative machinery productivity.

Postwar data are fragmentary. Labor productivity in the machinery industry is alleged to have risen by 15 percent in 1949; by 19 percent in 1950; by 14 percent in 1951; and by 10 percent in 1952, yielding an index figure of 171.7 for 1952 based on 1948.[73] However, the relationship of labor productivity in 1948 to the prewar level is not stated. For the Ministry of Machine and Instrument Construction, productivity in 1950 may be estimated at 189, based on 1940,[74] but since only about one tenth of the machinery industry is under the jurisdiction of this Ministry, it cannot be taken to typify the trend of labor productivity in all machinery manufacture.

Trends in man-hours expended per unit are available since 1939 for the following U.S. machinery industries (1939 = 100)[75]:

[71] *Monthly Labor Review*, May, 1942, p. 1072. Since hours worked declined from 1929 to 1939, output per man would have risen less than output per man-hour.

[72] *Ibid.*

[73] *USSR Information Bulletin*, February 10, 1950; *Trud*, January 27, 1951, p. 1; *ibid.*, January 29, 1952, p. 1; *ibid.*, January 23, 1953, p. 1.

[74] *Trud*, April 16, 1949, p. 2; *Planovoe khoziaistvo*, 1952, No. 1, p. 29.

[75] Mimeographed releases of the U.S. Department of Labor, Bureau of Labor Statistics.

General industrial equipment   81.0 (*1950*)
Household electrical appliances   87.1 (*1950*)
Railroad freight cars   90.4 (*1948*)
Selected metal-forming machinery   90.6 (*1949*)
Selected types of mining machinery   98.5 (*1949*)
Selected types of machine tools   104.9 (*1950*)

These figures suggest that there was a productivity increase in U.S. machinery manufacturing between 1939 and 1950, although they do not permit the ascertainment of a specific amount. It is not unlikely that there was a productivity increase in the Soviet industry as well, in view of the large increases claimed for the period from 1948 to 1952, but of course this may merely have represented ground lost during the war.

TABLE 57

TRENDS IN LABOR PRODUCTIVITY IN SOVIET MACHINERY
MANUFACTURING, 1932–37
(1932 = 100)

YEAR	TOTAL MACHINERY	RAILROAD CARS AND LOCOMOTIVES	TRACTORS	AGRICULTURAL MACHINERY	AUTOMOBILES
a. Based on Soviet production index					
1932	100	100	100	100	100
1933	122	115	128	123	144
1934	145	135	162	126	194
1935	n.a.[a]	n.a.	n.a.	n.a.	n.a.
1936	n.a.	179	249	206	235
1937	225	200	n.a.	n.a.	253
b. Based on the Machinery Index					
1932	100	100	100	100	100
1933	116	117	120	104	137
1934	131	137	148	115	162
1935	n.a.	n.a.	n.a.	n.a.	n.a.
1936	n.a.	96	210	183	226
1937	140	n.a.	n.a.	n.a.	267

[a] n.a. = information not available.

Table 57 summarizes the foregoing estimates of the Soviet labor productivity trend, by industry, from 1932 to 1937. While the disparity between the two total machinery indexes based on 1932 is not as great as when 1928 is used as a base (see Table 43), the Machinery Index-based labor productivity index indicates a substantially smaller productivity rise than the official index-based series. Table 57 indicates that, in general, the individual machinery indexes computed from official Soviet sources are consistent with the global machinery index computed from similar sources. The same is not true, however, of the series based on the Machinery Index, for three out of the four industry series show substantially higher rates of productivity increase during this period than does the global index.[76] These three—tractors, agricultural machinery, and automobiles—provided (in 1936) 52 percent of the gross value of all machinery included in the Machinery Index, while railroad cars and locomotives, for which the indicated productivity rise is less than for machinery as a whole, provided 23 percent of the gross value in the same year. It must be inferred that the remaining 25 percent of the items covered by the Machinery Index were in industries which experienced a relatively low productivity rise during this period.

With respect to the broader question of whether the official Soviet production index for machinery or the Gerschenkron Machinery Index provides a better basis for the measurement of labor productivity trend, the following observations may be made:

1. The official index, by pricing new commodities at current prices, offsets the dampening effect upon the rise of labor productivity caused by admission to the product mix of commodities with initially high unit labor requirements. The Machinery Index, through the use of "post industrialization" prices, permits the full dampening effect of the new commodities upon the index.[77] Since new commodities were of such importance in the Soviet machinery industry, particularly during the First Five Year Plan, this is probably the principal explanation of the different behavior of the indexes in Table 43 from 1928 to 1932, and perhaps until 1937 as well.

2. The use of "post-industrialization" rather than "pre-industriali-

---

[76] However, because of the discontinuance of wheel-type tractor production in 1937 while the plants were being converted to military production, the 1937 labor productivity index for this industry, based on the Machinery Index value of output, would have shown a substantial drop from 1936.

[77] Thus, if we denote by the symbol Ve the gross value of established products, by Vn the gross value of new products, by le the labor inputs for established products, and by ln the labor inputs for new products, the index in any year will equal $Ve + Vn/le + ln$. The use of current prices assigns a relatively high value to Vn, whereas the use of end-year prices assigns to Vn a value comparable to unit value for Ve. Since ln is the same regardless of the value assigned, it is clear that the greater Vn, the greater the value of the index.

zation" value weights tends to minimize the importance of those machinery branches in which labor productivity has risen most rapidly, assuming that prices are proportional to labor inputs. Thus, if labor productivity in various branches of machinery was increasing at varying rates, an index of labor productivity for all machinery weighted by end-year unit prices would show a smaller rate of growth than one weighted by base-year unit prices.

On the first count, it may be argued that the Machinery Index provides a more realistic basis for measuring the trend in labor productivity, even though the productivity gains achieved in individual branches of machinery production are hidden. On the second count, however, the prices employed by the Machinery Index appear to be less suitable for the purposes of measuring labor productivity than the *theoretical* pricing system of the official Soviet production indexes, i.e., constant 1926/27 prices.

At any rate, it is probably a combination of these two factors which accounts for the different behavior of the two total machinery indexes in Table 57 for the years 1932 to 1937. An index of labor productivity constructed as an aggregate of physical unit labor requirements, using (properly) base-year weights, would probably fall somewhere in between the total machinery indexes in Table 57. There would not be the upward bias imparted by the introduction of new commodities at current prices, nor the downward bias imparted by the use of end-year weights.

X

COTTON TEXTILE MANUFACTURING

THE INDUSTRY

THE fabrication of raw cotton into yarn and the weaving of yarn into cloth were treated as a single industry by the 1939 U.S. Census of Manufactures. This practice, which is at variance with that of Great Britain and other nations, stems from the integrated character of cotton textile manufacturing in the United States. Only 17.5 percent of the cotton yarn produced in 1939 was designed for sale, the balance being used internally by the producing establishments.[1] However, relatively few of the so-called integrated mills finished their own cloth, i.e., bleached and dyed it or imparted such special characteristics as shrink or crease resistance. It is estimated that in 1939 only 13 percent of the unfinished gray goods (cloth) produced was styled by the producing mill. Of the rest, 30 percent was used commercially without finishing, 9 percent went for sheets, pillowcases, and towels after being bleached only by the producing mill or by others for its account, while 48 percent was styled or finished by independent converters.[2] The 1939 Census treated dyeing and finishing as a separate industry, including the processing of all textiles with the exception of woolens and worsteds. Though cotton was the major fabric handled, the data do not permit of any precise segregation of wage earners engaged exclusively in its conversion.[3]

[1] U.S. *Census of Manufactures,* 1939, II, Part I, 288 ff.

[2] Jules Backman and M. R. Gainsburgh, *Economics of the Cotton Textile Industry,* p. 39.

[3] The finishing industry in 1939 converted 973 million linear yards of rayon and silk; 2,174 million linear yards of cotton and linen were bleached and finished, while 1,432 million linear yards of cotton and linen were dyed and finished. See U.S. *Census of Manufactures,* 1939, II, Part I, 351. The 1937 *Census of Manufactures* did separate the fabrics. In that year, the number of wage earners engaged in dyeing and finishing cotton cloth was 49,635, representing 66.2 percent of the number of wage earners engaged in the dyeing and finishing industry as a whole. (The comparable figure for 1935 was 60.7 percent.) See U.S. *Biennial Census of Manufactures,* Part I, p. 301. This was 10.2 percent of the combined labor force in the cotton manufacturing and finishing industries (the comparable figure for 1935 was 10.1 percent).

With respect to the structure of the Soviet cotton textile industry, it may be noted that there was also a considerable degree of vertical integration. It was estimated that in 1939 about 70 percent of the cotton cloth output was produced in combined spinning-weaving mills.[4] A more detailed breakdown for the year 1935 is shown in Table 58, from

TABLE 58

STRUCTURE OF THE SOVIET COTTON TEXTILE INDUSTRY, 1935[a]

TYPE OF ESTABLISHMENT	NUMBER OF ESTABLISHMENTS		NUMBER OF WAGE EARNERS	
	Absolute	Percentage of Total	Absolute	Percentage of Total
Total	533	100.0	466,384	100.0
Spinning	45	8.4	58,617	12.6
Spinning and thread	2	0.4	5,119	1.1
Spinning and weaving	66	12.4	174,247	37.4
Weaving	195	36.6	83,136	17.8
Weaving and finishing	12	2.2	23,133	4.9
Spinning, weaving, and finishing	18	3.4	73,891	15.8
Spinning and finishing	1	0.2	3,062	0.7
Finishing	24	4.5	18,013	3.9
Other	170	31.9	27,166	5.8

Source: P. A. Khromov, *Ocherki ekonomiki tekstil'noi promyshlennosti SSSR*, pp. 52–53.

[a] This table includes only large-scale industry.

which it appears that, measured by employment, more than half the capacity was in integrated establishments, although a considerable number of small mills engaged only in weaving.

The administrative structure of the Soviet industry prevailing in the thirties is important to an understanding of the various statistical data available. The allocation of output among the several administrative jurisdictions is shown in Table 59 for the year 1937. Most of the yarn and cloth was produced in establishments under the administrative jurisdiction of the Commissariat for Light Industry of the USSR and the various republic light industry commissariats. It will be seen, however, that census industry lines and administrative jurisdiction were not coterminous. For example, 83.1 percent of total yarn output was

[4] *Legkaia promyshlennost'*, 1939, No. 10, p. 39.

TABLE 59

PRODUCTION OF COTTON YARN AND CLOTH IN THE SOVIET UNION, 1937, BY ADMINISTRATIVE JURISDICTION[a]

JURISDICTION	YARN		CLOTH	
	Thousands of metric tons	Percentage of Total	Millions of linear meters	Percentage of Total
Total, USSR	533[b]	100	3447[b]	100
Cotton textile industry	443	83.1	3119	90.5
Commissariat for Light Industry of the USSR	342	64.2	2330	67.6
Commissariats for Light Industry of Republics	101	18.9	789	22.9
Knit-goods industry	36	6.8	n.a.[c]	n.a.
Commissariat for Light Industry of the USSR	7	1.3	n.a.	n.a.
Commissariats for Light Industry of Republics	29	5.5	n.a.	n.a.
Other Industries under the USSR and republic light industry commissariats	4	0.8	28[d]	0.8
Industrial cooperatives	n.a.	n.a.	79[e]	2.3
Other administrative units, including small-scale enterprises under local management and non-industrial cooperatives	50[f]	9.3	221	6.4

[a] Where not otherwise indicated, data are from *Legkaia promyshlennost'*, 1938, No. 2, p. 156.

[b] Ia. A. Ioffe, *SSSR i kapitalisticheskie strany*, p. 191.

[c] n.a. = information not available.

[d] This includes the output of the knit-goods industry under the jurisdiction of the USSR and republic light industry commissariats.

[e] *Legkaia promyshlennost'*, 1940, No. 2, p. 10. The figure given in the source is for 1938 rather than 1937, but it may be accepted as representative of the role of the industrial cooperatives in this industry in 1937.

[f] This figure also includes the yarn output of the industrial cooperatives, not separately available.

produced within the cotton textile industry (census definition) by plants supervised by the national and republic light industry commissariats, while an additional 6.8 percent fell under the knit-goods industry (census definition) establishments supervised by the same commissariats. The remaining 10.1 percent of the yarn output fell under other administrative units; what proportion of this percentage came from enterprises meeting the "large-scale industry" minimum census standards cannot be determined.[5]

The significance of administrative jurisdiction for our problem is as follows:

a. The labor section wage earner statistics exclude employees of industrial cooperatives, whereas the output of the cooperatives is included in the global production data. Some 29.6 thousand persons were engaged in the production of cotton textiles within the industrial cooperatives in 1938, some of whom were home workers.[6] Since many cooperative enterprises were more in the nature of handicraft than factory industry, they are omitted from the productivity comparison.[7]

[5] It is instructive to compare the data in Table 59 with the following planned data for 1941:

JURISDICTION	YARN		CLOTH	
	Thousands of metric tons	Percentage of total	Millions of linear meters	Percentage of total
Total planned output	699	100.0	4338	100.0
Commissariat for the Textile Industry	628	89.8	4250	98.0
Commissariat for Light Industry	50	7.2	....	....
Cooperatives	21	3.0	85	2.0
Commissariat for the Chemical Industry	......	....	3	0.0

Source: *1941 Plan*, p. 71.

The textile industry was put under a separate commissariat in 1939, but the knit-goods industry remained under the jurisdiction of the light industry commissariats, and the yarn output attributed to the latter undoubtedly reflects the yarn output of the knit-goods industry. The share of the cooperatives in total output, to judge by cloth, appears to have remained constant from 1937 to planned 1941. The implication of the data is that the portion of the output which in 1937 was produced by local industry or nonindustrial cooperatives was to be brought under central commissariat control in 1941; the only alternative is that this portion of the output does not appear in the *1941 Plan*.

[6] *Legkaia promyshlennost'*, 1940, No. 3, p. 10.

[7] A number of comparably small enterprises were undoubtedly omitted from the U.S. Census because of failure to meet the minimum production requirements. The omission of the Russian cooperative sector of the industry en bloc serves to raise the relative level of Russian productivity. However, in view of the relatively small role of the cooperatives in the total picture, the resultant error is not great.

b. The Soviet labor section wage earner data were limited in their coverage to enterprises meeting the minimum census requirement of 16 wage earners per establishment if mechanical power were available, or 30 wage earners in the absence of mechanical power. As of January 1, 1936, there were 533 establishments, employing 466.8 thousand wage earners, of census size in the cotton textile industry.[8] Of these, 264 establishments, employing 440.2 thousand wage earners, were under the administrative jurisdiction of national and republic commissariats,[9] while 269 smaller establishments, employing 26.6 thousand wage earners, were under other administrative organs. In addition, there was an indeterminate number of establishments below census size.

The global physical output data include the product of census and noncensus enterprises alike.[10] It would appear from Table 59 that about 6 percent of the 1937 output of yarn and cloth was produced in establishments under jurisdictions other than the national and republic light industry commissariats and the industrial cooperatives.[11] Part of the labor force, that employed in census enterprises, engaged in the production of the non-light industry commissariat portion of the product, was included in the labor section employment data, while wage earners in noncensus enterprises were excluded. The output attributable to the noncensus labor force cannot be derived. However, the error involved in failing to correct for this item is inconsequential.[12]

c. The labor force of those enterprises engaged primarily in the production of knit goods and secondarily producing some yarn for their own account was in all probability classified entirely under knit-goods production, rather than divided between knit goods and cotton textiles.[13] Therefore, the yarn output of the knit-goods industry should not be

[8] Table 58 and *Trud v SSSR*, 1936, p. 184.

[9] *Trud v SSSR*, 1936, p. 187.

[10] *Sotsialisticheskoe stroitel'stvo SSSR*, 1936, p. 705.

[11] The percentage for cloth is derived directly from the table. The yarn percentage is that portion attributed in the table to other administrative units, less the 3 percent planned contribution of the industrial cooperatives in 1941.

[12] This can be judged from available data on small-scale industry for 1933. In that year, although 131 cotton mills were classified as small-scale, compared with 501 classified as large-scale, the value of product of the small-scale enterprises was only 3,857 thousand 1926/27 rubles, compared with 3,138,840 thousand rubles produced in large-scale enterprises. *Sotsialisticheskoe stroitel'stvo SSSR*, 1935, p. 11.

[13] See *supra*, p. 29.

included with that of the cotton textile industry in assessing the latter's productivity.

To summarize the three foregoing points, 10.6 percent of total Soviet yarn output and 3.1 percent of cloth output in 1937 should be deducted from total production for the purpose of determining productivity in the cotton textile industry.[14]

A final problem in defining the industry concerns the statistical treatment of cotton finishing. This operation appears to have been treated in Russia as part of cotton textile manufacturing.[15] As Table 58 indicates, 3.9 percent of the wage earners employed in the industry in 1935 were in enterprises engaged solely in the finishing of cloth, while an indeterminate additional number performed similar work in factories engaged in some combination of spinning, weaving, and finishing. Because of greater concern in the United States for variegation of color and special material type, it is probable that a smaller proportion of the Soviet cotton textile labor force was engaged in finishing work than in the United States, where the ratio was 10 percent in 1935 and 1937. Arbitrarily, a figure of 7 percent, midway between the lower Russian limit and the U.S. figure, is assumed to represent the proportion of Soviet cotton textile wage earners engaged in the dyeing and finishing of cloth.

THE PRODUCT

The 1939 U.S. Census divided the product of the cotton textile industry into two major categories: cotton yarn and cotton broad-woven goods (over 12 inches in width). There were in addition several minor categories: cotton narrow fabrics and the various products of yarn doubling.[16] Physical output data are available for all but narrow cotton fabrics. However, for qualitative reasons the doubled yarn products cannot be aggregated either with single yarn or woven goods.

---

[14] This includes, for yarn, 6.8 percent produced by the knit-goods industry, 3 percent (estimate) by the industrial cooperatives, and 0.8 percent by other industries (mainly chemicals); for cloth, 2.3 percent produced by the industrial cooperatives and 0.8 percent produced by the knit-goods and other industries.

[15] See *Trud v SSSR,* 1936, p. 246.

[16] The doubled yarn products include cotton thread (50.5 million pounds), cotton twine (20.3 million pounds), cotton cordage and rope (30.3 million pounds), and tire cord on cones (97.1 million pounds). The total of these items, 198.2 million pounds, represented about 6 percent of the total single yarn produced during the year.

Russian production statistics make no separation of broad- and narrow-woven goods. For several years the output of cloth was given in both linear and square meters, the ratio of the latter to the former unit being 76 percent.[17] Since Russian looms averaged less than one meter in width, the output in linear meters should have exceeded that in square meters, even if fabrics equivalent to the U.S. narrow fabrics group (12 inches or less in width) had been excluded.[18] However, assuming that all cotton cloth, regardless of width, was included in the Russian production statistics, the error resulting from our inability to make a similar allowance for U.S. narrow-woven goods is minimized by the use of square rather than linear units of measurement for purposes of making the productivity comparison.[19]

Regular Soviet statistical yearbooks show thread as the only product of cotton doubling, in units of 200 meter reels rather than by weight, thus rendering it difficult to determine the quantity of yarn diverted into thread manufacture.[20] The *1941 Plan* contains some figures which may be interpreted to mean that about 20 percent of all cotton yarn planned for that year was to be subjected to some form of doubling.[21] However, this cannot be compared with the 6 percent figure cited above for the United States, for that represented doubled yarn and products other than cloth, whereas the Soviet figure represented doubled yarn to be woven, as well as in final form. The productivity comparison will run perforce in terms of single yarn output, with the assumption that yarn doubling absorbed in each country an equally proportionate share of the total labor force.

In aggregating yarn output, qualitative differences are conventionally eliminated by expressing the output in "counts," i.e., in units of length

---

[17] *Sotsialisticheskoe stroitel'stvo*, 1936, p. 195.

[18] In 1940, 64.4 percent of all Russian cotton looms were 80 centimeters in width, while 24.5 percent were 100 centimeters in width. See *Planovoe khoziaistvo*, 1940, No. 9, p. 78. The average width was said to be about 90 centimeters. See *Legkaia promyshlennost'*, 1940, No. 1, p. 48.

[19] It would be possible to make the U.S. adjustment on the basis of value of product. However, the value relationship is not necessarily expressive of the physical relationship between the two products; nor is it certain that the Soviet production statistics include all narrow fabrics. It appears preferable, therefore, not to attempt an adjustment. The resultant bias, if any, is in the direction of overstating Soviet productivity.

[20] *Sotsialisticheskoe stroitel'stvo SSSR*, 1936, p. 195.

[21] *1941 Plan*, p. 157.

per unit of weight. The U.S. count is the number of hanks of 840 yards each per pound of yarn,[22] whereas in the Soviet Union it is the number of kilometers per kilogram of yarn. There is a direct relationship between the fineness of the count and unit labor requirements. The average yarn count in the Soviet Union in 1937 was 39.3 (metric system),[23] while that for the United States in 1939 was estimated at 37 (22 under the U.S. system of counting).[24] If one judges by an analysis of U.S. and British experience, the difference in unit labor requirements between these two counts is so small[25] as to obviate the necessity of any adjustment on this score.

Comparing the quality of cloth is a more difficult problem because of the great diversity of the product. The only statistics common to both countries relate to the weight of cloth per square meter and indicate U.S. superiority of product in this respect.[26] However, weight per unit of area is not the sole determinant of quality (productivity); the density of the fabric is an important determinant of labor requirements, and this may differ from weight in the case of fine fabrics.[27] The available data do not allow of a computation of the combined effects of the two factors. It is therefore necessary to disregard possible differences in the quality of cloth in preparing the productivity estimate.[28]

The output of cotton yarn and cloth in the Soviet Union from 1928 to the planned level for 1941 is shown in Table 60. The figures purport

[22] Thus, if 840 yards weigh one pound, the yarn is No. 1. A count of 84,000 yards per pound would be No. 100, a very fine yarn.

[23] *Legkaia promyshlennost'*, 1940, Nos. 11–12, p. 14.

[24] L. Rostas, *Comparative Productivity in British and American Industry*, p. 131.

[25] See Anglo-American Council on Productivity, *Cotton Spinning*, pp. 58–61.

[26] According to the *1941 Plan*, p. 150, the output of woven goods in Russia was to average 12.23 kilograms per 100 linear meters. A corresponding estimate of 14.8 kilograms per 100 meters (broad-woven goods only) can be derived for the United States. See *Census of Manufactures*, 1939, II, Part I, 291, 302. The average U.S. linear meter was also wider than the Soviet linear meter, augmenting the discrepancy.

[27] In United Nations, Department of Economic Affairs, *Labour Productivity of the Cotton Textile Industry in Five Latin-American Countries*, the following formula was used to measure the combined effects of weight and density:

$$\left(\frac{\text{warp ends}}{\text{sq. inch}} + \frac{\text{picks}}{\text{sq. inch}}\right) \times \text{width of the fabric in inches} \times \frac{\text{yards}}{\text{pound}}.$$

[28] In an article by a Soviet textile engineer, the statement is made, without any supporting data, that the density of Soviet cloth output in 1938 exceeded that of the United States in 1935 by 15 to 20 percent. See *Legkaia promyshlennost'*, 1940, Nos. 11–12, p. 51.

Table 60

PRODUCTION OF COTTON YARN AND CLOTH IN THE SOVIET
UNION, 1928–41

YEAR	YARN (THOUSANDS OF METRIC TONS)	UNFINISHED CLOTH (MILLIONS OF LINEAR METERS)
1928	324[a]	2,778[f]
1929	354[a]	3,094[f]
1930	287[b]	2,515[g]
1931	314[b]	2,541[g]
1932	355[b]	2,694[f]
1933	367[b]	2,732[f]
1934	388[b]	2,733[f]
1935	384[a]	2,640[f]
1936	480[a]	3,270[f]
1937	533[a]	3,447[f]
1938	574[c]	3,491[h]
1939	607[d]	3,788[j]
1940	n.a.[l]	n.a.
1941	699[e] *(1941 Plan)*	4,338[k] *(1941 Plan)*

[a] Ia. A. Ioffe, *SSSR i kapitalisticheskie strany*, p. 191. This series is consistent, for overlapping years, with the series cited in note *b*.

[b] *Sotsialisticheskoe stroitel'stvo SSSR*, 1936, p. 195. It is indicated in the source (p. 705) that the data include the output of all industry, both large scale and small scale. However, in another source in which almost identical figures are cited for 1931 and 1932, the output of industrial cooperatives is specifically excluded. See *Sotsialisticheskoe stroitel'stvo SSSR*, 1934, p. 137, note to Table 7. It is assumed that for the later years, at least, the product of the industrial cooperatives is included, an assumption that is supported by the data in Table 59.

[c] Estimated from the 1939 output on the basis of a statement that, from 1938 to 1939, cotton yarn output rose by 32.6 thousand tons. See P. A. Khromov, "Proizvoditel'nost' truda v khlopchatobumazhnoi promyshlennosti SSSR," in Akademiia Nauk, Institut Ekonomiki, *Proizvoditel'nost' truda v promyshlennosti SSSR*, 1940, p. 282.

[d] The yarn output of the cotton textile industry for 1939, as distinct from the knit-goods and technical cloth industries and the industrial cooperatives, was 504 thousand tons. See *Planovoe khoziaistvo*, 1940, No. 9, p. 88. Assuming that this corresponded to the jurisdiction producing 443 thousand tons in 1937 (see Table 59), and that the ratio of this output remained constant from 1937 to 1939, the estimate of 607 thousand tons may be derived.

[e] *1941 Plan*, p. 71.

[f] Ioffe, *op. cit.*, p. 192. For the year 1932, this series is almost identical with that in *Sotsialisticheskoe stroitel'stvo SSSR*, 1936, p. 195 (although the series in the 1934 edition of the last-named publication, which specifically excluded the output of cooperatives, was less by 92 million meters). After 1932, however, the two series diverge, the figures in Ioffe exceeding those in *Sotsialisticheskoe stroitel'stvo SSSR* by the following amounts: 1933, 31 million meters; 1934, 60 million meters; and 1935, 66 million meters. The data for 1937 presented in Table 59 suggest that the production statistics in Ioffe repre-

Notes to Table 60 (*Continued*)

sent the total output of the entire economy, whereas those presented in various editions of *Sotsialisticheskoe stroitel'stvo* omit minor administrative branches and, moreover, have been inconsistent in their inclusiveness over time.

[g] *Trud v SSSR*, 1936, p. 184. This series is consistent with that in Ioffe, *op. cit.*, for the years 1928, 1929, and 1932.

[h] *Sotsialisticheskoe stroitel'stvo SSSR*, 1939, p. 73.

[j] P. A. Khromov, *Ocherki ekonomiki tekstil'noi promyshlennosti SSSR*, p. 129.

[k] *1941 Plan*, p. 71.

[l] n.a. = information not available.

to be global, i.e., to include the output of all sectors of the economy, including the cooperatives and small-scale industry.

The output of yarn for 1937, which will be employed in the productivity comparison, should be reduced by 10.6 percent and that of cloth by 3.1 percent, for reasons indicated above. The resultant figures are 476.5 thousand metric tons of yarn and 3,340 million linear meters of cloth. With respect to the translation of linear into square meters, it was noted above that, for several years for which production was given in both units of measurement, the output in square meters was 76 percent of the output expressed in linear meters. However, this may be too low, by virtue of the inclusion in the Soviet statistics of what would be classified as narrow fabrics in the United States. A leading Soviet authority on productivity indicated the propriety of a reduction factor of 20 percent between the two units of measurement;[29] if one accepts this factor, the relevant Soviet cloth output for 1937 was 2,672 square meters.

The 1939 U.S. output of cotton yarn was 1,427 thousand metric tons; of cotton cloth, 7,563 million square meters.

THE LABOR FORCE

By 1913 the labor force in Soviet cotton manufacture was at a level which at least equaled, and probably exceeded, the peak labor force under the prewar five year plans.[30] There was a sharp decline in the

[29] *Problemy ekonomiki*, 1939, No. 2, p. 49. The author of the statement was P. A. Khromov.

[30] The number of wage earners in cotton textile manufacture in 1913 has been variously placed at 566 thousand (P. A. Khromov, *Ocherki ekonomiki tekstil'noi promyshlennosti SSSR*, p. 129); 492 thousand (Waldemar Adermann, *Die russische*

number employed after World War I, but by 1926 the magnitude which was to be maintained during the following decade had been recovered. Thus, when the era of rapid industrialization was inaugurated in 1928, it was possible to meet the increased demand for cotton textiles without any over-all increase in manpower or, more accurately, womanpower.

The labor force data available for the years 1928 to 1936 are presented in Table 61. It will be noted that employment was slightly less on January 1, 1936, than on January 1, 1928. The difference between the labor section and industry section data is probably due largely to the exclusion from the former, and inclusion in the latter, of wage earners working for industrial cooperatives. The number of such wage earners was put at 29.6 thousand during 1938.[31]

The following additional data are available or may be estimated for subsequent years:

a. The number of wage earners as of December, 1936, for an undefined sector of the cotton manufacturing industry, was given as 385.4 thousand, with a planned labor force of 368 thousand for the first quarter of 1937.[32] The figures are useful only in indicating an intent to reduce employment from 1936 to 1937.

b. According to statistics compiled by Soviet trade unions, cotton manufacturing wage earner employment was 474.3 thousand on July 1, 1938, and 484.6 thousand on July 1, 1939.[33] The similar figure for October 1, 1934, was 530.3 thousand wage earners.[34] These data are not useful for our purposes[35] except to indicate the possibility of a decline in employment from 1934 to 1938.

c. The output per wage earner in cotton textile manufacturing for 1937 was given as 9,204 1926/27 rubles.[36] It is clear from the context that this figure was derived by dividing gross value of product as shown in the various issues of *Sotsialisticheskoe stroitel'stvo SSSR* by the num-

---

Baumwollindustrie nach dem Kriege, p. 47); and 480.4 thousand (*Sotsialisticheskoe stroitel'stvo SSSR*, 1936, p. 13).

[31] *Legkaia promyshlennost'*, 1940, No. 3, p. 10.

[32] *Ibid.*, 1937, No. 3, p. 84.

[33] Vsesoyuznyi Tsentral'nyi Sovet Professional'nykh Soiuzov, *Statisticheskii spravochnik*, III, 18.

[34] *Trud v SSSR*, 1935, p. 261.

[35] See *supra*, p. 38.

[36] Khromov, *Ocherki*, p. 127.

TABLE 61

THE LABOR FORCE IN SOVIET COTTON MANUFACTURING,
1928–36

(*In thousands of persons*)

YEAR	NUMBER OF EMPLOYEES, JANUARY 1[a]	NUMBER OF WAGE EARNERS, JANUARY 1 (LABOR SECTION)[b]	AVERAGE ANNUAL NUMBER OF WAGE EARNERS (LABOR SECTION)	AVERAGE ANNUAL NUMBER OF WAGE EARNERS (INDUSTRY SECTION)
1928	522.7	455.9	485.0[c]	489.2[f,g]
1929	550.4	489.9	n.a.[k]	........[g]
1930	489.9	439.4	n.a.	........[g]
1931	431.5	370.6	n.a.	........[g]
1932	494.6	417.4	412.2[d]	451.4[f,g]
1933	491.7	413.7	397.2[e]	440.2[f]
1934	475.6	412.9	420.4[e]	464.0[f]
1935	517.6	455.4	444.8[d]	475.0[j]
1936	516.8	448.3	n.a.	466.7[h]

[a] *Trud v SSSR*, 1936, p. 184.

[b] *Ibid.*, less the number of learners from *Sotsialisticheskoe stroitel'stvo SSSR*, 1936, p. 516.

[c] *Trud v SSSR*, 1936, p. 185, less the average of the number of learners at the beginning and at the end of the year from *Sotsialisticheskoe stroitel'stvo SSSR*, 1936, p. 516.

[d] *Trud v SSSR*, 1936, p. 185.

[e] *Ibid.*, 1935, p. 62.

[f] *Sotsialisticheskoe stroitel'stvo SSSR*, 1936, p. 13. The following figures appear in the 1935 edition (p. 236) of this statistical handbook: 1932—439.4; 1933—438.4.

[g] The following series for the years 1928–32 appears in *Sotsialisticheskoe stroitel'stvo SSSR*, 1934, p. 134:

1928—477.8	1931—380.3
1929—496.1	1932—425.1
1930—422.2	

This series was not linked in with that shown in the table because of obvious discrepancies in coverage for the overlapping years.

[h] Estimated as of July 1, 1936, from *Zhenshchina v SSSR*, 1937, p. 62. Monthly data for 1935 indicate that July 1 employment was 97.2 percent of average employment for the entire year. See *Trud v SSSR*, 1936, p. 185. The figure for 1936 can therefore be regarded as fairly close to average annual employment for the year.

[j] Estimated by A. D. Redding in an unpublished manuscript.

[k] n.a. = information not available.

ber of wage earners appearing in the same source, i.e., by an industry section wage earner figure.[37] (In both cases, only large-scale industry

[37] The same source cites a figure of 3,905 rubles for 1913, which can be derived precisely from *Sotsialisticheskoe stroitel'stvo SSSR*, 1936, p. 13; similarly with a figure of 6,750 rubles for 1932, cited in *Legkaia promyshlennost'*, 1939, No. 6, p. 46. Slightly

is included.) The gross value of output in cotton textile manufacturing under the jurisdiction of the national and republic commissariats of light industry was 4,178 million rubles in 1937.[38] The only possible difference between this figure and total value of product for large-scale industry would lie in the omission of that portion of the product produced by cooperative enterprises meeting the large-scale census requirements, and in the light of the relative unimportance of cooperative production in 1937 (see Table 59) this is not a significant error.[39] The 1937 labor force may thus be estimated at 454 thousand. Since this is an "industry section" figure, the corresponding "labor section" figure may be estimated at 425 thousand wage earners, using the ratio prevailing between the number of wage earners, according to the two concepts, in 1935.[40]

d. It is indicated in a Soviet source that output per wage earner in 1939 was 1,300 kilograms of yarn and 6,875 square meters of cloth, the figures having been calculated by dividing the total output, first of yarn, then of cloth, by the combined number of wage earners engaged in spinning and weaving.[41] The yarn output yields 467 thousand wage earners for 1939. The output of cloth in square meters is not available for 1939, though the use of the linear-square meter ratio from earlier years would yield a somewhat lower labor force for the year. The labor force concept employed was not indicated in the source.

Since this concludes the catalogue of post-1936 labor force figures that may be estimated for cotton manufacturing, the only course open

different figures for 1937 can be secured by applying to the data for 1932 and 1934 the percentage productivity increases cited in Khromov, *Ocherki,* p. 127, and *Planovoe khoziaistvo,* 1939, No. 3, p. 151. In each case, however, the difference is less than 1 percent.

[38] *Legkaia promyshlennost',* 1938, No. 1, p. 21.

[39] Moreover, it is not at all certain that the value of product of large-scale cooperative enterprises entered into the computation of annual value of product per wage earner. Even if it did, however, the gross value of product cited would be understated by a maximum of about 3 percent, this figure representing the contribution of all cooperative enterprise, both large and small scale.

[40] The difference between these two figures, 29 thousand, may be compared with the 29.6 thousand wage earners employed by the cooperatives in 1938. *Legkaia promyshlennost',* 1940, No. 3, p. 10.

[41] P. A. Khromov, "Proizvoditel'nost' truda v khlopchatobumazhnoi promyshlennosti SSSR," in Akademiia Nauk, Institut Ekonomiki, *Proizvoditel'nost' truda v promyshlennosti SSSR,* p. 286.

is to accept the estimate of 425 thousand wage earners for 1937. This implies a moderate decline in employment from 1935 to 1937, which is consistent both with the intention of the Russian planners and the trend that was manifested from 1935 to 1936 (see Table 61).

The next problem is that of securing separate labor force estimates for spinning and weaving. There is a Soviet statement to the effect that about half of the direct production workers were employed in weaving, the remainder presumably being engaged in spinning and finishing.[42] This ratio may be checked against several sets of employment data, which may be used for this purpose but not for estimating total employment, since they are confined to direct machine operators.

a. The output per man-hour in spinning was 64.4 kilo-numbers, or 1.6 kilograms, of yarn in 1935; the corresponding output of cloth was 7.88 meters.[43] The average number of days worked per wage earner in the industry that year was 258,[44] or 1,806 hours on the basis of the prevailing seven-hour day. From these data it may be estimated that there were 133 thousand wage earners engaged in spinning and 186 thousand engaged in weaving in 1935, a ratio of 42–58 percent.

b. The average annual output of cotton yarn per wage earner was 2,850 kilograms in 1936; of cotton cloth, 10,670 square meters.[45] Comparison of these figures with the output data in Table 60 yields employment of 168 thousand direct wage earners in spinning and 245 thousand in weaving, a ratio of 41–59 percent.

c. Production of cotton goods in 1938 has been listed at 3,200 kilograms of yarn per wage earner per annum and 7.3 linear meters of cloth per man-hour.[46] The estimated average number of hours worked by wage earners in 1938 is 1,829.[47] This yields 179 thousand wage earners engaged in spinning and 261 thousand engaged in weaving, a ratio of 41–59 percent.[48]

d. The number of direct production workers per 1,000 spindles in

[42] *Legkaia promyshlennost'*, 1940, Nos. 9–10, p. 37.

[43] Khromov, "Proizvoditel'nost' truda," p. 268.

[44] *Trud v SSSR*, 1936, p. 188.

[45] Khromov, "Proizvoditel'nost' truda," p. 286.

[46] *Legkaia promyshlennost'*, 1940, No. 1, p. 51.

[47] Estimated from the information that the annual output per wage earner in 1938 was 139 thousand kilo-numbers of yarn, and the hourly output, 76 kilo-numbers. See *Legkaia promyshlennost'*, 1940, No. 1, pp. 49–51.

[48] It is tempting to conclude that the total of these two figures, 440 thousand wage

1935 was 7.77; per loom, 0.44.[49] On September 15, 1934, there were 7,930,000 spindles and 216,000 looms in operation in the Soviet Union.[50] In calculating the ratio of wage earners to machines, the so-called shift coefficient was taken into consideration, i.e., the machine park was increased in proportion to the number of shifts per day that the machines were operated, averaging 1.83 in 1935.[51] The resultant labor force may be estimated at 113 thousand spinners and 174 thousand weavers, a ratio of 39–61 percent.

The persistence of a ratio of about 40 percent of wage earners engaged in spinning to 60 percent engaged in weaving in the foregoing estimates, as well as in similar calculations that can be made for other years, permits us to place some confidence in it. The only contradictory piece of evidence is the statement cited above, that about half of the production wage earners were engaged in spinning; and even there, if our assumed 7 percent of the labor force engaged in finishing is removed, this ratio becomes 46 to 54 percent.

If a 40–60 percent distribution is accepted for the Soviet Union, a startling contrast with the corresponding U.S. distribution emerges. The 1939 Census of Manufactures carries the following wage earner data (average for the year):

Cotton broad-woven goods	312,249
Cotton narrow fabrics	13,318
Cotton yarn	70,452
Cotton thread	13,298
Total	409,317

The labor force engaged in spinning cannot be separated directly from that engaged in weaving, since "broad-woven goods" includes the entire labor force of the integrated mills. Rostas has estimated that, of the above total, 221 thousand wage earners were engaged in spinning and 150 thousand in weaving.[52] The difference of 38 thousand between his figures and the Census total is accounted for by his omission of "narrow fabrics" and "thread" (26.5 thousand) and the estimated num-

---

earners, represented total wage earner employment in the industry. However, too little is known of the manner in which the productivity data were calculated to make this a safe procedure.

[49] Khromov, *Ocherki*, p. 132.

[50] *Sotsialisticheskoe stroitel'stvo SSSR*, 1936, p. 197. Data for 1935 are not available.

[51] *Trud v SSSR*, 1936, p. 188.

[52] Rostas, *op. cit.*, pp. 130, 131 *n*.

ber of wage earners engaged in yarn doubling. For our purposes, these excluded classes should be added in. If the total number of wage earners in "broad-woven goods" and "yarn" is distributed in the ratio of 60 to 40 percent, as estimated by Rostas for a portion of the two, "narrow fabrics" assigned to weaving, and "thread" to spinning, the following U.S. wage earner estimate for 1939 emerges:[53]

	WAGE EARNERS	PERCENTAGE
Spinning	243,000	59
Weaving	166,000	41
Total	409,000	100

The variance in the spinning-weaving labor force ratio between the two countries attests to the fact that spinning was relatively more efficient than weaving in Russia as compared with the relative efficiency of the two operations in the United States.[54]

The 1937 Soviet wage earner estimates must be augmented by learners and junior service personnel. The ratio of the two groups to wage earners on January 1, 1936, was 6.7 percent.[55] By the use of this ratio the following estimates are obtained:

Estimated number of wage earners, learners, and junior service personnel in USSR cotton textile manufacturing (including finishing), 1937	453,500
Less: estimated number in finishing	31,700
Wage earners in spinning and weaving	421,800
Spinners (40 percent)	**168,700**
Weavers (60 percent)	253,100

[53] A careful Soviet analysis of the 1935 U.S. labor force yielded the following results:

	WAGE EARNERS	PERCENTAGE
Spinning	170,000	45
Weaving	170,000	45
Doubling	30,000	8
Overhead	10,000	2
Total	380,000	100

See *Legkaia promyshlennost'*, 1940, No. 1, p. 50. If cotton doubling is added to spinning, a preponderant portion of the labor force is seen to have been engaged in spinning, though not to the same extent as the Rostas estimate would indicate. However, the Rostas estimate is based on a special Bureau of Labor Statistics study and is therefore preferred.

[54] Great Britain, with 53 percent in spinning and 47 percent in weaving in 1937, was intermediate between Russia and the United States.

[55] *Trud v SSSR*, 1936, p. 186.

COMPARATIVE PRODUCTIVITY

The foregoing sections may now be summarized:

	RUSSIA, 1937	UNITED STATES, 1939
Output of cotton yarn (thousands of metric tons)	476.5	1,427.0
Number of wage earners in spinning	168,700	243,000
Annual output of yarn per wage earner (kilograms)	2,825	5,872
Relative productivity (U.S. = 100)	48	100
Output of cotton cloth (millions of square meters)	2,672	7,563
Number of wage earners in weaving	253,100	166,000
Annual output per wage earner (square meters)	10,557	45,560
Relative productivity (U.S. = 100)	23	100

From 1937 to 1939, the Russians asserted that labor productivity in spinning rose by 6.5 percent and in weaving by 12.8 percent, both measured in physical output per wage earner.[56] The increase for the industry as a whole, measured in value of output per wage earner, was 17.3 percent.[57] No data are available for 1940. If the physical productivity claims, which cannot be checked against underlying data, are accepted as accurate, Soviet productivity in 1939, in relation to U.S. productivity in the same year, would have been 51 percent in spinning and 26 percent in weaving.

It is of interest to compare the foregoing figures with estimated productivity of British industry:[58]

PRODUCTIVITY AS A PERCENTAGE OF
U.S. PRODUCTIVITY, 1939

	Great Britain, 1939	USSR, 1937
Spinning	58–62	48
Weaving	38–40	23

A number of USSR-U.S. productivity comparisons derived from Soviet sources are shown in Table 62. Except for the starred items, the comparisons were made quite crudely, without regard for differences in industrial structure, methods of labor force measurement, or product quality. The reader will also note differences in the years specified;

[56] *Legkaia promyshlennost'*, 1940, Nos. 9–10, p. 37. This included only factories of "union significance," i.e., under the national light industry commissariat.

[57] Khromov, *Ocherki*, p. 127.

[58] Rostas, *op. cit.*, p. 131. This comparison was made in output per man-hour. A British productivity team put the spinning figure at only 42 percent in 1950. Anglo-American Council on Productivity, *Cotton Spinning*, p. 4.

for the United States, a year earlier than 1939 is used in all but one instance, and since U.S. productivity was rising at the time,[59] the relatives are understated in comparison with a 1939 base. The Soviet comparisons are chiefly of interest in pointing to a lower relative productivity in weaving.[60]

TRENDS IN SOVIET PRODUCTIVITY, 1928–39

The available data on trends in Soviet cotton manufacturing productivity are presented in Table 63. The index shown in column (1) represents the ratio of cotton cloth production to the number of wage earners in cotton manufacturing as a whole.[61] The remaining indexes are reproduced from Soviet sources.

The index in column (1) is based on annual output; those in columns (2) and (3), on hourly output. This may help to explain, for example, why the annual output index for 1935, which is scarcely above the 1928 level, diverged from the hourly index of weaving productivity. Raw material and yarn shortages contributed to low annual productivity,[62] while the productivity record for the time actually worked was better.

After 1932, the value index of productivity outran the others significantly. It is difficult to account for the magnitude of the divergence, since cotton manufacturing was an old industry, and the pricing of new products should not have constituted a major inflationary item for the production index on the basis of which the productivity index was calculated.

Perhaps the most surprising aspect of Table 63, however, is the more

[59] The Bureau of Labor Statistics index of output per man-hour in U.S. cotton manufacturing from 1935 to 1939 was as follows (1935 = 100):

YEAR	OUTPUT PER MAN-HOUR
1935	100.0
1936	110.0
1937	110.0
1938	110.2
1939	117.6

U.S. Department of Labor, Bureau of Labor Statistics, *Handbook of Labor Statistics,* 1950 ed., p. 170.

[60] In the case of the starred comparisons, adjustment for increased U.S. productivity from 1935 to 1939 and increased Soviet productivity from 1937 to 1938 brings the estimates fairly close to our own.

[61] The unavailability of separate labor force data for spinning and for weaving made it impossible to compute separate indexes.

[62] See Khromov, *Ocherki,* p. 138.

TABLE 62

SOVIET-MADE COMPARISONS OF USSR-U.S. COTTON TEXTILE
LABOR PRODUCTIVITY
(U.S. = 100)

YEARS COMPARED	UNIT OF MEASUREMENT	SOVIET INDEX
Spinning		
USSR, 1939—U.S., 1937	kilograms per annum	49[a]
USSR, 1939—U.S., 1937	kilograms per annum	50[b]
USSR, 1936—U.S., 1935	kilograms per annum	44[c]
*USSR, 1938—U.S., 1935[g]	kilograms per annum	50[d]
USSR, 1938—U.S., 1935	kilo-numbers per hour	62[d]
USSR, 1936—U.S., 1936	kilograms per annum	40[e]
USSR, 1939—U.S., 1939	not specified	63–67[f]
Weaving		
USSR, 1939—U.S., 1937	square meters per annum	38[a]
USSR, 1936—U.S., 1935	kilograms per annum	40[c]
*USSR, 1938—U.S., 1935[g]	meters per hour	42[d]
USSR, 1936—U.S., 1936	square meters per annum	37[e]
USSR, 1939—U.S., 1939	not specified	**40–45[f]**

[a] P. A. Khromov, "Proizvoditel'nost' truda v khlopchatobumazhnoi promyshlennost SSSR," in Akademiia Nauk, Institut Ekonomiki, *Proizvoditel'nost' truda v promyshlennosti SSSR*, p. 286. Output per wage earner was calculated by dividing first yarn and then cloth by the combined number of wage earners engaged in spinning and weaving. The U.S. data were from the 1937 Census of Manufactures. In the case of spinning, the Soviet author erroneously used as his output dividend only yarn produced for use within the establishment, neglecting yarn made for sale. The correct ratio for spinning is 40 percent.

[b] *Planovoe khoziaistvo*, 1940, No. 9, p. 88.

[c] *Problemy ekonomiki*, 1939, No. 2, p. 49.

[d] *Legkaia promyshlennost'*, 1940, No. 1, p. 48. These figures are the result of a careful comparison of hourly productivity data, adjusted for quality difference. They are the most sophisticated of the Soviet comparisons.

[e] *Legkaia promyshlennost'*, 1939, No. 7, p. 40.

[f] *Ibid.*, 1939, No. 12, p. 19.

[g] These estimates were made with much more care than the others.

rapid rise shown in hourly productivity for weaving than for spinning. Soviet investment policy under the first three five year plans favored spinning, in order to rectify a long-existing imbalance between spinning and weaving capacity.[63] The explanation seems to lie in the rela-

[63] In 1937, for example, 16 percent of yarn output was produced in plants constructed during the five year plans, compared with 9 percent of cloth output. For a detailed account of investment policy in the industry, see *Legkaia promyshlennost'* 1940, No. 1, p. 12.

TABLE 63

INDEXES OF SOVIET COTTON TEXTILE LABOR PRODUCTIVITY,
1928–39
(1928 = 100)

YEAR	(1) ANNUAL OUTPUT OF CLOTH PER WAGE EARNER[a]	(2) HOURLY OUTPUT PER WAGE EARNER		(3) ANNUAL OUTPUT PER WAGE EARNER IN 1926/27 RUBLES, SPINNING AND WEAVING[c]
		Spinning[b]	Weaving[b]	
1928	100.0	100.0	100.0	100.0
1929	n.a.[d]	108.5	115.4	115.3
1930	n.a.	117.4	135.5	108.5
1931	n.a.	n.a.	n.a.	121.5
1932	114.1	105.5	121.1	120.2
1933	120.1	n.a.	n.a.	128.7
1934	113.5	n.a.	n.a.	132.9
1935	103.6	105.1	123.9	139.9
1936	n.a.	120.4	146.1	169.6
1937	141.6	123.5	148.3	162.1
1938	n.a.	127.2	154.0	n.a.
1939	n.a.	131.6	167.0	190.3

[a] Calculated from Tables 60 and 61 by dividing the output of cloth by the total number of wage earners in the industry (labor section data).
[b] P. A. Khromov, *Ocherki ekonomiki tekstil'noi promyshlennosti SSSR*, p. 128.
[c] *Ibid.*, p. 127.
[d] n.a. = information not available.

tive technological backwardness of weaving at the commencement of the industrialization period, so that the incremental yields in productivity increases were greater per unit of capital investment than for spinning.[64] A Soviet writer commented that the greater productivity rise for weaving "was due chiefly to the fact that the tempo of decline of labor

[64] This hypothesis is borne out by similar findings made with respect to the cotton industry in Latin America: "In the case of spinning mills, the influence of the type of equipment is of very little importance, compared to the joint effect of all the other factors. . . . This is because modern machinery in the spinning mills differs very little from the old type of equipment, as regards both production per unit of equipment and the number of workers required per unit of equipment. . . . In the weaving mills, on the contrary, the influence of the type of equipment on labor consumption is of considerable importance." United Nations, Department of Economic Affairs, *Labour Productivity of the Cotton Textile Industry in Five Latin-American Countries*, p. 6.

expenditure per unit of equipment was less in spinning than in weaving," despite the greater investment in spinning.[65]

From 1928 to 1939, output per man-hour in U.S. cotton goods manufacturing increased by 53 percent, so that, judging by the data in Table 63, there was little difference in the rate of productivity growth experienced by cotton manufacturing in the two countries over this period.

FACTORS AFFECTING SOVIET PRODUCTIVITY

The relationship between labor and capital resources. A United Nations study of Latin-American cotton manufacturing yielded the conclusion that the principal cause of low productivity was the excessive supply of labor in relation to available capital. For example, "The most important reason for the employment of a superfluous number of workers is the production policy followed by some Chilean mills, whereby the greatest possible output must be obtained from the machinery, even if this means the employment of numerous workers and the lowering of the output of labor."[66]

There is reason to believe that the Soviet cotton textile industry in the thirties was characterized by similar conditions. As a consequence of the emphasis upon heavy industry, investments allotted to cotton manufactures were held very low.[67] The cotton labor force consisted in large part of women, who were drawn into the labor market by the decline in real wages suffered by the head of the family. There are occasional references to labor shortages, particularly just before the war, but to the extent that they were real, rather than part of the general propaganda drive which led to the imposition of strict labor controls, they were probably occasioned by excessive turnover and seasonal withdrawals from the labor market.

Of maximum, even uneconomic, exploitation of machinery there is considerable evidence. Three-shift operation was introduced in 1928[68] and apparently continued throughout the next decade.[69] Excessive

[65] Khromov, *Ocherki*, p. 131. From 1928 to 1939, the ratio of wage earners to spindles declined by 14 percent, the ratio of wage earners to looms by 36 percent. *Ibid.*, p. 132.

[66] United Nations, Department of Economic Affairs, *op. cit.*, p. 51 and *passim.*

[67] See Khromov, *Ocherki*, pp. 79–83.

[68] *Ibid.*, p. 138.

[69] In 1939, the average number of hours worked per spindle was 5,820, compared with an average of 2,086 hours worked per annum per wage earner, i.e., an average of 2.8 shifts per spindle. See *Planovoe khoziaistvo*, 1940, No. 9, p. 78.

machine speeds, often without adequate provision for repair, were encouraged.[70] Work loads, on the other hand, were relatively low. A British wartime study of the U.S. cotton industry revealed that American weavers tended from 32 to 60 looms, on the average, depending on the type of cloth and machinery.[71] Russian data indicate that, even on automatic looms in the most modern plants, 7 to 20 looms per weaver was the average work load, while on nonautomatic looms 4 to 6 looms was the average.[72] The inexperience of the Russian worker was certainly a factor; but it can be surmised that the Soviet factory manager was more concerned with keeping his machinery fully employed rather than his labor force. It was only during the war, when women were needed to man what were formerly men's jobs, that the emphasis changed.[73]

Technological factors. The greater modernity and mechanization of the U.S. machine park was another prime factor in U.S. superiority in productivity. In 1937, when the spinning mule had virtually been abandoned in the United States in favor of the more productive ring frame, 25 percent of Russian spindles were of the mule type.[74] The disparity in weaving was much greater. Whereas only 18.5 percent of the Russian looms were automatic in 1937,[75] the comparable figure for the United States was 39 percent.[76]

[70] Khromov, *Ocherki,* p. 141.

[71] United Kingdom, Ministry of Production, *Report of the Cotton Textile Mission to the United States of America,* p. 29.

[72] Khromov, *Ocherki,* p. 135.

[73] See Solomon Schwarz, *Labor in the Soviet Union,* p. 26.

[74] Khromov, *Ocherki,* p. 78. Russian investment in spindles was devoted largely to replacing mules by ring frames, with the result that there was little over-all increase in the spindle park from 1928 to 1939.

[75] *Ibid.,* p. 161. The Second Five Year Plan had set as a goal 40 percent mechanization by 1937, but actual achievement was far behind the goal.

[76] United Kingdom, Ministry of Production, *op. cit.,* p. 16. The significance of the automatic loom is illustrated by the following quotation: "The most striking difference between American and British mills in productivity in weaving is attributable to the wide use of automatic looms in America. There we saw pillow cottons weaving at more than 90 percent efficiency and 104 looms per weaver. Few firms in Britain would weave such cloths at more than 8 non-automatic looms per weaver, and 85 percent efficiency . . . our operative weavers are unanimously of the opinion that, with complements of looms per weaver even as high as 104, the weavers in American mills on automatic looms, with American controlled conditions, have no harder task than weavers on similar cloths running four, six, or eight non-automatic looms in Lancashire, under British conditions." Anglo-American Council on Productivity, *Cotton Weaving,* pp. 16–17.

The Russian cotton textile industry of the thirties was an old industry. At the end of 1934, 75 percent of the spindles in operation and 80 percent of the looms had been in place prior to 1917. On January 1, 1936, only 22.5 percent of the total cotton textile output was produced in plants which had been built or modernized subsequent to 1928, compared with a general industrial average of 79.8 percent.[77] Cotton textiles even lagged behind textiles in general: whereas on January 1, 1937, 39 percent of the capital invested in all textiles had been accumulated since 1928, the corresponding figure for cotton textiles was 24 percent.[78] One of the principal goals for the cotton textile industry was a relative increase in spinning capacity, for the lack of yarn often prevented capacity use of looms.[79] Yet as of 1940 it was reported: "Notwithstanding the construction of a number of large spinning mills . . . the lack of spinning capacity was not completely overcome. . . . The lack of yarn is one of the factors hindering increased production in the cotton industry."[80]

Breakage rates. The rate of breakage depends on a number of technical factors, including the twist and quality of yarn and its preparation as well as proper machine operation and the skill of the tender. There is an inverse correlation between the rate of yarn breakage and productivity.[81] The average yarn breakage rate per 1,000 spindle hours was 120–150 in Soviet textile mills in 1939,[82] the U.S. rate for comparable yarn being fixed at between 27 and 45.[83] It was pointed out that in consequence of this difference, Russian spinners spent only 15 to 20 percent of their time in cleaning and maintaining machinery and the

[77] Khromov, *Ocherki,* p. 80.

[78] *Legkaia promyshlennost',* 1939, No. 6, p. 46.

[79] Deficit spinning capacity was due to the availability of cheap English yarns in the pre-Soviet era, the loss of Esthonian yarn after World War I, and increased yarn requirements of the automobile and electrical industries.

[80] Khromov, *Ocherki,* p. 101.

[81] For example: "Under American conditions the number of spindles or looms tended per spinner or weaver will depend largely upon the number of yarn breakages. To reduce breakages, therefore, is broadly equivalent to reducing the labor force and production cost. Under the American automatic loom system such a reduction in cost will more than offset the higher cost of spinning due to the higher yarn twist." United Kingdom, Ministry of Production, *op. cit.,* p. 10.

[82] *Legkaia promyshlennost',* 1940, No. 1, p. 48.

[83] Khromov, *Ocherki,* p. 140. A British productivity team indicated that 30 per 1,000 spindle hours was an average postwar U.S. breakage rate and continued: "It would be considered very bad spinning to let the end breakage rate reach 50." Anglo-American Council on Productivity, *Cotton Spinning,* p. 38.

balance in repairing breaks, whereas U.S. spinners divided their time equally between the two tasks.[84] The situation in weaving was similar: average Russian breakage rates of 1.2 to 1.5 per machine hour prevailed, contrasted with U.S. rates of 0.34 to 0.42 for similar types of cloth.[85]

The labor force. On July 1, 1938, women constituted 67.4 percent of the number of wage earners in Soviet cotton textile manufacture.[86] The female portion of the U.S. cotton mill labor force in 1939 was 42.4 percent in the independent yarn mills and 36.6 percent in the integrated mills.[87] The higher proportion of women workers in the Soviet industry was a factor in lower productivity.

Labor turnover is another factor to be considered. A British mission made this comment on U.S. turnover: "There is a comparatively large turnover in the American mills due, partly, to the fact that labor is, on the whole, less stable, and, if circumstances warrant it, does not hesitate to move from one plant to another or from one industry to another."[88] However, there is a difference between this type of turnover and that which prevailed in the Russian industry. The American worker moved because he was laid off or in search of higher wages, and to a considerable extent this mobility tended to raise the marginal productivity of labor. Soviet labor mobility, however, was prompted largely by a desire to escape substandard living conditions or was the type of irrational mobility commonly found among new recruits to the industrial labor force, concentrated in large measure among the unskilled.[89] The peak of turnover in Soviet cotton manufacturing was reached in 1932, when the number of voluntary quits constituted 72 percent of the average

[84] *Legkaia promyshlennost'*, 1940, No. 1, p. 48.

[85] *Ibid*. The productivity significance of breakage rates in weaving is illustrated by the following: "The main work of the weaver, apart from supervision, centers on the taking-up of warp breakages. It is clear that even a small reduction in the warp-breakage rate would make it possible for the weaver to look after a larger complement of automatic looms. To reduce the breakage rate to half . . . would mean a very substantial increase in productivity through the possibility of greatly increasing the complement of machinery per weaver, without increased work." Anglo-American Council on Productivity, *Cotton Weaving*, p. 16.

[86] *Planovoe khoziaistvo*, 1939, No. 10, p. 114.

[87] Rostas, *op. cit.*, p. 139.

[88] United Kingdom, Ministry of Production, *op. cit.*, p. 38.

[89] For example, 80 percent of the persons leaving their jobs in a large Soviet textile mill in 1939 had less than two years of industrial experience. See Khromov, *Ocherki*, p. 143.

payroll workers for the year. The ratio fell to 43 percent in 1934 and rose again to 49 percent in 1936.[90] Subsequent data are not available, but even after the passage of stringent manpower legislation in 1940 and 1941, the problem of excessive turnover was far from solved.[91]

Among the other labor factors contributing to low Soviet productivity may be cited an excessive proportion of indirect labor[92] and seasonal withdrawals of part of the labor force.[93]

TABLE 64

EFFICIENCY OF SOVIET COTTON SPINDLE OPERATION, 1928–39

YEAR	IDLE TIME AS A PERCENTAGE OF SCHEDULED SPINDLE HOURS
1928	4.45
1929	4.21
1930	4.85
1931	n.a.[a]
1932	13.98
1933	8.34
1934	6.76
1935	4.84
1936	6.73
1937	9.98
1938	10.57
1939	8.30

Source: *Legkaia promyshlennost'*, 1940, Nos. 11–12, p. 12.
[a] n.a. = information not available.

Organizational and structural factors. The percentage of idle time in relation to the total number of scheduled spindle hours in the Soviet Union, for the years 1928 to 1939, is shown in Table 64. Average U.S. machine efficiency in 1950 was reported to be 91 percent, with a range

[90] *Legkaia promyshlennost'*, 1937, Nos. 8–9, p. 109.

[91] See N. S. Maslova, *Proizvoditel'nost' truda v promyshlennosti SSSR*, p. 71. It was reported, for example, that only 58 percent of the workers hired by cotton mills during 1946 remained on the job permanently. See *Planovoe khoziaistvo*, 1947, No. 3, p. 23.

[92] It was reported that in 1940 indirect factory labor constituted 18 to 20 percent of all Soviet wage earners, compared with 8 to 12 percent in the United States. See *Legkaia promyshlennost'*, 1940, No. 5, p. 30.

[93] Khromov, *Ocherki*, p. 142.

in practice from 88 percent to 95 percent.[94] By this criterion, the Russians would seem to have achieved a high rate of machine efficiency. However, there is no way of knowing the relative theoretical capacities from which the efficiency rates were computed.[95]

The scale of enterprise does not appear to have been a retarding factor in the growth of productivity in Soviet cotton manufacture. For many years, the industry had been characterized by large producing units. Already in 1913, for example, 78 percent of the industry's labor force was employed in factories with staffs of over 1,000 persons.[96] The tendency toward a large scale of manufacture was particularly marked in spinning, smaller enterprises playing a more important role in weaving. As of 1939, there was probably a greater degree of concentration in Soviet than in U.S. cotton manufacturing.[97]

PRODUCTIVITY TRENDS SINCE 1939

There are no data which permit of an estimate of the change in Soviet cotton productivity from 1939 to 1940. Operating to augment annual output per wage earner was the lengthening of the standard working day from seven to eight hours that occurred in 1940; but hourly productivity may have suffered in consequence. At any rate, in view of the course of productivity in this industry during the preceding decade, any change from 1939 to 1940 must have been a moderate one.

Although the physical facilities of the Soviet cotton manufacturing industry, centralized in Moscow and the Ivanovo province to the east, were largely unscathed during the war, a sharp drop in productivity occurred nonetheless. Output per wage earner in both spinning and weaving was described as "significantly lower" in 1945 than in 1940, the decline being greater in weaving. The major causes cited were lack of raw materials and fuel and the employment of unqualified workers,

[94] Anglo-American Council on Productivity, *Cotton Spinning,* p. 55.

[95] It may also be noted that a higher ratio of operators to machinery tends, *ceteris paribus,* to result in a higher rate of operating efficiency.

[96] Khromov, *Ocherki,* pp. 52–53.

[97] For example, only 38.2 percent of U.S. wage earners in integrated mills and 7.2 percent in independent yarn mills worked in enterprises employing over 1,000 wage earners in 1939. See Rostas, *op. cit.,* p. 138. The corresponding figure for Soviet large-scale industry was 86.3 percent, a figure which would not have been reduced materially by the inclusion of small-scale enterprises.

which led to high breakage rates and low machine speeds.[98] The 1946 level of spinning productivity was given as 89.2 percent of the prewar level; and that of weaving, as 67.2 percent.[99] For the industry as a whole, 92 percent of the 1940 productivity level was achieved by 1948,[100] but the prewar level had not yet been reached by March, 1949.[101]

During the first four years of the first postwar five year plan, the increase in productivity was stated to have been 19 percent for spinning and 41 percent for weaving.[102] If productivity in 1945 had not been greatly below that in 1946, the data would point to the attainment of the 1940 level of productivity by the end of 1950. However, since the Soviet claims cannot be verified by recourse to output and labor force data, this conclusion must remain uncertain.

Output per man-hour in U.S. cotton textile manufacturing was 100.7 percent of 1939 in 1945.[103] A rough calculation based on the 1947 Census of Manufactures indicates a decline in productivity from 1939 to 1947 on the order of 12 percent in yarn mills and 11 percent in cotton broad woven fabrics.[104] There are no adequate data for subsequent years.

[98] Maslova, op. cit., p. 62; Planovoe khoziaistvo, 1947, No. 3, p. 14.

[99] Planovoe khoziaistvo, 1947, No. 3, pp. 21, 23. The method by which productivity was measured was not indicated.

[100] Tekstil'naia promyshlennost', 1948, No. 11, p. 3.

[101] Trud, March 24, 1949, p. 1.

[102] Tekstil'naia promyshlennost', 1950, No. 3, p. 6.

[103] Monthly Labor Review, December, 1946, p. 900.

[104] U.S. Census of Manufactures, 1947, II, 155 ff.

XI

SHOE MANUFACTURING

THROUGHOUT the prewar planning period, Soviet shoe manufacturing continued to be a handicraft industry to a greater degree than virtually any other manufacturing industry. During the fiscal year 1926/27, only 30 percent of all shoes were produced under factory conditions, the remainder being produced either in small workshops or under the traditional putting-out system.[1] A number of large factories were created by concentrating the equipment of smaller plants; two of the largest Soviet enterprises, the Parizhskaia Kommun and Burevestnik plants in Moscow, were created in this manner. However, the small shop remained an important producing unit. In 1940, 41 percent of all wage earners in manufacturing and 15 percent of the product (by value) were classified as small scale by current census definitions.[2] There were some 12,271 of these small establishments operating during this year, employing an average of 12 wage earners and producing an average gross product of 26,000 rubles. It will be recalled that the 1939 U.S. Census excluded such establishments as those with an annual gross product of less than $5,000; or those engaged mainly in performing work for individual customers, with a gross product of less than $10,000; or those engaged in neighborhood industries and hand trades employing little or no power machinery. Even at the nominal ruble value of 5.3 to the dollar prevailing in 1940, the average annual gross product of Soviet small-scale manufacturing was below the minimum U.S. Census requirement. If a more realistic purchasing power parity rate were substituted and the additional Census stipulations were also taken into account, it is likely that the U.S. counterparts of most of the small shoe enterprises in the Soviet Union would have been excluded from the

---

[1] A. M. Gornostai-Polskii, *Osnovy ekonomiki kozhevenno-obuvnoi promyshlennosti*, p. 69.

[2] *Ibid.*, p. 247. For the census definitions, see *supra*, p. 40.

Census.[3] The ensuing discussion will be confined to the large-scale sector of Soviet shoe manufacturing.

Within this sector, there were three major groups of enterprises, each displaying peculiar productivity characteristics:

a. By far the most efficient portion of the industry was under the direct administrative jurisdiction of the national light industry commissariat. In 1936 it included only 15 enterprises,[4] employing 39,000 wage earners,[5] and producing 51.5 million pairs of shoes,[6] i.e., 1,320 pairs of shoes annually per wage earner.

b. State-owned enterprises under the jurisdiction of republic and local administrative agencies were smaller and less efficient. They employed 43,000 wage earners in 1936 and produced about 1,190 pairs of shoes per wage earner during the year.[7]

c. Cooperative enterprises were far less efficient than the state-owned.

---

[3] It might be argued that, since small enterprises were of far greater relative importance in Russia than in the United States, the omission of the small-scale sector of the Soviet industry would have the effect of distorting the productivity comparison. This argument is valid if what is sought is comparative labor time per pair of shoes produced in each country, regardless of the method of production. It is at least of equal interest, however, to determine relative productivity under factory conditions in each country, a measure which is secured by omitting the small handicraft enterprises in both countries. Since, for Russia, output per wage earner in small-scale shoe shops was only about 25 percent of that in larger establishments in 1940, it is apparent that the inclusion or exclusion of the small shops would result in widely varying conclusions.

[4] *Kozhevenno-obuvnaia promyshlennost'*, 1936, No. 8, p. 15.

[5] *Trud v SSSR*, 1936, p. 226. This figure is as of January 1.

[6] *Kozhevenno-obuvnaia promyshlennost'*, 1937, No. 1, p. 2.

[7] This estimate is based on the assumption of an unchanged output structure among the various administrative groups in large-scale shoe manufacture from 1935 to 1936. The relevant 1935 data are as follows:

	MILLIONS OF PAIRS OF SHOES	PERCENTAGE OF TOTAL
Large-scale industry, total	90.5	100
National enterprises	38.3	42
Republic and local enterprises	36.8	41
Cooperative enterprises	15.4	17

Sources: *Kozhevenno-obuvnaia promyshlennost'*, 1937, No. 2, p. 2; *ibid.*, 1937, No. 8, pp. 8–9.

This estimate places productivity in the republic and local enterprises at 80 percent of that in national enterprises in 1936. A figure of 90 percent may be derived for 1940. See Gornostai-Polskii, *op. cit.*, p. 225.

Their share of total output varied between 15 and 18 percent during the years 1932 to 1937.[8] Their average output per wage earner for 1935 may be estimated at 246 pairs of shoes[9] and their average employment in 1940 at 78 wage earners.[10] The U.S. shoe manufacturing enterprises of Census size averaged 221 wage earners in 1939. All Russian large-scale shoe manufacturing, including the cooperatives, had an average employment of 145 wage earners in 1940; without the cooperatives, this figure rises to 477.[11] Thus by including the Soviet cooperatives in the productivity comparison, we secure a comparison between industries which are as alike in terms of concentration of employment as the data permit. Omission of the Soviet cooperative sector would introduce a large bias in the direction of higher relative Soviet productivity.

Available statistics on Soviet shoe output to 1940 are shown in Table 65. The differences among the various series presented therein are as follows:

a. Series A is limited to large-scale enterprises under the jurisdiction of national and local light industry commissariats.[12]

b. Series B and C, though derived from different sources, appear to be identical, the conflicting data for 1935 being attributable to the pre-liminary character of the figure in Series B. These series include, in addition to the industry covered in Series A, the large-scale enterprises of the industrial cooperatives and (very minor) of commissariats other than that for light industry.[13]

c. Series E appears to differ from Series B and C by virtue of the inclusion of the output of small-scale enterprises and of rebuilt shoes;[14]

---

[8] See *Kozhevenno-obuvnaia promyshlennost'*, 1933, No. 1, p. 6; *ibid.*, 1935, No. 10, p. 593; *ibid.*, 1937, No. 2, p. 2; *ibid.*, 1937, No. 8, pp. 8–9.

[9] Estimated from Tables 65 and 70.

[10] Gornostai-Polskii, *op. cit.*, p. 247.

[11] *Ibid.*

[12] This can be deduced from productivity data in Gornostai-Polskii, *op. cit.*, pp. 206, 225.

[13] That the data are limited to large-scale enterprise is evident from *Sotsialisticheskoe stroitel'stvo*, 1936, p. 206, n. 1. That cooperatives are included may be surmised from *ibid.*, pp. 703, 705.

[14] This can be demonstrated for the year 1933. In that year, 80.3 million pairs of new shoes and, in addition, 10 million pairs of rebuilt shoes, were produced in large-scale industry (Series C). See *Sotsialisticheskoe stroitel'stvo*, 1936, p. 206, n. 3. The difference between this total, 90.3 million pairs, and the 99.4 million pairs shown in Series E must have come from small-scale industry.

TABLE 65

PRODUCTION OF SHOES IN THE LARGE-SCALE SECTOR OF THE
SOVIET SHOE MANUFACTURING INDUSTRY, 1928–40[a]

(*In millions of pairs of shoes*)

YEAR	SERIES A[b]	SERIES B[e]	SERIES C[f]	SERIES D[h]	SERIES E[j]
1928	23.6	29.6	n.a.	n.a.	n.a.
1929	n.a.[c]	48.8	n.a.	n.a.	48.8
1930	65.6	75.4	n.a.	n.a.	n.a.
1931	77.0	86.7	n.a.	n.a.	n.a.
1932	78.2	84.7	n.a.	86.9	n.a.
1933	65.9	80.2	80.3	n.a.	99.4
1934	58.1	75.5	75.5	n.a.	n.a.
1935	69.2	85.5	90.5	n.a.	n.a.
1936	96.6	n.a.	125.0	n.a.	n.a.
1937	133.9[d]	n.a.	164.3[g]	182.9	n.a.
1938	138.8	n.a.	n.a.	n.a.	213.0
1939	146.5	n.a.	n.a.	n.a.	n.a.
1940	150.2[d]	n.a.	n.a.	n.a.	220.0[k]

[a] Excludes rubber and felt footwear.

[b] A. H. Gornostai-Polskii, *Osnovy ekonomiki kozhevenno-obuvnoi promyshlennosti,*
p. 206.

[c] n.a. = information not available.

[d] Gornostai-Polskii, *op. cit.,* p. 74. This source presents an output series which is
consistent with that shown in Series A up to 1936, but which contains the following
figures for subsequent years: 1937—137.8; 1940—189.8. It would appear that the
1940 figure contains the output of the cooperatives, whereas the earlier figures do not.

[e] *Sotsialisticheskoe stroitel'stvo,* 1936, p. 206. The figure for 1935 is marked "preliminary."

[f] *Kozhevenno-obuvnaia promyshlennost',* 1937, No. 8, p. 8.

[g] Ia. A. Ioffe, *SSSR i kapitalisticheskie strany,* p. 195.

[h] *Sotsialisticheskoe stroitel'stvo,* 1939, p. 75.

[j] *Ibid.,* p. 73.

[k] University of Birmingham, *Bulletins on Soviet Economic Development,* No. 1, p. 8.
No source is given for this figure. However, it is consistent in trend with the data in
Series A.

it may be surmised that Series D includes the output of rebuilt shoes
but not of small-scale enterprises.[15]

[15] The principal evidence for this lies in the fact that, for the year 1937, Series D
exceeds Series C by 18.6 million pairs of shoes, compared with the total of 21.3
million pairs of rebuilt shoes produced in 1940 (see Table 66). The fact that for
1934 Series B and D differ insignificantly does not destroy the validity of the hypothesis,
since it is evident from *Sotsialisticheskoe stroitel'stvo,* 1936, p. 206, that prior to 1933
either no attempt was made to account for rebuilt shoes or the magnitude of their
production was not sufficient to be worth noting.

A better notion of the significance of rebuilt shoe output may be gained from Table 66, where 1940 shoe production is shown broken down by administrative jurisdiction.[16] Some 75 percent of all rebuilt shoes were produced in the industrial and invalid cooperative system.

TABLE 66

OUTPUT OF SHOES IN THE SOVIET UNION, 1940,
BY ADMINISTRATIVE AGENCY

(*In millions of pairs*)

	TOTAL	NEW	REBUILT
Commissariat of Light Industry	154.4	151.5	2.9
Commissariat of Local Industry	5.0	3.9	1.1
NKVD	4.1	3.6	0.5
Industrial cooperatives	36.4	21.9	14.5
Invalid cooperatives	5.6	4.2	1.4
Other	5.6	4.7	0.9
Total	211.1	189.8	21.3

Source: A. M. Gornostai-Polskii, *Osnovy ekonomiki kozhevenno-obuvnoi promyshlennosti*, p. 79.

However, they presumably constituted a part of the output of large-scale enterprise, and since the labor force engaged in their production is included in the denominator of the productivity ratio, they should be included in the numerator.[17]

For the year 1939, the only Soviet output statistic available is that for the limited sector of the industry covered by Series A in Table 65. However, by assuming the constancy of the ratio prevailing between Series A and Series D in 1937, an estimate of 200 million pairs of shoes for all large-scale industry may be obtained for 1939.[18]

The 1939 output of shoes in the United States was 435.3 million pairs.

[16] These data are probably limited to large-scale industry, which would explain why the total output shown for 1940 in Table 66, 211.1 million pairs, exceeds the total in Table 65, Series E.

[17] It cannot be said a priori that rebuilt shoes were more or less costly in labor time than new shoes, and data are lacking. It may be surmised that lack of leather constituted the economic rationale for rebuilt shoe production, rather than the saving of labor.

[18] Interpolating on a straight line basis between 1938 and 1940 for Series E would leave for 1939 some 16 to 17 million pairs of shoes as the output of small-scale industry, about 8 percent of total product. In terms of value of product, small-scale

THE PRODUCT

In the case of shoes, more than for almost any other of the commodities with which we are concerned in this study, the use of relative quantities, uncorrected for qualitative differences, is likely to result in misleading conclusions. This point was made forcefully some years ago by E. C. Snow in a presidential address before the Royal Statistical Society:

The fact that the proportions of footwear described as women's and men's in the United States and the United Kingdom are approximately the same in the two countries does not by any means demonstrate that the products themselves are comparable. There may be considerable difference in the nature of the production within the type. Although in the huge output of the United States there are naturally many women's shoes of types suitable for this country, the fact that over a large part of the States it is universal to wear rubber overshoes in the winter means that the proportion of the sub-types within the type (e.g., light, medium, heavy, etc.) differ substantially. Whether the footwear produced is "light" or "heavy" has distinct bearing upon the "output per head," and we really require knowledge of this character before we can draw reliable conclusions.[19]

Following are some of the factors which tend to vitiate direct quantitative comparison of shoe output between Russia and the United States:

Class of consumer. The variation of shoe cost, by class of consumer,

industry contributed 15.3 percent of total output in 1940. See Gornostai-Polskii, *op. cit.,* p. 247. This discrepancy may be due either to an overstatement in the estimated physical output for large-scale industry or to lower unit values for small-scale, rather than for large-scale, production of shoes. The latter possibility may have reflected a large element of repair work by small-scale establishments, which would have affected value of output without coming into the physical output statistics. If it were assumed that the relative share of small-scale industry in 1939 output, in physical terms, was 15.3 percent, the relative Soviet productivity level estimated below would be reduced by three percentage points.

Theoretically, the output data should be adjusted for the production of the Narodnyi Komissariat Vnutrennikh Del SSSR (NKVD—People's Commissariat of Internal Affairs of the USSR), since its labor force was probably excluded from the regular labor force statistics. However, no estimate will be attempted because of the relatively small output of the NKVD. It is assumed that the labor force of local industry commissariats and the "other" administrative units shown in Table 66 were included in the labor force statistics shown in Table 70, below, though here again there may be a discrepancy for reasons stated in Abram Bergson, "A Problem in Soviet Statistics," *The Review of Economic Statistics,* November, 1947, pp. 238–39.

[19] See E. C. Snow, "The International Comparison of Industrial Output," *Journal of the Royal Statistical Society,* 1944, Part I, p. 53.

TABLE 67

PRODUCTION OF SHOES IN THE UNITED STATES,
BY CLASS OF CONSUMER, 1939[a]

CLASS OF CONSUMER	NUMBER OF PAIRS	GROSS VALUE OF OUTPUT	GROSS VALUE PER PAIR	OUTPUT OF EACH CLASS AS PERCENTAGE OF TOTAL
Total output	435,258,128	$731,816,076[b]	$1.68	100.0
Men: Dress	76,636,981	182,166,659	2.38	17.6
Work	28,124,504	48,553,025	1.73	6.5
Youths and boys	17,316,169	24,778,307	1.43	3.9
Women	168,776,620	335,126,882	1.99	38.8
Misses and children	46,091,283	50,290,097	1.09	10.6
Infants	24,631,553	17,649,709	0.72	5.7
Other	73,681,018	73,251,397	0.99	16.9

Source: U.S. Department of Commerce, Bureau of the Census, *Census of Manufactures,* 1939, II, Part II, 48.

[a] Excludes rubber footwear.

[b] A value of $991,798, representing leggings, puttees, and footwear made in other industries and for which quantities are not available, is omitted.

for the United States in 1939 is shown in Table 67. Although not explicitly stated in the Census, all classes of shoes appear to have been made of leather, with the exception of the "Other" group, which consisted of a wide variety of types and materials, including canvas, satin, wood sandals, and combinations of leather and other materials. Comparable Soviet data for a year reasonably close to 1939 are not available; the nearest approximations are the data shown in Table 68, classifying the output of four factories during the first quarter of 1937. These factories, however, were four of the five largest shoe producing enterprises in the Soviet Union, their combined output constituting about one quarter of all Soviet shoe production in 1936.[20] The Skorokhod plant, in Leningrad, itself accounted for about 14 percent of total output. The only additional piece of relevant information available is that, of an undefined total output, 1940 Soviet output included 70 million pairs of men's shoes and 57 million pairs of women's shoes.[21]

[20] Estimated from *Kozhevenno-obuvnaia promyshlennost,* 1937, No. 1, p. 2.

[21] Gornostai-Polskii, *op. cit.,* p. 236. It is not indicated whether this is limited to leather shoes or whether it includes fabric shoes as well.

TABLE 68

DISTRIBUTION OF SHOE OUTPUT, BY CLASS OF CONSUMER,
FOR FOUR LARGE SOVIET FACTORIES, FIRST QUARTER, 1937
(*Percentage of total*)

CLASS	SKOROKHOD	PARIZHSKAIA KOMMUN	PROLETARSKAIA POBEDA NO. 2[a]	BUREVEST- NIK[a]
Total output	100	100	100	100
Men's calf	20	32	..	20
Women's calf	8	19	27	..
School and preschool calf	27		..	..
Textile and combined leather-textile	37	26	..	..
Sandals	8		..	..
Children's oilcloth with rubber soles		23	..	..

Source: *Kozhevenno-obuvnaia promyshlennost'*, 1937, No. 6, p. 6.
[a] Total distribution not given.

From these scanty data, a distribution of Soviet shoe output has been constructed and compared with that of the United States (see Table 69). The Soviet data are more accurately described as being an hypothetical rather than an estimated distribution. Using U.S. 1939 unit gross value as weights, the resultant 12 percent excess of U.S. over Soviet "weighted value" cannot properly be considered as being an accurate expression of differences in labor inputs per unit flowing from the factors under consideration, but merely as being an index of the direction of the bias. Therefore, it does not seem appropriate to adjust the quantitative data on this account; but the reader is given notice that a bias exists in the direction of understating relative U.S. productivity and is one that may be of considerable magnitude.

Quality differences. Even within each consumer type, there are innumerable differences in quality which affect labor requirements. "Individual operations on a high-grade shoe may require over 50 percent more time than on a medium-grade shoe. Furthermore, some styles require operations not called for in other styles, causing considerable variations in labor-time requirements."[22] For example, in 1936, a sample

[22] Boris Stern, "Labor Productivity in the Boot and Shoe Industry," *Monthly Labor Review*, February, 1939, p. 276.

TABLE 69

DISTRIBUTION OF SOVIET AND UNITED STATES SHOE OUTPUT,
BY CLASS OF CONSUMER

| | SOVIET UNION[a] | UNITED STATES, 1939[b] | |
| | | | |
TYPE OF SHOE	Percentage of total	Percentage of total	Value per unit
Men's leather	25	24	$2.20
Women's leather	20	39	1.99
Youth's and children's leather	20	20	1.05
Other	35	17	0.99

[a] These data are more in the nature of hypotheses than estimates. They are based on Table 68, as well as on general information regarding Soviet shoe production. For example, there is little doubt that nonleather shoes constituted a larger proportion of total output in the USSR and that relatively more women's leather shoes were produced in the United States. The excess of men's over women's leather shoes shown for the USSR appears to be justified by the 1940 datum available, although the great preponderance of men's shoes during this particular year may have reflected a step-up in military production.

[b] Based on the U.S. Department of Commerce, Bureau of the Census, *Census of Manufactures*, 1939, II, Part II, 48.

of 23 U.S. plants revealed that the number of men's shoes produced per man-hour ranged from 0.521 to 2.597; the number of women's shoes (15 plants), from 0.351 to 1.063.[23] As between Russia and the United States, not even a rough approximation of the direction of any bias can be secured.

Style and variety. Intrinsic differences in quality aside, style and variety may be quite costly in terms of labor requirements. There were, and presumably continue to be, serious deficiencies in the selection of shoes available to the Russian consumer. Not only were many types of specialized shoes completely unavailable, but complete size lines of standard items were rare.[24] In the United States, on the other hand, product differentiation led to a great variety of lines and styles,[25] pre-

[23] *Ibid.* No conclusions should be drawn from these figures as to the relative cost of men's and women's shoes, since the samples were not homogeneous with respect to manufacturing process.

[24] See, for example, *Kozhevenno-obuvnaia promyshlennost'*, 1937, No. 7, p. 14.

[25] We may cite as authority a Soviet engineer familiar with the U.S. industry: "What is one's major impression of the American shoe industry? It is the wide variety

sumably contributing to the augmentation of consumer welfare. This factor cannot be quantified, but it obviously resulted in relatively greater labor input per unit of shoe output.

THE LABOR FORCE

The available Soviet labor force statistics for the period from 1928 to 1940 are presented in Table 70. The most complete series is that limited to the sector of the industry under the jurisdiction of the national and republic light industry commissariats; for years for which both series are available, this series tended to approximate the labor section data shown in the general statistical handbooks.

Since the output of cooperatives is to be included in Soviet output, for comparative purposes it is necessary to estimate the 1939 figure for the industry section series, which included wage earners in the employ of cooperatives. In 1935, the industry section series was 213.3 percent of the corresponding figure for wage earners under the light industry commissariats; in 1940, the ratio had fallen to 179.4 percent, indicating the relatively greater importance of state-owned industry in total employment. By interpolation on a linear basis, the 1939 percentage may be estimated at 186.1 percent and the corresponding global number of wage earners at 216.6 thousand. By addition of the estimated number of learners and junior service personnel,[26] the appropriate Soviet labor force figure for 1939 was 236.3 thousand, of whom 127.1 thousand were in state-owned industry and 109.2 thousand in the cooperatives.

The appropriate U.S. labor force for 1939 was as follows:

Boot and shoe cut stock and findings[27]	18,845
Footwear	218,028
Total	236,873

of shoes produced. No consumer need say that it is difficult for him to satisfy his tastes on the shoe market. Styles, models, colors, size and type of heels, upper styles, patterns, stitching, perforation—all are extremely varied." *Kozhevenno-obuvnaia promyshlennost'*, 1935, No. 5, p. 236.

[26] On the basis of the relative number of these as of January 1, 1936. See *Trud v SSSR,* 1936, p. 223.

[27] A portion of the labor force of this industry should ideally be segregated to take into account wage earners engaged in the production of cut stock and findings sold to repair shops. However, the Census provides no data from which such an adjustment could be made.

TABLE 70

THE LABOR FORCE IN THE SOVIET LARGE-SCALE
SHOE INDUSTRY, 1928–40

(*In thousands of wage earners*)

YEAR	NUMBER ON JANUARY 1, IN- CLUDING LEARNERS, EXCLUDING COOP- ERATIVES (LABOR SECTION DATA)[a]	AVERAGE ANNUAL NUMBER UNDER NATIONAL AND REPUBLIC LIGHT INDUSTRY COMMISSARIATS[b]	AVERAGE ANNUAL NUMBER, INCLUD- ING COOPERATIVES (INDUSTRY SECTION DATA)
1928	26.5	33.7	39.3[e]
1929	40.4	n.a.[c]	74.0[f]
1930	65.7	78.1	141.9[f]
1931	94.0	92.7	155.8[f]
1932	93.9	87.1	206.1[e]
1933	91.5	n.a.	177.5[e]
1934	80.2	n.a.	157.6[e]
1935	74.5	76.4	163.0[g]
1936	91.9	n.a.	n.a.
1937	n.a.	124.8	n.a.
1938	n.a.	126.6	n.a.
1939	n.a.	116.4	n.a.
1940	n.a.	117.2[d]	210.3[d]

[a] *Trud v SSSR,* 1936, p. 223.

[b] A. M. Gornostai-Polskii, *Osnovy ekonomiki kozhevenno-obuvnoi promyshlennosti,* p. 206.

[c] n.a. = information not available.

[d] The number of wage earners in large-scale industry under the light industry commissariats was elsewhere put at 116.0 thousand for this year; other large-scale industry, at 94.3 thousand; small-scale industry, at 147.7 thousand. See Gornostai-Polskii, *op. cit.,* p. 247. The discrepancy of 1.2 thousand between the figure given by this source and the figure in the table is probably due to inclusion in the latter of wage earners under other commissariats engaged in the production of shoes.

[e] *Sotsialisticheskoe stroitel'stvo,* 1936, p. 15.

[f] *Ibid.,* 1935, p. 259.

[g] Based on an unpublished manuscript by A. D. Redding.

COMPARATIVE PRODUCTIVITY

The foregoing data may be summarized as follows:

	RUSSIA, 1939	UNITED STATES, 1939
Output of shoes (millions of pairs)	200.0	435.3
Number of wage earners (thousands)	236.3	236.9
Annual output of shoes per wage earner	846	1,837
Relative productivity (U.S. = 100)	46	100

A Soviet estimate placed Russian shoe output per wage earner (in kind) at half the U.S. level in 1937;[28] another placed it at 40 percent (in gross value of product) for the same year.[29] In neither case was the method of computation indicated.

TABLE 71

ANNUAL OUTPUT OF SHOES PER WAGE EARNER
IN ENTERPRISES UNDER THE SHOE TRUST OF THE USSR,
1938 AND 1939
(*In pairs of shoes*)

ENTERPRISE	1938	1939
Skorokhod	1,536	1,885
Parizhskaia Kommun	1,410	1,596
Burevestnik	1,534	1,787
Mikoian	1,307	1,665
Tbilisi	911	1,266
Sverdlovsk	926	1,366
Kuznetsk	1,174	1,382
Moskovskaia model'naia	206	232
Kaliazinsk model'naia	154	178
Leningradskaia model'naia	228	270
Rostovskaia model'naia	186	299
Average	1,222[a]	1,470[a]

Source: A. M. Gornostai-Polskii, *Osnovy ekonomiki kozhevenno-obuvnoi promyshlennosti*, p. 225.

[a] These averages appeared as stated in the Russian source. They are not simple arithmetic averages, and there is no induction of how they were computed.

The productivity performance of individual Soviet enterprises is shown in Table 71.[30] The sharp dividing line between the so-called model or fancy shoe plants and those producing ordinary shoes re-emphasizes the need for caution in interpreting shoe productivity based on quantity of output alone.

[28] *Kozhevenno-obuvnaia promyshlennost'*, 1939, No. 5, p. 11.

[29] *Ibid.*, p. 10.

[30] The Tbilisk, Sverdlovsk, and Kuznetsk plants were constructed during the Second Five Year Plan; the other plants were built earlier. That the newer plants were no more efficient than the old was attributed to the fact that they incorporated neither technological nor organizational novelties. See Gornostai-Polskii, *op. cit.*, p. 225.

TRENDS IN SOVIET PRODUCTIVITY

Several indexes of the trend of Soviet labor productivity from 1928 to 1940 are shown in Table 72. State-owned industry exhibited a marked

TABLE 72

INDEXES OF PRODUCTIVITY IN LARGE-SCALE SOVIET
SHOE MANUFACTURE, 1928–40
(1928 = 100)

	STATE-OWNED INDUSTRY		ALL LARGE-SCALE INDUSTRY	
YEAR	Physical output per wage earner[a]	Value of output per wage earner[b]	Physical output per wage earner[c]	Value of output per wage earner
1928	100.0	100.0	100.0[e]	100.0[j]
1929	n.a.[d]	99.6	87.6[e]	89.1[k]
1930	120.0	103.3	70.5[e]	80.9[k]
1931	118.6	101.1	74.0[e]	77.4[k]
1932	120.0	101.7	54.6[e]	60.5[j]
1933	n.a.	108.1	60.0[e]	66.7[j]
1934	n.a.	112.7	63.6[e]	69.2[j]
1935	130.0	116.6	73.7[e]	n.a.
1936	n.a.	n.a.	n.a.	n.a.
1937	153.3	n.a.	87.5[f]	n.a.
1938	156.6	n.a.	92.6[g]	n.a.
1939	179.6	n.a.	110.2[g]	n.a.
1940	183.1	n.a.	119.9[h]	124.8[l]

[a] A. M. Gornostai-Polskii, *Osnovy ekonomiki kozhevenno-obuvnoi promyshlennosti,* p. 206. Excludes the production of rebuilt shoes.

[b] *Trud v SSSR,* 1936, p. 223.

[c] All figures exclude the production of rebuilt shoes.

[d] n.a. = information not available.

[e] Calculated from Table 65, Series B and C, and Table 70.

[f] Production data from Table 65, Series C; labor force estimated from Table 70 on the assumption of a linear increase in the ratio of wage earners in state-owned industry to wage earners in large-scale industry from 1935 to 1940.

[g] Labor force estimated as in note *f, supra.* Output estimated by assuming a constancy of the 1937 ratio between Series A and C in Table 65.

[h] Production data from Gornostai-Polskii, *op. cit.,* p. 74 (this figure is interpreted as referring to the output of all large-scale industry). Labor force taken from Table 70.

[j] Calculated from *Sotsialisticheskoe stroitel'stvo,* 1936, p. 15.

[k] Value of product from *Socialist Construction in the USSR,* 1936; labor force data from Table 70.

[l] Gornostai-Polskii, *op. cit.,* p. 247.

difference in this respect from the cooperatives. A guess may be hazarded that the productivity of the cooperatives was diluted in large measure by the continuous process of reclassifying enterprises from small to large scale, particularly during the first half of the decade. That this affected the cooperatives in particular is evident from the following facts: the number of large-scale shoe enterprises rose from 1,290 in 1932 to 1,707 in 1933;[31] nevertheless, on July 1, 1934, there were only 145 enterprises in the state-owned sector of large-scale industry.[32] Moreover, it may also be surmised that capital investment was directed largely toward the state-owned sector.

Working time. One of the principal difficulties involved in translating annual into hourly output per wage earner is the insufficiency of data on overtime hours worked in Soviet industry. For shoe manufacturing, however, it is stated that overtime work constituted 0.97 percent of all working time in 1938, 2.7 percent in 1939, and 5.5 percent during the first half of 1940.[33] On the assumption that there was little overtime work prior to 1939, the reduction in the working day from eight to seven hours sometime during the years 1928–30 would mean that the index figure for 1938 was understated by 14 percent, in hourly productivity terms. However, the eight-hour day was reinstituted in June, 1940, and this, combined with overtime during the first half of the year, would mean rough equality for an index number calculated in annual and hourly output per wage earner. Since the eight-hour day was retained after the war, overtime would have caused an index of hourly productivity to lag behind one of annual productivity.

FACTORS AFFECTING PRODUCTIVITY

Technological. Although relatively little new investment was allocated to Soviet shoe manufacturing during the prewar plans,[34] the fact

---

[31] *Sotsialisticheskoe stroitel'stvo*, 1934, p. 29; *ibid.*, 1935, p. 11.

[32] *Trud v SSSR*, 1935, p. 80.

[33] *Kozhevenno-obuvnaia promyshlennost'*, 1940, No. 8, p. 12.

[34] In 1937, although the Soviet shoe and leather industry produced 2 percent (by value) of all industrial products, only 0.1 percent of the output of the machinery industry was devoted to equipment for it. See Gornostai-Polskii, *op. cit.*, p. 88. Some 21 new shoe factories were to be built during the Second Five Year Plan, scheduled by 1937 to be producing 28 percent of the output of state-owned enterprise. In fact, only 6 plants had been or were being built by 1937, and their share of total output was only 9 percent. See *Kozhevenno-obuvnaya promyshlennost'*, 1937, No. 6, p. 31.

that technological progress was slow in the U.S. shoe industry made for a smaller productivity difference than might have been anticipated.[35] An American observer of the pre-World War I Russian shoe industry noted in 1913 that "the use of machinery of American origin began in 1899 and of the equipment now installed in the 49 factories, about 60 percent is American, 30 percent German, and 10 percent French."[36] The Skorokhod plant, in Leningrad (financed by German capital), was described as having "a multiple-storied modernly constructed brick building, the equipment is installed according to American plan, and the entire system of manufacture follows, as far as practicable, American methods."[37] Thus, the Soviets inherited a relatively modern large-scale shoe industry. Their problem lay in the thousands of handicraft establishments, which even in 1940 were still important producers.[38]

The labor force. On July 1, 1936, 58.1 percent of the labor force in Soviet shoe manufacturing consisted of women;[39] by 1940, the percentage had risen to about 66 percent.[40] The labor force in U.S. shoe manufacturing included only 40 percent of women in October, 1939.[41]

The Soviet labor force was subject to great dilution during the war. On January 1, 1942, the percentage of women in the Moscow Burevestnik shoe plant was 76 percent; on January 1, 1943, it was 86.6 percent. Of all wage earners in nationally managed shoe plants on the latter date, 42 percent had been newly hired during 1942.[42] There is no information on the postwar situation, though undoubtedly these extreme wartime ratios were reduced.

[35] The position of the U.S. industry was described in the following terms: "The extent of mechanization and machine standardization in existence in 1923, the nature of the technology used in the industry, and the nature of the product manufactured are factors largely responsible for the slowing down in the trend toward higher man-hour productivity in the shoe industry. In spite of the higher degree of mechanization, shoe manufacturing is still in the stage of semiautomatic development." Stern, *op. cit.,* pp. 273–74.

[36] U.S. Department of Commerce and Labor, *Shoe and Leather Trade in Russia,* p. 3.

[37] *Ibid.,* p. 4.

[38] There were in 1940 some 12,270 small-scale shoe manufacturing enterprises with total employment of 147.7 thousand wage earners. See Gornostai-Polskii, *op. cit.,* p. 247.

[39] *Zhenshchina v SSSR,* 1937, p. 62.

[40] Gornostai-Polskii, *op. cit.,* p. 219.

[41] U.S. Department of Labor, Bureau of Labor Statistics, *Handbook of Labor Statistics,* 1947 ed., p. 19.

[42] *Legkaia promyshlennost',* 1943, No. 6, p. 3.

The war resulted in the destruction of 70 percent of the capacity of the Soviet state-owned shoe industry.[43] The Skorokhod plant was destroyed by artillery fire after most of its machinery and personnel had been evacuated.[44] By the end of 1946, however, this plant was reported once more to be the largest producing unit in the country, having a planned capacity in 1948 equal to that in 1940 and a planned 1950 labor productivity to exceed that of 1940 by "not less than 10%."[45]

Of other major plants, labor productivity in Proletarskaia Pobeda No. 2 (Leningrad) was reported to have achieved the following levels, compared with 1940, measured in value of output per wage earner: 1945—75 percent; 1946—97.1 percent; and 1947—107 percent.[46] Daily output of shoes per wage earner at Burevestnik (Moscow) was, based on 1940, 70 percent in 1945 and 86 percent during the first four months of 1947.[47]

Nationally administered shoe enterprises as a whole were said to be producing 4.9 pairs of shoes a day per wage earner in April, 1947, compared with 4.8 pairs in 1940.[48] But for the entire shoe industry, it was conceded that 1949 labor productivity remained considerably below the prewar level.[49] Nor was the 1950 output target achieved. It may be surmised that, at the very most, the Soviet shoe industry had in 1950 reached the 1940 level of labor productivity, the probabilities leaning toward a somewhat lower figure.

Man-hour productivity increased by 5.7 percent in U.S. shoe manufacturing between 1939 and 1950.[50] With maximum assumptions regarding Soviet productivity, i.e., with a 9 percent productivity increase from 1939 to 1940, as indicated in Table 72, and with 1950 productivity equal to that of 1940, Soviet productivity in 1950 would still have been less than half the U.S. level. In all probability, it was below the comparative estimate for 1939.

[43] *Ibid.*, 1946, No. 1, p. 14.   [44] *Ibid.*, 1945, No. 9, p. 3.
[45] *Ibid.*, 1946, Nos. 7–8, p. 7.   [46] *Ibid.*, 1947, No. 3, p. 5.
[47] *Ibid.*, 1947, No. 7, p. 2.   [48] *Ibid.*
[49] *Ibid.*, 1949, No. 5, p. 1.
[50] U.S. Department of Labor, Bureau of Labor Statistics, *Trends in Man-hours Expended per Pair: Footwear,* p. 4.

XII

BEET SUGAR PROCESSING

THE INDUSTRY AND THE PRODUCT

THE sugar beet provides Russia with virtually its entire supply of sugar. Prior to the Revolution, a considerable amount of imported cane sugar was refined, but since then the industry has been based on domestically grown beets. In the late thirties Russia became the world's largest producer of beet sugar.

Sugar beet manufacture had reached a fairly well-developed stage in the pre-Soviet economy. During the crop years from 1910–11 to 1914–15, there were 236 sugar factories in operation, on the average, of which 197 were located in the Ukraine, in the main source of the beet supply.[1] The same locational pattern persisted under the Soviets; of 186 sugar manufacturing establishments operating during the crop year 1935–36, 146 were located within the Ukraine.[2] However, there has been an effort to expand the production of beets and the manufacture of beet sugar into Eastern European Russia and Asia.[3]

The comparison of productivity in Soviet and U.S. sugar manufacturing is complicated by important structural differences in the industries of the two countries. The U.S. beet sugar plants normally carry the process of manufacture through to the production of refined granulated sugar suitable for final consumption. The so-called sugar refineries in the United States are engaged exclusively in the processing of cane sugar and do not ordinarily handle beet sugar. Another peculiarity of the U.S. industry is that beet sugar is generally sold only in granulated form, such other products as powdered, loaf, and bit sugar being produced in the cane sugar refineries.[4]

The Russian beet sugar manufacturing industry is divided into two

---

[1] Ewsey Rabinowitsch, *Die russisch-ukrainische Zuckerindustrie seit dem Weltkriege,* p. 6.

[2] *Sakhar,* 1936, No. 3, pp. 69–72.

[3] Naum Jasny, *The Socialized Agriculture of the USSR,* pp. 580–83.

[4] Works Progress Administration (hereinafter cited as WPA), National Research Project, *Productivity and Employment in Selected Industries: Beet Sugar,* p. 13.

parts: the production of granulated sugar and the processing of granulated sugar into other forms, so-called refining. More than half the sugar in the prewar period was marketed directly by the beet processing plants either in the form of refined granulated or of syrup, equivalent to the output of U.S. beet sugar plants.[5] The remainder of the granulated sugar was transferred to the refineries[6] (in the Russian sense) for conversion into forms demanded by the consumer.[7] The proportion of granulated sugar undergoing "refinement" tended to vary with the sugar crop: in good years, the refineries could handle less than half the total output of the beet processing plants, whereas in bad years the same refining capacity manufactured a larger proportion of total output.[8]

[5] Beet sugar cannot be used commercially in a raw state because of its unpleasant taste, and it may be assumed that, qualitatively, the Russian product is the equivalent of the U.S. product. It has been stated that the Soviet granulated sugar sold is 99.7 percent chemically pure sugar. See Gosudarstvennyi Nauchnyi Institut, *Bolshaia sovetskaia entsiklopediia*, L, 346–52.

[6] It is stated that "refined sugar factories of the USSR use only the white sugar," (*ibid.*), which may be interpreted to mean that all the sugar shipped from the beet processing plants has actually been refined in the American sense. However, even if sugar is shipped without having undergone final refinement, i.e., washing and filtering to remove syrup, the savings in labor inputs thus made by the Soviet processing plants are minor and not of sufficient magnitude to vitiate a comparison with the work of U.S. beet sugar plants.

[7] Soviet refineries, at least before the war, operated entirely on the basis of purchased granulated sugar. See *Sakhar,* 1940, No. 1, p. 13. Of 192 sugar plants operating in 1939, 184 belonged to the so-called Sugar Trust and 8 to the Sugar Refining Trust. See *ibid.,* 1940, No. 2, p. 4. However, some refineries may have been operated by the Sugar Trust, for in 1935 there were 16 refineries in operation. See *Otchet o rabote sakharnoi promyshlennosti za 1933–1935 gg.,* Moscow, 1936, p. 351 (hereinafter referred to as *Rabote sakharnoi promyshlennosti*).

The Soviet sugar refining industry primarily had its origin in the demand by consumers for very hard lump or bit sugar, which is held between the teeth when drinking tea. Most of the so-called refined sugar was sold in this hard bit form, only a minor amount being sold as whole loaf and powdered sugar. See *ibid.,* pp. 87, 303, 351.

[8] The percentage of granulated sugar undergoing "refinement" from 1930 to 1936 was as follows:

YEAR	PERCENTAGE
1930	14
1931	16
1932	53
1933	35
1934	35
1935	35
1936 (*Plan*)	38

Sources: *Sotsialisticheskoe stroitel'stvo SSSR,* 1936, p. 226; *Sakhar,* 1936, No. 1, p. 10.

It is clear that the U.S. beet sugar industry is comparable, in terms of the operations it performs, to that portion of the Russian industry engaged in the production of granulated sugar, excluding the "refineries." This is not to say, of course, that these two industries are alike in all respects. For example, there may be differences in regard to labor required for the production of sugar by-products—beet pulp and molasses—particularly the latter, which in some U.S. plants is subjected to the so-called Steffens process to extract additional sugar.[9] There may also be differences in sugar packaging which affect labor inputs. To adjust for differences of this nature, however, would require productivity data of a fineness available for neither country.

The output of Soviet granulated sugar from 1928 to 1938 is shown in Table 73. The 1939 output of granulated beet sugar in the United States was 1,472,169 metric tons.[10]

LABOR FORCE

The available Soviet labor force statistics for sugar manufacturing are assembled in Table 74. "Labor section" data are available only for the years 1931 to 1934, when they ranged from 5 to 7 thousand wage earners fewer than the corresponding "industry section" data. In both cases, the sugar refineries are included and, to judge by the magnitude of the data, the labor force engaged in beet procurement and out-of-plant transport as well.[11]

The data in the last three columns of Table 74 are derived from a special publication of the Sugar Trust, at the time an administrative

---

[9] See WPA, *Productivity and Employment in Selected Industries: Beet Sugar*, pp. 183–87.

[10] U.S. *Census of Manufactures*, II, Part I, 178–81. In addition, an insignificant quantity of raw sugar was produced for sale.

[11] The inclusion of extra-plant personnel was due to the fact that the Sugar Trust, in order to ensure an adequate supply of beets during the sugar campaign, supervised state farms producing beets, provided and manned central collection points for the product of State and collective farms, and operated railroad branch lines to the sugar plants because of the poor roads and the unavailability of trucks. Horse-drawn vehicles were widely used as well. On January 1, 1936, the Sugar Trust was operating 738 kilometers of wide-gauge and 1,028 kilometers of narrow-gauge railroad spurs. See *Rabote sakharnoi promyshlennosti*, p. 33. The personnel manning the beet collection points and the railroad lines amounted to 18.5 thousand in 1934, of whom 15 thousand were wage earners. See *ibid.*, p. 70.

TABLE 73

PRODUCTION OF SUGAR IN THE SOVIET UNION, 1928–38

YEAR	OUTPUT (THOUSANDS OF CENTNERS)[a]
1928	12,826[b]
1929	8,230[b]
1930	15,070
1931	14,862
1932	8,268
1933	9,953
1934	14,035
1935	20,316
1936	19,984
1937	24,211
1938	25,071

[a] The data from 1928 to 1935 are from *Sotsialisticheskoe stroitel'stvo SSSR*, 1936, p. 226, and relate to sugar "weighed" at the factory. The data from 1936 to 1938 are from L. V. Opatski, "Proizvoditel'nost' truda v sakharnoi promyshlennosti SSSR," in Akademiia Nauk, Institut Ekonomiki, *Proizvoditel'nost' truda v promyshlennosti SSSR*, p. 299, and relate to sugar "manufactured." In 1935, "weighed" sugar output constituted 99.2 percent of "manufactured" sugar output (*Rabote sakharnoi promyshlennosti*, pp. 300–303), so that the error involved in the use of the different concepts is small. A centner is equal to 100 kilograms.

[b] These data actually cover the crop years 1928–29 and 1929–30. Since most of the sugar beets grown in a year are processed before the end of the same calendar year, it is appropriate to relate the data to the portion of the crop year from September to December, i.e., to the first-named calendar year.

subdivision of the Commissariat for the Food Industry.[12] Prior to 1934, these data also included out-of-plant personnel, but beginning in 1934 such personnel were shown separately. It is appropriate to use the more restricted labor force concept for comparison with the U.S. industry, for the Census of Manufactures excluded outside trucking personnel[13] from the total of factory wage earners.

The scope of the Sugar Trust data and the manner of their collection are not specified in the source. They may be compared with the

[12] From 1936 to 1938, the data are from a monograph on the sugar industry but are based on statistics of the Sugar Trust.

[13] In the United States, most beets were transported to the processing plants by truck rather than by rail. See WPA, *Productivity and Employment in Selected Industries: Beet Sugar*, p. 114.

TABLE 74

THE LABOR FORCE IN SOVIET SUGAR MANUFACTURING, 1928–38

(*In thousands*)

YEAR	AVERAGE ANNUAL NUMBER OF WAGE EARNERS, INCLUDING REFINERIES (INDUSTRY SECTION)	AVERAGE ANNUAL NUMBER OF WAGE EARNERS, INCLUDING REFINERIES (LABOR SECTION)	AVERAGE ANNUAL NUMBER OF WAGE EARNERS IN GRANULATED SUGAR PLANTS, EXCLUDING PROCUREMENT AND TRANSPORT	AVERAGE ANNUAL NUMBER OF WAGE EARNERS, INCLUDING PROCUREMENT AND TRANSPORT	
				Granulated sugar	*Refineries*
1928	75.3[a]	n.a.	n.a.	n.a.	n.a.
1929	n.a.[b]	n.a.	n.a.	n.a.	n.a.
1930	n.a.	n.a.	n.a.	n.a.	n.a.
1931	n.a.	66.9[d]	n.a.	n.a.	n.a.
1932	69.3[a]	64.5[d]	n.a.	55.0[g]	10.3[h]
1933	66.9[a]	60.1[e]	n.a.	54.7[g]	8.6[h]
1934	83.1[a]	78.1[e]	55.0[f]	70.0[g]	11.1[h]
1935	n.a.	n.a.	59.1[f]	n.a.	13.8[h]
1936	n.a.	n.a.	66.4[f]	n.a.	n.a.
1937	95.2[c]	n.a.	73.0[f]	n.a.	n.a.
1938	n.a.	n.a.	77.0[f]	n.a.	n.a.

[a] *Sotsialisticheskoe stroitel'stvo SSSR,* 1936, p. 17.

[b] n.a. = information not available.

[c] L. V. Opatski, "Proizvoditel'nost' truda v sakharnoi promyshlennosti SSSR," in Akademiia Nauk, Institut Ekonomiki, *Proizvoditel'nost' truda v promyshlennosti SSSR,* p. 297. This figure may be presumed to be identical in concept with those for earlier years by virtue of the fact that, at the same place, figures for 1928 and 1932 are cited which are identical with those shown in the table.

[d] *Sotsialisticheskoe stroitel'stvo SSSR,* 1934, p. 325.

[e] *Trud v SSSR,* 1935, p. 63.

[f] The data for 1934 and 1935 are from *Rabote sakharnoi promyshlennosti,* p. 70; those for 1936 to 1938 are estimated from Opatski, *op. cit.,* p. 296. The latter source yields for 1935 a figure which is identical with that shown in the table.

[g] *Rabote sakharnoi promyshlennosti,* pp. 332–33.

[h] *Ibid.,* p. 92.

TSUNKHU data for years in which both were available, covering the entire sugar industry as follows:

YEAR	INDUSTRY SECTION SERIES	LABOR SECTION SERIES	SUGAR TRUST SERIES
1932	69.3	64.5	65.3
1933	66.9	60.1	63.3
1934	83.1	78.1	81.1

The Sugar Trust series[14] for each year occupies a point intermediate in magnitude between the two TSUNKHU series and is sufficiently close to the labor section series to warrant its use in comparing productivity.[15] To the number of wage earners in 1938, 77 thousand, we may add the estimated number of learners and junior service personnel,[16] yielding the figure of 85.7 thousand. The comparable figure for U.S. beet sugar manufacturing in 1939 was 10.4 thousand wage earners.[17]

COMPARATIVE PRODUCTIVITY

The foregoing data may now be summarized:

	RUSSIA, 1938	UNITED STATES, 1939
Output of granulated sugar (metric tons)	2,507,100	1,472,169
Number of wage earners	85,700	10,400
Output of sugar per wage earner (metric tons)	29.3	141.6
Relative productivity (U.S. = 100)	21	100

A Soviet comparison of both countries for 1937 yielded a relative productivity ratio of 26 percent for Russia.[18] Since U.S. productivity rose from 1937 to 1939, while Soviet productivity declined from 1937 to 1938, this is not inconsistent with our figure of 21 percent.[19]

TRENDS IN SOVIET PRODUCTIVITY

Three indexes of labor productivity in Soviet sugar manufacturing from 1928 to 1938 are presented in Table 75. With respect to the first two indexes, it will be noted that, except for the years 1935 and 1936,

[14] The entire sugar industry appears to have been under the jurisdiction of the Commissariat for the Food Industry, of which the Sugar Trust was a constituent part, so that no difference between the Sugar Trust and TSUNKHU data is to be anticipated on this score. See *Trud v SSSR*, 1935, pp. 90–91.

[15] The Sugar Trust series is an average of monthly payroll counts and is therefore a full year rather than an active period average. See *Rabote sakharnoi promyshlennosti*, pp. 70–71.

[16] The estimate is based on the relative numbers of such personnel employed in 1935. *Ibid.*, p. 70.

[17] U.S. *Census of Manufactures*, II, Part I, 178.

[18] L. V. Opatski, "Proizvoditel'nost' truda v sakharnoi promyshlennosti SSSR," in Akademiia Nauk, Institut Ekonomiki, *Proizvoditel'nost' truda v promyshlennosti SSSR*, p. 314.

[19] The Soviet comparison was made in substantially the same fashion as our own, the only difference being failure to include learners and junior service personnel in the Soviet labor force data used for comparative purposes.

TABLE 75

INDEXES OF LABOR PRODUCTIVITY IN SOVIET SUGAR
MANUFACTURING, 1928–38

(1928 = 100)

YEAR	OUTPUT PER WAGE EARNER (IN PHYSICAL UNITS)[a]	UNIT LABOR REQUIREMENTS PER 100 CENTNERS OF BEETS PROCESSED[b]	OUTPUT PER WAGE EARNER (1926/27 RUBLES)[c]
1928	100.0	100.0	100.0
1929	114.2	112.8	n.a.[d]
1930	114.4	n.a.	n.a.
1931	n.a.	n.a.	n.a.
1932	90.2	97.3	75.9
1933	109.1	109.9	79.1
1934	120.4	122.4	88.6
1935	162.5	139.7	n.a.
1936	142.1	160.3	n.a.
1937	156.8	158.8	139.5[e]
1938	154.0	151.2	n.a.

[a] For the years 1932 to 1938, the index was calculated on the basis of the data in Tables 73 and 74. The labor force series employed covered the average annual number of wage earners in beet sugar manufacture, excluding procurement and transport, from 1934 to 1938, chained to the more inclusive series for the two preceding years. For the years 1928 to 1932, the index was constructed on the basis of man-day requirements per 100 centners of sugar produced, derived from *Sakhar*, 1931, Nos. 15–16, p. 71, and *Rabote sakharnoi promyshlennosti*, pp. 316–17, and linked to the series for the subsequent years in 1932. The man-day requirements series can be extended up to 1935, as follows: 1933—108.1; 1934—120.9; 1935—154.0. Thus, for 1933 and 1934 the two series are virtually identical; only for 1935 is there substantial divergence.

[b] The data are from L. V. Opatski, "Proizvoditel'nost' truda v sakharnoi promyshlennosti SSSR," in Akademiia Nauk, Institut Ekonomiki, *Proizvoditel'nost' truda v promyshlennosti SSSR*, pp. 294, 296, and *Rabote sakharnoi promyshlennosti*, pp. 316–17. The labor force in procurement and transportation is included in the index. The original data are given in man-days per 1,000 centners of sugar beets processed.

[c] Calculated from *Sotsialisticheskoe stroitel'stvo SSSR*, 1936, p. 17. This index includes sugar refining as well as beet processing.

[d] n.a. = information not available.

[e] Opatski, *op. cit.*, p. 297.

there is substantial correspondence between them. While differences in the two indexes resulting from changing percentages of beet sugar content and changing percentages of the proportion of the sugar extracted are to be expected, the differences shown here appear to be too great to be explained by these factors. However, for the period as a whole both indexes yield an over-all productivity increase in excess of 50 percent.

The third index, based on value of output per wage earner, includes sugar refining and therefore is not strictly comparable with the others. However, both the direction and magnitude of the differences are surprising. The principal source of the discrepancy was prior to 1932, for from 1932 to 1937 the productivity increase shown by the value index exceeds that shown by the physical indexes. The statistical origin of the discrepancies cannot be ascertained. Nor are data available for the years 1939 and 1940.

FACTORS AFFECTING PRODUCTIVITY

Plant and equipment. The beet sugar industry enjoyed only a low investment priority during the first three five year plans. Consequently, it operated largely with old equipment. Of 192 plants in operation during the 1939 campaign, 175 had been built prior to World War I. Those constructed between 1928 and 1939, mainly outside the traditional locus of the industry—the Ukraine—served to increase the capacity of the industry by only 18 percent.[20] Modernization investment was also relatively modest; for example, the percentage of the industry's capital as of January 1, 1935, that had been invested between 1918 and 1934 was 11.4 percent, compared with 35.3 percent for all food processing and 45.8 percent for manufacturing and mining.[21] A critical evaluation of sugar industry equipment in 1940 emphasized the lack of modern machinery, particularly in beet cutting and in in-plant transportation.[22]

The sugar yield of beets. The output of sugar per unit of beet input is a variable, depending on the sugar content of the beet and the proportion of sugar extracted. It was found that "the labor actually expended in a plant bears a closer relationship to the quantity of beets sliced than to the tonnage of sugar produced by that plant."[23]

The sugar content of the beet depends partly on cultivation practice, partly on the weather. The average sugar content of the Soviet beet

[20] *Sakhar,* 1940, No. 2, p. 17.
[21] Opatski, *op. cit.,* p. 295.
[22] See *Sakhar,* 1940, No. 2, p. 4; *ibid.,* 1940, No. 3, p. 4; *ibid.,* 1940, No. 4, p. 4.
[23] WPA, *Productivity and Employment in Selected Industries: Beet Sugar,* p. 78.

crop from 1932 to 1938 was 16.6 percent, with a high of 18.06 percent in 1935.[24] The U.S. average for the years 1932 to 1935 was 16.6 percent,[25] indicating that sugar content was not a relevant factor in explaining productivity differences. The proportion of sugar extracted varies with the physical and chemical condition of the beets, the mechanical efficiency of the plant, and the skill of the labor employed. The loss in conversion appears to have been higher in Russia than in the United States,[26] explaining a portion, though a minor one, of the observed difference in productivity.

Organizational factors. Beet sugar manufacture is a highly seasonal industry, since it is dependent on the supply of beets, which cannot be satisfactorily stored and must be processed soon after harvesting. The campaign, or production period, begins when the first beets arrive at the factory, and thereafter operations are carried on for twenty-four hours a day until the supply is exhausted. Management is faced with the problem of recruiting a peak labor force for a short period of time[27] and with ensuring an adequate flow of beets. In neither the United States nor Russia did the supply of labor appear to provide any prob-

[24] Opatski, *op. cit.,* p. 308.

[25] WPA, *Productivity and Employment in Selected Industries: Beet Sugar,* p. 153.

[26] The loss of sugar in the Soviet Union, as a proportion of sugar content, was as follows:

YEAR	PERCENTAGE	YEAR	PERCENTAGE
1932	2.87	1936	2.63
1933	2.56	1937	2.96
1934	2.57	1938	3.33
1935	2.46		

See *Rabote sakharnoi promyshlennosti,* pp. 328–29; Opatski, *op. cit.,* p. 296.

Similar data for the United States are as follows:

YEAR	PERCENTAGE
1932	1.4
1933	1.5
1934	1.7
1935	1.4

See WPA, *Productivity and Employment in Selected Industries: Beet Sugar,* p. 80.

[27] The average length of the sugar campaign in the United States was 70 days in the thirties, though the fluctuating demand for sugar resulted in considerable variation regarding this average. WPA, *Productivity and Employment in Selected Industries: Beet Sugar,* pp. 9, 170. The Soviet campaign was typically longer and reflected a fuller utilization of available facilities. In 1935 the campaign lasted 102 days, longer periods being indicated for 1938 and 1939. See *Rabote sakharnoi promyshlennosti,* p. 305; *Sakhar,* 1939, No. 7, p. 14.

lem during prewar years, but in Russia, particularly in the earlier years, the supply of beets caused difficulties.[28]

Between campaigns, a staff of employees is retained to prepare the sugar for shipment and repair equipment. One of the causes of lower Russian productivity has been the retention by Russian plants of larger off-season staffs than was customary in the United States. The ratio of average monthly employment during the off-season (January to July, inclusive) to employment in the peak seasons was 25 percent in the United States in 1939, compared with 57 percent in Russia in 1937.[29]

POSTWAR TRENDS IN PRODUCTIVITY

The sugar manufacturing facilities of the Ukraine were destroyed or damaged during the war and required extensive reconstruction.[30] The reported output of sugar in 1950 was 24 million centners,[31] indicating that plant capacity had been substantially restored by that date. The mechanical power at the disposal of the industry in 1949 approximated that in 1940, despite the fact that not all the war-damaged plants had been rebuilt, indicating a greater degree of mechanization accompanying reconstruction.[32]

In U.S. beet sugar manufacturing, output per wage earner increased by 13.5 percent from 1939 to 1950.[33] A Soviet productivity increase of like, or even greater, magnitude during a similar period is by no means inconceivable. However, if Soviet productivity in 1950 were to have reached, say, one third of the United States level for the same year, the Soviet increase from 1938 to 1950 would have had to have been on the order of 60 percent, i.e., more than the rise in productivity from 1928 to 1938. While lack of data prevents the formulation of firm conclusions, a guess may be hazarded that an achievement of this magnitude was unlikely, and that therefore relative Soviet productivity in 1950 remained under one third of the United States level and, in all probability, not far from the ratio estimated above.

[28] Opatski, *op. cit.*, p. 296.

[29] Opatski, *op. cit.*, p. 319. The Russian seasons are one month later than those of the United States, i.e., from February to August and from September to January.

[30] *Sakharnaia promyshlennost'*, 1949, No. 8, p. 11.

[31] *Ibid.*, 1951, No. 1, p. 1.

[32] *Ibid.*, 1949, No. 6, p. 1; *ibid.*, 1949, No. 4, p. 1.

[33] U.S. Department of Labor, Bureau of Labor Statistics, *Productivity Trends in Selected Industries*, Bulletin No. 1046, p. 3.

PART III
SUMMARY AND CONCLUSIONS

XIII

INTERTEMPORAL AND INTERNATIONAL PRODUCTIVITY COMPARISONS

SOVIET PRODUCTIVITY TRENDS, 1928–40

THE industry indexes of productivity trend developed in the foregoing chapters are assembled in Table 76. Except for the machinery industries, they represent changes in annual volume of physical output per wage earner. The individual indexes have been summarized in Table 77, using (*a*) 1928 Soviet employment weights and (*b*) 1936 Soviet employment weights. A separate calculation shows the effect of inclusion in the index of four machinery groups for the years 1932 to 1936.[1]

The difference in the results obtained through the use of 1928 and 1936 employment weights is very small. The principal shift in weights between these two years was a reduction in the relative importance of cotton textiles, which was compensated for by increasing the relative weights of shoes, steel, and coal. The computed indexes show a considerably smaller productivity rise than the official Soviet index, which is also shown in Table 77.[2]

The computed indexes in Table 77 indicate that during the decade 1928–38 Soviet industrial labor productivity rose at a rate, compounded annually, of about 6 percent per annum. However, the rate of growth was far from uniform within the period. The level of productivity in 1932 was not far above that of 1928, the sharpest rise coming from 1932 to 1936.

The Soviet productivity experience may best be evaluated against the

---

[1] From 1932 to 1937, the productivity index for all machinery manufacturing, based on the Gerschenkron Machinery Index, rose by 40 percent (see Table 43, p. 144). This is less than the average for industry without machinery as shown in Table 77, and less than the average of the four industry groups shown in Table 76.

[2] Some of the admitted uncertainties of the Gerschenkron Machinery Index (see Alexander Gerschenkron, *A Dollar Index of Soviet Machinery Output, 1927–28 to 1937*, Chap. 4), made it advisable to exclude productivity estimates based on that index from the computed productivity indexes of Table 77.

Table 76

INDEXES OF THE TREND OF PRODUCTIVITY IN SELECTED SOVIET MINING AND MANUFACTURING INDUSTRIES, 1928–40

(1928 = 100)

YEAR	COAL MINING	IRON ORE MINING	CRUDE OIL AND GAS EXTRACTION	IRON AND STEEL	COTTON CLOTH	SHOES	BEET SUGAR	RAILROAD LOCOMOTIVES AND CARS (1932 = 100)	TRACTORS (1932 = 100)	AGRICULTURAL MACHINERY (1932 = 100)	AUTOMOBILES[a] (1932 = 100)
1928	100.0	100.0	100.0	100.0	100.0	100.0	100.0				
1929	107.8	123.0	n.a.[b]	111.8	n.a.	87.6	114.2				
1930	126.9	145.0	n.a.	123.7	n.a.	70.5	114.4				
1931	124.6	118.0	157.0	110.1	n.a.	74.0	n.a.				
1932	119.8	124.5	141.0	100.5	114.1	54.6	90.2	100	100	100	100
1933	134.7	142.2	154.0	105.6	120.1	60.0	109.1	117	120	104	137
1934	153.3	181.7	144.0	136.6	113.5	63.6	120.4	137	148	115	162
1935	168.9	232.1	166.0	172.1	103.6	73.7	162.5	n.a.	n.a.	n.a.	n.a.
1936	195.2	298.1	n.a.	227.5	n.a.	n.a.	142.1	96	210	183	226
1937	188.6	318.6	n.a.	246.8	141.6	87.5	156.8	n.a.	n.a.	n.a.	267
1938	195.8	n.a.	200.0	n.a.	n.a.	92.6	154.0	n.a.	n.a.	n.a.	n.a.
1939	n.a.	n.a.	n.a.	n.a.	n.a.	110.2	n.a.	n.a.	n.a.	n.a.	n.a.
1940	212.6	n.a.	n.a.	n.a.	n.a.	119.9	n.a.	n.a.	n.a.	n.a.	n.a.

[a] Includes complete vehicles only.
[b] n.a. = information not available.

perspective of developments in other nations. During the forty years from 1899 to 1939, the average annual rate of productivity increase in U.S. manufacturing was about 2 percent per man and 2.75 percent per man-hour.[3] Higher rates were attained during shorter periods; e.g., the old Bureau of Labor Statistics index of manufacturing productivity indicated an annual rate of growth in productivity of 4 percent from 1919 to 1939.[4] Productivity in British manufacturing increased at the rate of 1.4 percent per annum from 1907 to 1937 and at the rate of 2.4 percent from 1924 to 1937.[5] For some individual years after World War II, the British economy experienced very high rates of productivity advance: 6 percent in 1948, 5 percent in 1949, and 8 percent in 1950, but this was due to very special circumstances and is unlikely to continue.[6] A recent study of the Canadian economy, which "is at an earlier stage of economic development than the other two countries [the United States and Great Britain] both in respect to its industrial structure and (in 1935) in *per capita* income," and which, therefore, might be expected to show a higher rate of productivity increase, revealed that from 1931 to 1941, gross national product per employed person rose by 3.8 percent per annum, the rate of productivity increase in manufacturing being somewhat lower.[7] Long-run productivity statistics are not available for other countries, but the guess may be hazarded that the Soviet rate of productivity increase from 1928 to 1938 has been unmatched.[8]

To what extent can the indexes in Table 77 be regarded as representative of the course of productivity in Soviet industry as a whole?

[3] Solomon Fabricant, *Employment in Manufacturing, 1899–1939*, p. 331.

[4] U.S. Department of Commerce, Bureau of the Census, *Historical Statistics of the United States*, p. 71.

[5] L. Rostas, *Comparative Productivity in British and American Industry*, p. 42.

[6] United Nations, Economic Commission for Europe, *Economic Survey of Europe in 1950*, p. 57.

[7] A. Maddison, "Productivity in Canada, the United Kingdom, and the United States," *Oxford Economic Papers* (New Series), October, 1952, p. 235; *idem*, "Productivity in an Expanding Economy," *The Economic Journal*, September, 1952, p. 584.

[8] Nineteenth-century U.S. statistics are not sufficiently reliable or extensive to permit the calculation of firm labor productivity estimates. A very crude estimate can be obtained by juxtaposing Person's index of manufacturing production with Fabricant's wage earner series; the result is a rate of productivity growth of slightly less than 3 percent per annum from 1870 to 1880 and of less than 2 percent for the following decades. See U.S. Department of Commerce, Bureau of the Census, *Historical Statistics of the United States*, 1945, pp. 64, 179.

TABLE 77

INDEXES OF PRODUCTIVITY IN SOVIET INDUSTRY, 1928–38
(1928 = 100)

YEAR	CALCULATED FROM PHYSICAL PRODUCTIVITY INDEXES FOR INDIVIDUAL INDUSTRIES,[a] USING			OFFICIAL SOVIET INDEX OF OUTPUT PER MAN-YEAR IN LARGE-SCALE INDUSTRY[c]
	1928 employment weights[b]	*1936 employment weights*[b]	*1936 employment weights, including four machinery branches*	
1928	100.0	100.0		100.0
1929	111.9	109.6		112.9
1930	116.4	115.1		123.9
1931	118.3	114.6		133.3
1932	110.4	106.0	106.0	136.8
1933	119.8	115.6	117.0	148.7
1934	127.7	127.1	130.1	164.6
1935	138.0	141.5	143.7	186.0
1936	161.0	166.5	166.2	225.8
1937	173.6	177.2		245.9
1938	179.3	182.9		272.9

[a] The lacunae in Table 76 were filled in for the purpose of constructing this index, as follows:

Iron ore mining: It was assumed that there was no change in productivity from 1937 to 1938.

Crude oil and gas: Data for the years 1929 and 1930 were linked in from an index of annual value of output per wage earner. The figure for 1936 was chained in from an index of physical output per wage earner at the Baku oil fields. The figure for 1937 was interpolated between 1936 and 1938 on a straight-line basis.

Steel: The figure for 1938 was linked in on the basis of an index of annual value of iron and steel output per wage earner.

Cotton cloth: The data for the years 1929–31 were linked in from an index of annual value of cotton goods output per wage earner. The figures for 1936 and 1938 were linked in on the basis of an index of hourly output of cloth per wage earner.

Shoes: The figure for 1936 was interpolated on a straight-line basis.

Sugar: The figure for 1931 was interpolated on a straight-line basis.

Machinery: The figures for 1935 were interpolated on a straight-line basis.

NOTES TO TABLE 77 (*Continued*)

ᵇ The following Soviet employment weights were employed:

	January 1, 1928	*January 1, 1936*
Coal mining	246.0	427.6
Iron mining	21.7	38.6
Crude oil and gas	35.6	42.7
Iron and steel	167.8	318.5
Cotton textiles	455.9	448.3
Shoes	39.3*	163.0*
Sugar	75.3*	95.2*
Railroad locomotives and cars		135.0*
Tractors		42.3
Agricultural machinery		71.8*
Automobiles (complete vehicles only)		56.2*
Total	1041.6	1839.2

All figures except those starred are labor section type data. Where labor section data were either not available or where they were clearly inappropriate (e.g., in the case of shoe manufacturing, where the omission of the cooperative sector of industry resulted in a serious understatement), industry section data, representing average annual employment, were substituted. The industry section data substitutes are starred. The source of the data is either *Trud v SSSR*, 1936, or *Sotsialisticheskoe stroitel'stvo*, 1936.

ᶜ This index is from Table 1.

An independent production index computed by Donald Hodgman, on the basis of 137 product series, yields a productivity index figure of about 155 (1928 = 100) for the year 1937 and implies a 5 percent annual rate of productivity growth for the period from 1928 to 1937.[9] Irving H. Siegel has estimated that general industrial productivity in 1940 was about 175 percent of the 1928 level.[10] The official Soviet index is seen from Table 77 to be considerably higher than our own.

As a partial check upon representativeness, rates of productivity growth have been calculated for a larger number of industries, based on the official Soviet production indexes, which run in terms of gross value of output in 1926–27 rubles. These are shown in Table 78, column (1), together with the rates for the industries included in Table 77, based on the indexes contained therein. The following averages were

[9] Donald R. Hodgman, "Industrial Production," in Abram Bergson (ed.), *Soviet Economic Growth*, pp. 229, 232.

[10] Irving H. Siegel, "Labor Productivity in the Soviet Union," *Journal of the American Statistical Association*, March, 1953, p. 72.

TABLE 78

AVERAGE ANNUAL RATES (COMPOUNDED) OF GROWTH IN LABOR PRODUCTIVITY IN SOVIET INDUSTRY, 1928–37

INDUSTRY	(1) BASED ON SOVIET PRODUCTION INDEXES[a]	(2) BASED ON COMPUTED INDEXES SHOWN IN TABLE 77	(3) WAGE EARNERS EMPLOYED, JANUARY 1, 1936 (THOU- SANDS)[f]
Mining and heavy industry			
*Basic chemicals[b]	15.9	n.a.[c]	200.5
Machinery and metalworking	14.2	2.5[d]	1,785.0
Iron and steel	12.7	10.6	318.5
*Electric power stations[b]	11.3	n.a.	57.3
Coal mining	8.6	7.3	427.6
Oil extraction	8.6	7.2 (*1938*)	42.7
Iron ore mining	n.a.	13.7	
Light industry			
*Silk[b]	12.9	n.a.	21.9
*Paper[b]	10.7	n.a.	44.3
*Woodworking[b]	8.3	n.a.	309.6
*Linen[b]	7.1	n.a.	95.4
*Wool[b]	5.7	n.a.	68.9
Cotton textiles	5.5	3.9	448.3
Sugar	1.6	5.1	90.6
Shoes	n.a.	1.4[e]	91.9

[a] Computed from data in *Sotsialisticheskoe stroitel'stvo,* 1936, pp. 38–39, and *Planovoe khoziaistvo,* 1939, No. 3, p. 151.

[b] Industries not included in Table 76.

[c] n.a. = information not available.

[d] Based on the Gerschenkron Machinery Index, Table 43.

[e] Decline in productivity.

[f] *Trud v SSSR,* 1936.

secured from Table 78, column (1), using January 1, 1936, employment, shown in Table 78, column (3), as weights:

	AVERAGE ANNUAL PERCENTAGE RATE OF PRODUCTIVITY INCREASE, 1928–37
All industries in Table 78	11.3
All industries in Table 78, except machinery and metalworking	8.9[11]
All heavy industry in Table 78	13.2
All heavy industry in Table 78, except machinery and metalworking	11.4
All light industry in Table 78	6.5
All nonstarred industries in Table 78, excluding machinery and metalworking[12]	8.1
All starred industries in Table 78	10.3

These figures, which, it must be emphasized, are based on the official Soviet production indexes with all their deficiencies, show that the average annual rate of productivity for the starred industries exceeded that for the nonstarred industries (excluding machinery and metalworking), despite the fact that five out of seven in the former group were classified as light industry, which is seen from the above data to have had a smaller productivity rise than heavy industry. This can be attributed to the following factors: (*a*) if the chemicals industry is excluded, the average of the starred industries falls from 10.3 to 8.4 percent; (*b*) the cotton textile industry has one of the lowest rates of productivity growth of any of the industries included and was weighted heavily by virtue of its large employment. This suggests that failure to include the chemicals industry in our index of labor productivity change, and the inclusion in the index of cotton textiles as one of the chief representatives of consumer goods manufacturing, may have tended, by this test, to result in an understatement of the increase in productivity from 1928 to 1938. However, our inability to include the bulk of machinery and metalworking in our index may be even more serious, although the rate of increase shown for these industries in Table

[11] Machinery and metalworking accounted for 46 percent of the employment weights and therefore dominated the average.

[12] Nonstarred industries were included in Table 76 and entered into the index in Table 77; starred industries were not included therein.

78 must be taken with more than the customary grain of salt, by virtue of the probable excessive inflation in the Soviet index of machinery output.[13] On the other hand, the omission of all branches of food processing, with the exception of sugar, offset to a certain extent the exclusion of machinery, since the indications are that productivity in food processing remained low during the period with which we are concerned.

COMPARATIVE SOVIET-UNITED STATES PRODUCTIVITY, 1937–39

The estimates of comparative Soviet-United States productivity developed in the foregoing chapters are summarized in Table 79. It will be recalled that, with the exception of the machinery items, the estimates are based on annual output per wage earner expressed in physical units. The year of comparison for the United States is 1939, while for Russia the last prewar year for which firm estimates could be made has been chosen, on an industry by industry basis.

The productivity relatives in Table 79 yield the following average results, under alternative weighting schemes:

	SOVIET PRODUCTIVITY AS A PERCENTAGE OF U.S. PRODUCTIVITY
Unweighted, excluding machinery	38
Unweighted, including five machinery groups	40
Weighted by Soviet employment,[14] excluding machinery	39
Weighted by Soviet employment, including five machinery groups	40
Weighted by U.S. employment, excluding machinery	42
Weighted by U.S. employment, including machinery	42

The range of the estimates is small. Because of the relatively small weights involved, the average is little affected by the inclusion or exclusion of the five machinery industries studied,[15] although four out of five

[13] Gerschenkron, *op. cit.*, p. 11.

[14] The employment weights in all cases are those which were employed in making, for the year of the comparison, the productivity comparisons in the industry studies.

[15] The automobile employment weights were for the manufacture of complete vehicles only and exclude the production of bodies and parts.

TABLE 79

COMPARATIVE LABOR PRODUCTIVITY IN MINING AND MANUFACTURING, SELECTED INDUSTRIES, FOR THE UNITED STATES IN 1939 AND FOR THE SOVIET UNION IN STATED YEARS

(Soviet productivity as a percentage of U.S. productivity)

	SOVIET PRODUCTIVITY PERCENTAGE	YEAR OF SOVIET COMPARISON
Coal mining	40	1938
Iron mining:		
All industry	34	1937
Open cut only	54	1937
Underground only	51	1937
Crude oil and natural gas	48	1938
Iron and steel:		
Pig iron	42	1937
Steel ingots and rolled steel	43	1937
Cotton textiles:		
Yarn	48	1937
Cloth	23	1937
Shoes	46	1939
Beet sugar	21	1938
Machinery:		
Railroad locomotives and cars	47	1936
Tractors	58	1936
Agricultural machinery	50	1936
Heavy construction machinery	15	1936
Automobiles		
(complete vehicles only)	50[a]	1937

[a] This figure refers only to the manufacture of complete vehicles and excludes the production of bodies and parts. The figure is also subject to other limitations which are discussed *supra.*, pp. 168–71. A considerably lower figure was obtained by comparing output per wage earner in units of physical production.

of the industries were significantly above the industrial average in comparative productivity.[16]

There are presented in Table 80 data relating to coverage, as measured by Soviet employment and gross value of product, from which it

TABLE 80

COVERAGE OF SOVIET MINING AND MANUFACTURING
REPRESENTED BY THE INDUSTRY ESTIMATES IN TABLE 79

YEAR	PERCENTAGE OF TOTAL SOVIET WAGE EARNER EMPLOYMENT	PERCENTAGE OF TOTAL SOVIET VALUE OF PRODUCT
a. Excluding machinery		
1928	28.2[a]	30.4
	42.4[a]	
1934	20.3[b]	17.5
	24.6[c]	18.5[d]
b. Including five machinery branches		
1928	51.6[c]	31.3[e]
1934	23.5[b]	22.7[d]
1936	29.2[c]	n.a.[f]

[a] The lower figure is based on industry section statistics; the higher figure, on labor section statistics.

[b] Based on industry section statistics.

[c] Based on labor section statistics.

[d] It was assumed for iron mining, shoe manufacture, and sugar manufacture that the gross value of product for the industry in relation to total gross value of product was constant from 1934 to 1936.

[e] Excludes locomotives and railroad cars.

[f] n.a. = information not available.

appears that the coverage declined significantly with time, i.e., that our sample of industries would have been more representative in 1928 than in 1936.[17]

[16] Some very rough comparisons of over-all Soviet-U.S. productivity made by Soviet economists were as follows: Russia, 1936–United States, 1929, 37 percent (*Planovoe khoziaistvo*, 1938, No. 4); Russia, 1936–United States, 1929 (excluding lumbering), 41 percent (*ibid.*); Russia, 1936–United States, 1936, 42.8 percent (*ibid.*, 1938, No. 2, p. 72); Russia, 1937–United States, 1937, 40.5 percent (*ibid.*, 1939, No. 3, p. 154).

[17] The difference between the degree of coverage indicated by industry section and labor section employment statistics for 1928 is not due to a difference in the absolute number of wage earners covered by our index of productivity (excluding

Measured by 1939 U.S. data, the coverage is as follows:

	EMPLOYMENT[18] (PERCENT)	VALUE ADDED (PERCENT)
Industries in Table 79, excluding machinery	19	17
Industries in Table 79, including five machinery groups	25	23

The various measures of coverage indicate that the aggregate productivity comparisons include from one fifth to one half of mining and manufacturing, depending on the year and the coverage concept employed. The representativeness of this sample cannot be determined from the size alone, however. The principal lacunae are as follows: chemicals; the remaining machinery industries; the armament industries; the manufacture of consumer durable goods and other metalware; nonferrous metals; the wool, silk, and rayon industries; the needle trades; pulp, paper, and lumber manufactures; and the graphic trades.

Some comparative productivity data, culled from Soviet sources and of dubious merit, are presented in Table 81. With the exception of the figure for sulphuric acid, these data were calculated in terms of value of product per wage earner. None of the figures, save that for electrical machinery,[19] suggests that our sample of industries yields too low a comparative ratio.

---

machinery, the figures were 1.041 million wage earners according to the industry section data and 1.075 million according to the labor section data), but rather to the difference between total employment as indicated by the two series: 3.699 million under the industry section concept and 2.536 million under the labor section concept. This difference may be attributed in part to the inclusion of industrial cooperative employees in the industry section statistics; if cooperative employment bore the same relationship to total employment in 1928 as in 1933 (it was in all probability an even higher percentage in 1928), the industry section wage earner total, less the cooperatives, would be reduced to 3.277 million in 1928. Since the cooperatives were of less significance among the industries covered by our index than in industry as a whole, the percentage of coverage would be increased, probably to about 33 percent.

The degree of coverage shown by the gross value data is lower than employment coverage primarily by virtue of the importance in our index of coal mining, which (in 1934) had a gross output per wage earner only one third as great as the average for all industry.

[18] Employment and labor force data are from U.S. Department of Commerce, Bureau of the Census, *Census of Manufactures,* 1939, and *idem, Mining Industries,* 1939.

[19] This ratio is based on a comparison of U.S. 1929 dollar value of output per wage earner and Russian 1936 ruble value, equated at the rate of 2.86 rubles to the dollar. In estimating comparative productivity for other machinery groups, the same source

TABLE 81

SOVIET COMPARISONS OF SOVIET–UNITED STATES
PRODUCTIVITY FOR INDUSTRIES NOT COVERED IN TABLE 79

INDUSTRY OR PRODUCT	YEAR OF COMPARISON	SOVIET PRODUCTIVITY AS A PERCENTAGE OF U.S. PRODUCTIVITY
Chemicals	Russia, 1936—U.S., 1937	45[a]
Chemicals	Circa 1938 for both countries	36[b]
Sulphuric acid	Russia, 1937—U.S., 1937	40[c]
Electrical machinery	Russia, 1936—U.S., 1929	84[b]
Machine tools	Russia, 1935—U.S., 1929	33[b]
Paper	Russia, 1935—U.S., 1929	31[d]
Graphic trades	Russia, 1935—U.S., 1929	30[d]

[a] *Planovoe khoziaistvo*, 1939, No. 3, p. 151.
[b] Akademiia Nauk, Institut Ekonomiki, *Proizvoditel'nost' truda v promyshlennosti SSSR*, pp. 10–11, 204.
[c] *Problemy ekonomiki*, 1939, No. 2, p. 41.
[d] *Planovoe khoziaistvo*, 1936, No. 11, p. 62.

SOVIET PRODUCTIVITY IN 1950[20]

The dearth of postwar Soviet statistics renders it impossible, in the case of most of the industries under consideration, to do more than present a general impression of productivity changes from 1937–39 to 1950.

Coal mining. By 1950, Soviet coal mining productivity had not yet reattained the prewar level. At a rough estimate, it may be placed at 95 percent of the 1940 level. In the United States there was a substantial rise in productivity from 1939 to 1950, with the result that, in the latter year, Soviet productivity may have fallen to as low as 30 percent of the U.S. level.

Iron ore mining. In all likelihood Soviet 1950 productivity in this

employed conversion rates ranging from 3.9 rubles per dollar for agricultural machinery to 4.9 rubles per dollar for machine tools. It is not clear why so high a ruble rate was used for electrical machinery, and it is obvious that the use of a rate in line with the other machinery groups would reduce the indicated comparative level of Soviet electrical machinery productivity.

[20] The data on which the following conclusions are based are set out in the individual industry chapters, above.

industry exceeded the prewar level. Annual output per wage earner in the United States rose by 24.7 percent from 1939 to 1950, making it unlikely that the prewar productivity gap between the two nations had been narrowed.

Crude oil and gas. No information is available for this industry.

Iron and steel. The Russians have claimed that productivity in this industry rose by 33 percent from 1940 to 1950, a claim which an American student of the Soviet iron and steel industry regards as by no means impossible.[21] Scattered Russian statistics for individual steel mills raise some doubt about the probability of this achievement, however. United States steel productivity rose by about 34 percent between 1939 and 1950, on the basis of unofficial estimates, so that even if the full Soviet claims are conceded, the prewar comparative U.S.-Soviet level of productivity remained unchanged.

Cotton textiles. The best estimate for the Soviet industry is that productivity was about the same in 1940 and in 1950. United States productivity statistics are not available after 1940, but what evidence there is also points to there having been no drastic change from 1939 to 1950.

Shoe manufacturing. At the outside, Soviet shoe productivity in 1950 may have regained the 1940 level (which would put it at 9 percent about 1939), the probability being that a somewhat lower figure for 1950 may be nearer the truth. The U.S. shoe output per man-hour rose by 5.7 percent from 1939 to 1950.

Beet sugar manufacturing. Labor productivity in U.S. beet sugar manufacture increased by 13.5 percent from 1939 to 1950. A Soviet productivity increase of like, or even greater, magnitude during the same period is not inconceivable. It is possible, therefore, that the Soviet industry had raised by a few percentage points the low prewar productivity ratio of 21 percent.

Machinery. Large productivity increases in machinery manufacturing have been claimed by the Russians for the years 1949 to 1952. However, it is not possible to relate the 1950 productivity level to a prewar base.

The Russian industrial productivity index number of 137 in 1950,

[21] Gardner Clark, "Comments," in Abram Bergson (ed.), *Soviet Economic Growth,* p. 224.

based on 1940, is difficult to assess in terms of the results for the various industries. Of the major industries concerning which there is some information, Soviet productivity appears to have risen substantially only in machinery and in iron and steel. Coal mining and cotton textiles, both large employers of labor, were either at or below their 1940 productivity levels in 1950, and a similar pattern seems to hold for light industry in general.

A 1950 index number of 137 implies an average rate of productivity growth of 3 percent per annum for the decade as a whole. The official Soviet index shows an average annual rate of about 12 percent per annum from 1946 to 1950, offsetting a drastic wartime productivity decline. This may be compared with our estimate (see Table 77) of an annual rate of productivity growth of about 10 percent from 1934 to 1938, the prewar plan years of greatest productivity advance. For the same period, the official Soviet productivity index showed an increase of 13.6 percent per annum.

On the assumption that there was no change in the proportion of wage earners in large-scale industry to the total nonagricultural labor force from 1940 to 1950, the index of production developed by Hodgman indicates a 22 percent increase in productivity between the two years.[22] Under this assumption, however, the official Soviet production index yields a 1950 productivity figure of 142, compared with the claim of 137, indicating that the wage earner–total employment ratio was not stable and suggesting that the Hodgman index-based figure should be reduced to 118.

There is considerable question regarding the course of U.S. productivity from 1939 to 1950. The 1947 U.S. Census of Manufactures indicated an annual rate of productivity increase in manufacturing of about 1 percent between 1939 and 1947, but industry studies made by the Bureau of Labor Statistics indicate that the rate of growth thereafter may have increased somewhat.[23] Thus, if the Soviet claims are accepted at face value, by 1950 the Russians had substantially narrowed the prewar U.S.-Soviet productivity gap. If, however, as seems more reasonable,

[22] Donald R. Hodgman, "Industrial Production," in Abram Bergson (ed.), *Soviet Economic Growth*, p. 241.

[23] John C. Davis, "Productivity Trends and Some Economic Implications," in L. R. Tripp (ed.), *Industrial Productivity*, pp. 15–18.

the 1940–50 Soviet productivity increase is taken at 18 percent, following the Hodgman index, then the comparative productivity ratio would have undergone little change by 1950.[24]

[24] It will be recalled from *supra,* p. 55, that if output per man-hour were employed rather than output per man-year, a correction factor of at least 16 percent in favor of the United States would be in order because of an increase in the Soviet working week from 1937–39 to 1950.

XIV

FACTORS BEHIND THE PRODUCTIVITY TRENDS AND DIFFERENCES

INTERINDUSTRY VARIATION IN SOVIET PRODUCTIVITY CHANGE

THE average rate of productivity change is compounded of a wide variety of rates for the various mining and manufacturing industries, as a comparison of Tables 76 and 77 will quickly reveal. In order to determine whether there is any relationship between capital investment and the industry rate of productivity change, the computed rates shown in Table 78 are compared, in Table 82, with data on capital investment. There appears to be some correlation between the two series, the principal exception being shoe manufacturing, with a fairly high investment rate and a decline in productivity from 1928 to 1937. This may be due to the fact that, whereas the productivity data relate to all large-scale industry, the capital statistics are probably restricted to the state-owned sector, in which productivity rose by 4.5 percent per annum from 1928 to 1938. Investment data are not available for iron ore mining and oil extraction, but it may be noted that in the case of iron ore, at least, a high degree of mechanization was claimed for 1939.[1]

INTERINDUSTRY VARIATION IN COMPARATIVE PRODUCTIVITY

The data in Table 79 indicate some sharp interindustrial differences in comparative productivity. In the production of beet sugar, cotton cloth, and heavy construction machinery, Soviet labor productivity was far below that of the United States; in iron and steel manufacture, cotton spinning, shoe manufacturing, oil extraction, and some machinery groups, the difference was much smaller.

An obvious question is whether the observed differences can be explained in terms of the relative quantities of capital available per wage earner. Motive power can be used as a rough index of the quantity

[1] *Planovoe khoziaistvo,* 1939, No. 1, p. 82.

TABLE 82

AVERAGE ANNUAL RATES (COMPOUNDED) OF GROWTH
IN LABOR PRODUCTIVITY FOR INDIVIDUAL SOVIET MINING
AND MANUFACTURING INDUSTRIES, 1928–37,
COMPARED WITH CAPITAL INVESTMENT

INDUSTRY	RATE OF PRODUC-TIVITY GROWTH	PROPORTION OF TOTAL CAPITAL INVESTED FROM 1928 TO 1935, AS OF JANUARY 1, 1935
Iron ore mining	13.7	n.a.[e]
Steel manufacture	10.6	93.6[f]
Crude oil and gas	7.2[a]	n.a.
Coal mining	7.3	[50][g]
Sugar refining	5.1	32.6[f]
Cotton cloth manufacturing	3.9	12.9[f]
Shoe manufacturing	. . .[b]	56.9[f]
Automobiles	21.7[c]	80–100[g]
Tractors	20.4[d]	80–100[g]
Agricultural machinery	16.3[d]	80–100[g]
Railroad locomotives and cars	. . .[b]	n.a.

[a] For the years 1928–38.

[b] Decline in productivity.

[c] For the years 1932–37.

[d] For the years 1932–36.

[e] n.a. = information not available.

[f] *Sotsialisticheskoe stroitel'stvo*, 1936, p. 49. The percentages represent the ratio of the capital fund of factories newly built or completely rebuilt during the First and Second Five Year Plans to total capital fund in place on January 1, 1935.

[g] *Planovoe khoziaistvo*, 1939, No. 1, p. 82. This source divides industries into three categories: (*a*) those completely new or reconstructed, where the capital of the new or reconstructed (post-1928) plants constitutes 80–100 percent of the industry's total capital; (*b*) industries in which there is completion of basic technical reconstruction, particular aspects being incomplete (I have arbitrarily assigned a figure of 50 percent to this category); and (*c*) industries which had not undergone technical reconstruction.

of equipment. It has been argued that "there is a close relationship between horse-power per head and output per head,"[2] although no such relationship was found by Rostas in his U.S.-British comparisons.[3] To

[2] United Nations, *Economic Bulletin for Europe*, III, No. 1, 24.

[3] L. Rostas, *Comparative Productivity in British and American Industry*, p. 54, states: ". . . there is no correlation between horse-power per unit of output and output per worker, i.e., industries where horse-power per unit of output is higher in

test this relationship, comparative data on motive power per wage earner have been assembled in Table 83. Defining labor-intensive industries as those with a relatively low ratio of motive power to wage earners, and defining capital-intensive industries as those with a relatively high ratio, the industries have been ranked in the order of ascending capital-intensiveness, the U.S. figures being used as a standard.[4]

The number of shifts worked by an industry is obviously an important datum in evaluating the capital–labor ratio, since multishift work has the effect of raising the amount of capital available per wage earner at any given time. There are no shift data available for the United States circa 1939, but Soviet shift coefficients as of 1935 have been applied to the Soviet capital–labor ratios in Table 83 and are shown together with the unadjusted ratios. Since there was undoubtedly multishift work in 1939 in some of the U.S. industries contained in Table 83, e.g., iron and steel, beet sugar processing, and oil extraction, the U.S. capital–labor ratios are understated by comparison with the weighted Soviet capital–labor ratios. However, on an over-all basis, there was undoubtedly more multishift work in 1935 Russia than in the 1939 United States.

For industry as a whole there is a considerable discrepancy between the comparative motive power and the comparative productivity ratios when the Russian motive-power data are unweighted for shift and close correspondence when shifts are taken into account. If the U.S. data were weighted for shifts, the comparative capital–labor ratio would undoubtedly be smaller than the 38 percent shown in Table 83; but, on the other hand, the growth of Soviet motive power available per worker from 1934 to 1937 or 1938 would provide an offsetting factor.[5]

With respect to the individual industries, the hypothesis may be advanced that a backward economy should enjoy a comparative labor

---

the United States are not identical with industries where United States output per worker is also relatively high."

[4] If the industries were ranked by Soviet capital-intensiveness, the principal displacements would be iron ore mining, which was relatively less capital-intensive in Russia, and, in the case of the weighted capital—labor ratios, coal mining.

[5] From 1932 to 1937, motive power per wage earner is alleged to have risen by 89 percent in Soviet industry. See *Sotsialisticheskoe stroitel'stvo*, 1939, p. 23. The increase from 1932 to 1934 was 31 percent. See *Sotsialisticheskoe stroitel'stvo*, 1936, p. 28. It may thus be estimated that horsepower installed per wage earner in 1937 was 2.2 unweighted or 3.5 weighted for multishift operation.

Table 83

MOTIVE POWER PER WAGE EARNER IN SOVIET INDUSTRY (1934) AND UNITED STATES INDUSTRY (1939)

(In horsepower)

INDUSTRY	(1) UNITED STATES 1939[a]	(2) SOVIET UNION 1934[b]	(3) SOVIET UNION, 1934, WEIGHTED BY 1935 SHIFT COEFFI- CIENT[d]	(4) SOVIET UNION, UNWEIGHT- ED, AS A PERCENT- AGE OF THE UNITED STATES	(5) SOVIET UNION, WEIGHTED, AS A PER- CENTAGE OF THE UNITED STATES	(6) COMPAR- ATIVE PRODUC- TIVITY[e]
Shoe manufacturing	0.7	0.2	0.3	28	43	46
Cotton textiles	4.8	1.1	2.0	23	42	23–48
Coal mining	9.0	1.9	4.5	21	50	40
Beet sugar processing	21.0	2.0	4.0	10	19	21
Iron and steel	24.6	6.5	12.5	26	51	43
Iron ore mining	28.5	2.8	5.9	10	21	34
Oil extraction	32.2	18.4	30.9	57	96	48
All manufacturing	6.4	1.5[e]	2.4[e]	24	38	38–42

[a] U.S. Department of Commerce, Bureau of the Census, *Census of Manufactures,* 1939, I, 275 ff.; U.S. Department of Commerce, Bureau of the Census, *Mineral Industries,* 1939, Vol. I. The data in the source are in terms of horsepower available (horsepower of prime movers plus that of electric motors driven by purchased electricity).

[b] *Sotsialisticheskoe stroitel'stvo,* 1936, pp. 28–30. The data are given as of December 31, 1934. They are expressed in kilowatts, which have been converted at the rate of 1 kilowatt = 1.34 horsepower. Soviet motive power statistics represent the sum of the power of prime movers and electric motors, less electric generators, and thus appear to be comparable with those of the United States.

[c] Includes mining.

[d] Weighted by the following "shift coefficients":

Shoe manufacturing	1.39
Cotton textiles	1.83
Coal mining	2.38
Beet sugar processing	1.98
Iron and steel	1.93
Iron ore mining	2.11
Oil extraction	1.68
All industry	1.61

Source: *Trud v SSSR,* 1936, p. 79. A "shift coefficient" is defined as the ratio of the total number of man-days worked to the number of man-days worked on the most numerous shift, which would generally be the first day shift.

[e] From Table 79.

productivity advantage in labor-intensive industries, for there the advanced economy is least able to make its superior technological and capital resources felt. However, there are at least two qualifications that may be made: (*a*) this assumes a "normal" path of economic development, in which heavy and light industry develop apace; if the growth of heavy industry is forced at the expense of light industry, the productivity gap in capital-intensive heavy industry may narrow very quickly; (*b*) there may be instances of rigid technical coefficients, where the possibility of substituting labor for capital is small, in which event productivity might be relatively high for a capital-intensive industry.

For this hypothesis to be borne out by Russian-U.S. data, the productivity ratios in column (6) of Table 83 should rank from high to low, which is obviously not the case. The iron and steel industry may perhaps be regarded as falling under exception (*a*), above, and oil extraction under exception (*b*). The hypothesis does appear to provide a key to the high rate of comparative productivity in shoe manufacturing versus the low rate in sugar beet processing. Both industries, in the Soviet Union, were relatively stagnant technologically during the thirties, but the shoe industry was heavily labor-intensive,[6] whereas beet sugar manufacture (measured by U.S. standards) was fairly capital-intensive.

If the industries in Table 83 are ranked by the unweighted ratio of Soviet to U.S. horsepower per wage earner (Table 84), a clear tendency toward a positive relationship between the horsepower ratios and the productivity ratios appears. The case is not so clear when the ranking is by the weighted Soviet capital–labor ratios, but it will be recalled that the U.S. capital–labor ratio is unweighted for multishift work. However, the sample is too small to permit of conclusive generalization, particularly in view of the conflicting findings cited above.

A number of other factors relating to capital use have been adduced on various occasions to explain observed differences in labor productivity: the size of the market, the size of the plant, the degree of product standardization, among others. Though all of these undoubtedly play a role in the determination of relative productivity, it appears unlikely that any single factor would yield a precise correlation with the produc-

---

[6] Of 31 U.S. industries examined by Rostas, *op. cit.*, pp. 69–70, only cigar manufacturing had a lower ratio of motive power per wage earner than shoe manufacturing.

TABLE 84

RELATIONSHIP BETWEEN HORSEPOWER PER WAGE EARNER
AND COMPARATIVE PRODUCTIVITY IN SOVIET AND
UNITED STATES INDUSTRY

INDUSTRY	UNWEIGHTED RATIO OF SOVIET TO U.S. HORSEPOWER PER WAGE EARNER (PERCENT)	WEIGHTED RATIO OF SOVIET TO U.S. HORSEPOWER PER WAGE EARNER (PERCENT)	RATIO OF SOVIET TO U.S. LABOR PRODUCTIVITY (PERCENT)
Beet sugar manufacture	10	19	21
Iron ore mining	10	21	34
Coal mining	21	50	40
Cotton textile manufacturing	23	42	23–48
Iron and steel manufacturing	26	51	43
Shoe manufacturing	28	43	46
Oil extraction	57	96	48

Source: Table 83.

tivity of labor.[7] In view of the formidable nature of the task involved in making such comparisons for the United States and Russia on a reasonably precise basis, it will not be attempted here.[8]

THE SOVIET GOAL OF HIGH LABOR PRODUCTIVITY

Emphasis upon capital investment and technology as prime determinants of labor productivity should not be allowed to obscure the fact that the supply and skill of labor and the ability of management efficiently to organize the factors of production are also significant elements. I would argue, however, that, in the typical backward area undergoing industrialization, the latter group of factors is subordinate to the former in causing the growth of production and productivity. Labor shortages are not apt to constitute a major deterrent to production—indeed, it is the relative abundance of labor in relation to capital

[7] For example, see the findings of Rostas, *op. cit.*, pp. 58–63; Solomon Fabricant, *Employment in Manufacturing, 1899–1939*, pp. 25–26; International Labor Office, *Methods of Labor Productivity Statistics*, Chap. 2.

[8] Largely on an intuitive basis, it may be remarked that difference in plant size and market scope would probably not be important factors, whereas product standardization, operating to the advantage of the United States in heavy industry and to the advantage of Russia in the consumer goods industry, might well prove significant.

which may well constitute a serious obstacle to industrialization and the concomitant rise in the productivity of labor.[9] The rapidity of Soviet industrialization, the lack of amenities for the urban dweller, particularly housing, and the force of the ideological drive toward capital growth in heavy industry counteracted the seemingly logical policy on the part of factory management to economize capital with little regard to labor cost.

The Soviet planners placed great importance upon increased labor productivity, for the plant department as well as for the entire economy. The productivity targets, in my opinion, were operational goals and not mere genuflection to Marxist value theory.[10] The quest for higher labor productivity, in the face of the orthodox prescription with regard

[9] This theme runs through the recent United Nations, Department of Economic Affairs report, *Labour Productivity of the Cotton Textile Industry in Five Latin-American Countries.* For example, in describing Brazilian textile manufacturing, the report states (p. 18): "The factor which affects productivity most is superfluous personnel. . . . The superfluous labor in the old mills of Brazil is not entirely due to the incapacity of the managers to recognize this excess, but to the perpetuation of traditional work patterns which date from the end of the last or the beginning of the present century. . . . The tradition and social ties mentioned above spring from deeper and more fundamental economic factors. One is the excess of working population in relation to the country's capacity to invest in projects which create new employment opportunities. This factor occurs in most of the Latin-American countries and is of considerable importance when the increasing of the industry's productivity is envisaged." Again (p. 18): "An Ecuadorian mill could have ten times as many workers as a United States mill, without there being any difference in the relation of the cost of labor to that of the finished product." In Mexico (p. 81), "the crux of the problem . . . arises from the existence of a surplus of population in relation to the scanty capital which can be invested in industry and other activities."

[10] Some quotations from authoritative sources may be adduced in support of this assertion: "The index of labor productivity is a most important index in the national economic plan. Therefore, the control of plan fulfillment is a central problem of labor statistics. . . . For planning and statistical work, for operating leadership, starting with the enterprise and ending with the entire economy, it is necessary to have general, summary indexes of labor productivity." A. I. Ezhov, *Kurs promyshlennoi statistiki,* p. 67. "In those branches of industry where technical norms are well established and where conditions of production permit an accurate accounting of labor time spent per unit of product, it is expedient to control the fulfillment of the plan of output per worker, to use an index calculated in terms of units of working time. In factory planning, the basic production plan contains detailed estimates of the labor cost program of each department and shop. Thus an accounting of expenditure of working time is intimately related to labor planning in the higher echelons of factory plan administration." E. L. Granovskii and B. L. Markus, *Ekonomika sotsialisticheskoi promyshlennosti,* p. 478.

to appropriate capital–labor ratios in underdeveloped economies,[11] may nevertheless have been entirely rational in that it helped create an artificial limitation on the use of labor,[12] encouraged the installation of modern equipment, and caused a rapid deepening of capital intensity in a limited group of heavy industries essential for industrialization.[13] Emulation of the U.S. technological model, "catching up with and exceeding the most advanced capitalist nation," may well have been the shortest road to the maximization of long-run output.[14]

[11] The orthodox theoretical prescription for allocating capital resources has been stated as follows: "The general rule is that nations engaged in reconstruction or development should economize in the use of scarce capital by concentrating on capital-light investments. . . . The correct criterion for obtaining the maximum return from limited resources is marginal productivity—or, from the point of view of society as a whole, social marginal productivity (SMP), taking into account the total net contribution of the marginal unit to national product, and not merely that portion of the contribution (or of its costs) which may accrue to the private investor . . . of course, the relative abundance of different factors is a significant determinant of the SMP of each. Where capital is relatively scarce (compared with another area) its SMP will be higher and each investment will have to meet the more stringent test of a higher opportunity cost. In consequence, China will and should in general specialize in industries and use techniques requiring a lower capital : labor ratio than the United States." Alfred E. Kahn, "Investment Criteria in Development Programs," *Quarterly Journal of Economics,* February, 1951, pp. 38–39.

[12] For a discussion of the economics of labor supply in Soviet industry, see Joseph Kershaw, "Agricultural Output and Employment," in Abram Bergson, (ed.), *Soviet Economic Growth,* p. 294, and the comments by Abram Bergson (p. 308) and Richard Moorsteen (p. 310). I am inclined to agree with Bergson that the existence of a sizeable volume of surplus labor in agriculture was "highly plausible," the chief obstacle to its industrial employment being the lack of urban living amenities. However, when labor was needed it was secured, even under the most adverse conditions. See John Scott, *Behind the Urals* (New York, 1942).

[13] I have argued this point at greater length in an as yet unpublished manuscript dealing more generally with the problems of labor productivity in underdeveloped areas.

[14] Joseph S. Berliner, "Comments," in Bergson, *op. cit.,* p. 216, argues that "short of computing a production function for Soviet industry, then, output per worker should at least be presented in conjunction with output per unit of capital for purposes of comparison. Indeed, unless one accepts a labor theory of value, on purely theoretical grounds it makes sense to demand a productivity figure for all factors of production, that is, output per unit of capital, output per unit of fuel, output per unit of cotton thread, and so forth." Apart from the practical difficulties involved in obeying this injunction, it may be noted that output per man or per man-hour provides a more satisfactory means of gauging capital accumulation and technological progress than output per machine-hour. Except in the presence of fixed technical coefficients, total output per machine-hour can be altered by increasing the application of labor without

LABOR SKILLS

The lack of labor skills constituted a serious obstacle to the growth of Soviet labor productivity. During the initial years of the planning period it was necessary quickly to train millions of new recruits for the mass, semiskilled trades and to begin the longer task of building up a supply of skilled workers and technicians. The figures in Table 85, where trainees are related to the total labor force, indicate the year 1932 as the divide insofar as the semiskilled worker problem was concerned, and it is perhaps no coincidence that labor productivity fell sharply in some industries at this time. Many workers were undoubtedly placed directly at the work bench with no preliminary status as trainees,[15] but the data are probably indicative of changes in the pressure of the training burden. For individual industries, particularly heavy industry, the training peak was much higher than that indicated in Table 85: 19.6 percent of all wage earners in steel manufacture were trainees in 1932, and 19.2 percent of all wage earners were trainees in machinery and metalworking.[16]

Table 85 also shows the proportion of young people in the labor force. Training was undoubtedly facilitated by the recruitment of so large a portion of the labor force from the younger age groups, which could adapt themselves more easily to industrial conditions. On January 1, 1934, near the period of peak training load, 37.7 percent of all industrial wage earners were 23 years of age and under. For some of the skilled trades, the percentage was higher.[17]

The training of engineers and other technical personnel was a slower

---

additional capital investment or technological change, whereas output per man-hour is raised primarily through new capital investment and modernization.

[15] The following quotation purports to portray the nature of the training program in Russia during the early planning period: "The biographies of the large majorities of Soviet workers provide excellent illustrations of how quickly people grew under such conditions. Yesterday's unskilled worker, never having seen a machine, worked in the space of a year as assistant operative, and in two or three years operated complicated machinery independently; he often continued to study, and passed his technical examination, prepared to be an instructor, foreman, technician." Gosudarstvennyi Nauchnyi Institut, *Bolshaia sovetskaia entsiklopediia*, p. 1127.

[16] *Sotsialisticheskoe stroitel'stvo*, 1936, p. 516.

[17] For example, 39 percent of all molders, 49 percent of turners, 43 percent of milling machine operators, 49 percent of turret lathe operators, 47 percent of all skilled workers in aviation and automobile plants. See *Molodezh SSSR*, p. 127.

TABLE 85

TRAINEES AND YOUTHS IN THE SOVIET LABOR FORCE, 1928–36

YEAR	TRAINEES AS A PERCENTAGE OF THE TOTAL NUMBER OF WAGE EARNERS IN INDUSTRY[a]	PERSONS 23 YEARS OF AGE AND UNDER AS A PERCENTAGE OF THE NUMBER OF WAGE EARNERS IN INDUSTRY[b]
1928	5.6	26.3
1929	5.0	n.a.[c]
1930	4.6	24.7
1931	9.1	n.a.
1932	12.1	n.a.
1933	9.9	n.a.
1934	5.5	37.7
1935	4.5	34.1
1936	4.6	n.a.

[a] *Sotsialisticheskoe stroitel'stvo*, 1936, p. 516.

[b] *Molodezh SSSR*, p. 123. The figure shown for 1928 is as of July 1, 1927; for 1930—January 1, 1930; for 1934—January 1, 1934; for 1935—July 1, 1935. Up to January 1, 1934, the data included persons 22 years of age and under; beginning with that date, the age was raised to 23 years, so that the percentages for 1934 and 1935 are subject to a slight inflation on this account.

[c] n.a. = information not available.

process and in the long run probably constituted a more serious drag upon productivity. During the First Five Year Plan, 291 thousand persons graduated from the so-called technicums, and during the Second Five Year Plan 623 thousand graduated.[18] Qualified engineering graduates numbered 14.5 thousand in 1932 and 25.4 thousand in 1938, compared with total employment of 20.2 thousand engineers in 1927–28.[19]

In 1940, the vocational training of youth was concentrated in the State Labor Reserves, operating through a network of special training schools. Under this system, persons entering the semiskilled trades were given six months' training, while those entering the skilled trades received two years of special schooling. From 1940 to 1950, the State Labor Reserves graduated some 5.8 million boys and girls into indus-

[18] *Sotsialisticheskoe stroitel'stvo*, 1939, p. 124. The technicums are intermediate vocational schools, similar in some respects to vocational high schools in the United States.

[19] Gregory Bienstock, Solomon M. Schwarz, and Aaron Yugow, *Management in Russian Industry and Agriculture*, p. 110.

try;[20] during the same period, the net increment to the industrial labor force was 7.0 million persons.[21] However, there appears to have been a recent trend away from this type of training. The number of graduates of the system in 1952, 326,000, was the lowest since the inception of the program. In some schools the period of training is being lengthened, while in general there is greater emphasis on regular vocational high schools.[22] It is not clear whether this represents dissatisfaction with the type of training provided by the State Labor Reserves or a change to a more traditional type of vocational training now that the war and reconstruction emergency periods are receding.

[20] Solomon M. Schwarz, *Labor in the Soviet Union,* pp. 77–83.
[21] Warren W. Eason, "Population and Labor Force," in Abram Bergson (ed.), *Soviet Economic Growth,* p. 110.
[22] U.S. Department of Labor, *Notes on Labor Abroad,* April, 1953, pp. 14–15.

XV

FUTURE PROSPECTS FOR SOVIET PRODUCTIVITY CHANGE

THE subject of long-run trends in labor productivity has been explored with any degree of thoroughness only by Solomon Fabricant. His analysis of industrial development in the United States leads him to the hypothesis that with industrial growth there is a deceleration in the rate at which labor productivity increases, and that the path of productivity may not be that of a smooth exponential curve, but rather may be linear and steeply positive during the early stages of an industry's growth and mildly positive once industrial maturity is reached.[1]

It is questionable whether the American experience is applicable to the Russian economy, or indeed to any economy undergoing "late" industrialization. Because of the emphasis placed upon heavy industry by the Soviet planners, there was a very uneven rate of capital growth among industries. Some of Russia's older industries, such as cotton and wool manufacturing and sugar refining, were technologically backward in 1939 and have probably not progressed greatly since then. Other industries, both old and new, were catapulted into modernity by the borrowing of techniques from abroad. The Russian automobile industry, for example, was from the beginning a relatively efficient assembly-line operation, installed by American engineers and following closely contemporary methods in the United States. Therefore, the relevant concept of maturity in Russia is not temporal, but rather technological, maturity. The initial sharply positive rate of productivity increase may have been built into the new industries, and it is likely that only the backward consumer goods industries are still on the lower reaches of the productivity curve.

It is a reasonable assumption that, in the absence of war, the rate of productivity growth for those Soviet industries which had been newly

[1] Solomon Fabricant, *Employment in Manufacturing, 1899–1939,* Chap. 3.

developed during the planning period would have declined. In fact, the year 1936 appears to be a hinge in the growth slope for coal and iron and steel productivity in particular and for manufacturing in general, the latter to a less marked degree. This is not true, however, of the cotton textile, shoe, and sugar industries, the two first-named industries continuing a fairly constant rate of productivity advance beyond 1936 and the latter exhibiting sharp annual variations in productivity, depending to a great extent on crop conditions.

On the basis of the Soviet experience, the hypothesis may be advanced that a nation undergoing industrialization at a relatively late stage of world economic development is able, for those industries for which a high rate of capital investment can be maintained, rapidly to narrow the gap in output per worker that separates it from the more advanced nations by the installation of new capital equipment. However, these initial gains can carry it up only to a certain point, beyond which further gains may depend to a much greater extent on industrial management, labor skills, and the whole gamut of factors which are customarily emphasized in comparing the differences in productivity among advanced industrial nations.

The productivity targets in the Fifth Five Year Plan appear to belie this hypothesis. The Plan calls for a 50 percent increase in industrial labor productivity for the period 1950–55, or an annual average rate of 8.5 percent (compounded annually). This is to be achieved through a 70 percent increase in industrial production, the number of industrial wage earners rising by only 13 percent for the entire period, the lowest rate of labor force growth of any of the five year plan periods.[2] It is claimed that during 1951 and 1952, industrial productivity rose by 10 percent and 7 percent, respectively (Table 1), which is consistent with the five year plan target.

Perhaps the major factor arguing for the possibility of an achievement of the productivity rise planned is the degree of capital intensification envisaged by 1955. It has been estimated, for example, that electric power consumption per worker in Soviet industry is to rise from 6,080 kilowatt hours in 1950 to 10,340 kilowatt hours in 1955.[3]

[2] These data are from the "Draft Directives for Development of the Soviet Economy under the Fifth Five Year Plan," New York *Times,* August 23, 1952, pp. 6–7.

[3] Gregory Grossman, "Some Current Trends in Soviet Capital Formation," unpublished manuscript, 1953, p. 17.

However, it is by no means a foregone conclusion that the ambitious productivity figures will be attained. Moreover, there is some question as to the meaning of the global productivity percentages. It will be recalled that from 1928 to 1938, when the official Soviet productivity index indicated an average annual increase of 10.6 percent per annum, our estimate, based on industry studies, was 6 percent annually for the period. Presumably the inflationary bias due to the use of 1926–27 prices in computing the official production index was responsible for at least a part of the inflation in the official index of productivity. The change-over to current prices on January 1, 1949, and the calculation of labor productivity in the new prices under the Fifth Five Year Plan should eliminate the inflationary element. What prices the 1951 productivity results were calculated in is not clear, though January 1, 1952, prices were used for 1952.[4] It is possible that the progressive decline in the claimed annual increase in labor productivity from 12 percent in 1950 to 10 percent in 1951 to 7 percent in 1952 (Table 1) represents the influence of the new pricing system, though it is necessary to add that a continued rate of productivity growth equal to that of 1952 would not be consistent with the Fifth Five Year Plan target.

Table 86 contains a comparison of the rates of labor productivity increase claimed for five major industries during 1951 and 1952, the first two years of the Fifth Five Year Plan, with comparable industry rates for the period 1928–37 computed (a) on the basis of the official production index and (b) on the basis of the productivity indexes in Table 76. For the year 1952, in particular,[5] the claimed productivity advances were well below both sets for the period 1928–37, except for machinery, which exceeded the productivity increase calculated on the basis of the Gerschenkron index. This sample of industries, which does not include any of the "light" industries, is too small to provide a firm basis for generalization. Nevertheless, it does provide some indication that future productivity gains will be below the prewar rates.[6]

[4] It is stated specifically that the planning and measurement of labor productivity during 1952–55 would be on the basis of January 1, 1952, prices. See *Soviet Studies*, V (July, 1953), 84–89.

[5] It is possible again that the generally lower productivity advances shown for 1952 were the result of the introduction of the new system of planning prices, coupled with price reductions during 1952. *Ibid.*

[6] Because of the reconstruction factor, the productivity increases during the years 1946–50 do not constitute a satisfactory clue to potential future gains.

The question that comes to mind when one reviews the history of labor productivity in the Soviet Union is this: Will Soviet labor productivity attain the level prevailing in the United States within a reasonable time in the future? There are so many imponderables involved in answering this question that prudence dictates refraining from even a guess. However, some simple hypothetical projections can provide insight into what is involved in "catching up" with the United States.

TABLE 86

SOVIET PRODUCTIVITY CLAIMS FOR SELECTED INDUSTRIES, 1951 AND 1952, COMPARED WITH ESTIMATED PRODUCTIVITY INCREASES FOR THE YEARS 1928–37

| | PERCENTAGE INCREASE | | | |
INDUSTRY	1951[a]	1952[b]	Based on the Soviet production index, 1928–37[c]	Our estimate, 1928–37[c]
Coal mining	8	4	8.6	7.3
Oil extraction	9	5	8.6	7.2
Iron and steel	9	8	12.7	10.6
Machinery	14	10	14.2	2.5
Chemicals	9	8	15.9	n.a.[d]

[a] *Trud,* January 29, 1952, p. 1.
[b] *Ibid.,* January 23, 1953, p. 1.
[c] Table 78.
[d] n.a. = information not available.

In selecting specific rates at which to project growth, the experience of other nations is at best an imperfect guide. Contemporary Soviet industry as a whole, for example, cannot be equated to any stage of industrial development in the United States because of tremendous differences among industries. For coal mining, one would have to go back well before the turn of the century to find a time when U.S. labor productivity was as low as that of Soviet coal mining today; for blast furnace products, to around 1925; for steel mill products, to 1900; for most machinery items, to the 1920's; and for cotton and sugar, to a time for which U.S. statistics are not available. On the other hand, Russian 1937–39 productivity was above that of Great Britain in 1937 for some machinery items and for coal mining and was not far behind in many other industries.[7]

Estimated long-run rates of productivity increase in the United States, Great Britain, and Canada have been cited above. The commonly given rate of 2.5 percent for U.S. manufacturing apparently failed to materialize from 1939 to 1947; Fabricant has been quoted as believing that during this period the annual rise in output per man-hour was on the order of 1 percent.[8] However, there appears to have been an increase in the rate since 1947, and a future rate of 2 percent per annum is not improbable.[9]

Despite the Fifth Five Year Plan targets, it does not seem likely that Soviet industrial productivity is likely in the long run to exceed the estimated average annual rate of increase of 6 percent for the decade 1928–38. Indeed, the indications are that this rate will not be equaled over any lengthy period of time. On the other hand, in view of relatively low Soviet productivity in light industry and the considerable lag in heavy industry compared with the United States, a somewhat higher rate than that projected for the United States appears reasonable. Several alternative percentages are projected for the Soviet Union against a 2 percent annual productivity increase for the United States; and assuming that the prewar comparative USSR-U.S. productivity ratio of about 40 percent prevailed in 1950, the following results are obtained:

ANNUAL PERCENTAGE RATES OF PRODUCTIVITY INCREASE, COMPOUNDED (BASED ON USSR = 40 PERCENT U.S. IN 1950)	SOVIET PRODUCTIVITY AS A PERCENTAGE OF U.S. PRODUCTIVITY	
	1960	1970
1. United States, 2; Russia, 3	44	49
2. United States, 2; Russia, 4	49	59
3. United States, 2; Russia, 5	53	71
4. United States, 2; Russia, 6	59	86

[7] This follows from Rostas's conclusion (L. Rostas, *Comparative Productivity in British and American Industry*, p. 27) that in manufacturing, during the period 1935–39, "average productivity—as measured by physical output per worker—was at least twice (about 2.2 times) as high in the United States as in Britain."

[8] *Business Week*, May 5, 1951, p. 66.

[9] "Assuming the continuation of a defense economy similar to that presently in effect, it seems doubtful, from developments now foreseeable, that output per man-hour for the economy as a whole will increase during the next few years at a rate much faster than the approximately 2 percent average annual increase of the past." John C. Davis, "Productivity Trends and Some Economic Implications," in L. R. Tripp (ed.), *Industrial Productivity*, p. 20.

It must be emphasized that these ratios are hypothetical and are not presented as forecasts. United States productivity could, in fact, rise as rapidly, or more rapidly, than Soviet productivity, in which case the initial difference would widen. On the other hand, even if Soviet productivity rose at what I should regard as the outside limit of 6 percent per annum for twenty years, and if U.S. productivity continued at the "normal" rate of 2 percent, there would still be a difference between the levels in the two countries at the end of twenty years. The projections are useful only in bringing home the implications of a difference in labor productivity as great as that which prevails between the United States and the Soviet Union and in providing one indication of the magnitude of the task facing the Russians in their quest for a level of industrial efficiency equal to that of the United States.

BIBLIOGRAPHY

UNITED STATES GOVERNMENT PUBLICATIONS

U.S. Department of Commerce. Mineral Yearbook. Washington, D.C., various years.

—— National Income and Product of the United States. Washington, D.C., 1951.

U.S. Department of Commerce, Bureau of the Census. Census of Manufactures. Washington, D.C., 1929, 1937, 1939, and 1947.

—— Historical Statistics of the United States. Washington, D.C., 1949.

—— Manufacture and Sale of Farm Equipment and Related Products. Washington, D.C., 1940.

—— Mining Industries. Washington, D.C., 1939.

—— Statistical Abstract of the United States. Washington, D.C., 1947.

U.S. Department of Commerce and Labor. Shoe and Leather Trade in Russia. Special Agent Series No. 68, Washington, D.C., 1913.

U.S. Department of Labor, Bureau of Labor Statistics. Handbook of Labor Statistics. Washington, D.C., various editions.

—— Notes on Labor Abroad. Washington, D.C.

—— Productivity and Unit Labor Cost in Selected Manufacturing Industries. Washington, D.C., 1942.

—— Productivity Trends, Bituminous-Coal Mining. Washington, D.C., 1952.

—— Productivity Trends in Selected Industries. Bulletin No. 1046, Washington, D.C., 1951.

—— Trends in Man-Hours Expended per Pair: Footwear. Washington, D.C., May, 1952.

—— Trends in Man-Hours Expended per Unit: Selected Types of Construction and Mining Machinery. Washington, D.C., May, 1952.

—— Trends in Output per Man-Hour: Mining. Washington, D.C., Aug. 1950.

Works Progress Administration, National Research Project. Mechanization, Employment, and Output per Man in Bituminous-Coal Mining. Washington, D.C., 1939.

—— Production, Employment, and Productivity in 59 Manufacturing Industries. Washington, D.C., 1939.

—— Productivity and Employment in Selected Industries: Beet Sugar. Washington, D.C., 1938.

—— Technology, Employment, and Output per Man in Iron Mining. Washington, D.C., 1940.

Works Progress Administration, National Research Project. Technology, Employment, and Output per Man in Petroleum and Natural-Gas Production. Washington, D.C., 1939.

SOVIET GOVERNMENT PUBLICATIONS

Central Administration of Economics and Social Statistics of the State Planning Commission of the USSR. Socialist Construction in the USSR. Moscow, 1936.

Gosudarstvennyi Nauchnyi Institut. Bolshaia sovetskaia entsiklopediia (The Large Soviet Encyclopedia). One-volume edition, Moscow, 1948.

Gosudarstvennyi plan razvitiia narodnogo khoziaistva SSSR na 1941 god (State Plan for the Development of the National Economy of the USSR for 1941). This volume was issued as a series of appendices to a decree of the Council of People's Commissars and the Central Committee of the Communist Party, Jan. 17, 1941.

Ioffe, Ia. A. SSSR i kapitalisticheskie strany (The USSR and Capitalist Countries). Moscow, 1939.

Molodezh SSSR. See Tsentral'noe Upravlenie Narodno-Khoziaistvennogo Ucheta.

Narodnoe khoziaistvo SSSR (National Economy of the USSR). Sbornik No. 3, Moscow, 1950.

1941 Plan. See Gosudarstvennyi plan razvitiia narodnogo khoziaistva SSSR na 1941 god.

Slovar'-spravochnik. See Tsentral'noe Statisticheskoe Upravlenie Gosplana SSSR.

Socialist Construction in the USSR. See Central Administration of Economics and Social Statistics.

Sotsialisticheskoe stroitel'stvo SSSR. See Tsentral'noe Upravlenie Narodno-Khoziaistvennogo Ucheta.

Trud v SSSR. See Tsentral'noe Upravlenie Narodno-Khoziaistvennogo Ucheta.

Tsentral'noe Statisticheskoe Upravlenie Gosplana SSSR. Slovar'-spravochnik po sotsial'no-ekonomicheskoi statistike. 1944, 1948 editions, Moscow.

Tsentral'noe Upravlenie Narodno-Khoziaistvennogo Ucheta. Molodezh SSSR (Youth of the USSR). Moscow, 1936.

—— Sotsialisticheskoe stroitel'stvo SSSR (Socialist Construction in the USSR). 1934, 1935, 1936, 1939 editions, Moscow.

—— Trud v SSSR (Labor in the USSR). 1935, 1936 editions, Moscow.

—— Zhenshchina v SSSR (Women in the USSR). Moscow, 1937.

Vsesoyuznyi Tsentral'nyi Sovet Professional'nykh Soiuzov. Statisticheskii spravochnik. Vol. III, Moscow, 1939.

Zhenshchina v SSSR. See Tsentral'noe Upravlenie Narodno-Khoziaistvennogo Ucheta.

SECONDARY SOURCES

Adermann, Waldemar. Die russische Baumwollindustrie nach dem Kriege. Berlin, 1929.

Akademiia Nauk, Institut Ekonomiki, P. A. Khromov (ed.). Proizvoditel'-nost' truda v promyshlennosti SSSR (Labor Productivity in the Industry of the USSR). Moscow, 1940.

American Iron and Steel Institute. Annual Statistical Report. Philadelphia, various years.

American Petroleum Institute. Petroleum Facts and Figures. New York, various years.

Anglo-American Council on Productivity. Cotton Spinning. London, 1950.

——— Cotton Weaving. London, 1950.

——— Iron and Steel. London, 1952.

——— Simplification in British Industry. London, 1950.

——— Simplification in Industry. London, 1949.

Arakelian, A. A. "Proizvoditel'nost' truda v chernoi metallurgia SSSR," in Akademiia Nauk, Institut Ekonomiki, Proizvoditel'nost' truda v promyshlennosti SSSR.

Backman, Jules. Statement before the Wage Stabilization Board. New York, 1950.

Backman, Jules, and M. R. Gainsbrugh. Economics of the Cotton Textile Industry. New York, 1946.

Bardin, I. P., and N. P. Bannyi. Chernaia metallurgiia v novoi piatiletke (Ferrous Metallurgy in the New Five Year Plan). Moscow, 1947.

Barger, Harold, and Sam H. Schurr. The Mining Industries, 1899–1939: A Study of Output, Employment, and Productivity. New York, 1944.

Barna, T. "Note on the Productivity of Labor," Bulletin of the Oxford University Institute of Statistics, Vol. VIII, No. 7 (1946).

Baykov, Alexander. The Soviet Economic System. Cambridge, 1946.

Belenkii, V. L. Indeksy proizvoditel'nosti truda (Indexes of Labor Productivity). Moscow, 1930.

Bergson, Abram. "A Problem in Soviet Statistics," The Review of Economic Statistics, November, 1947.

——— Soviet Economic Growth. Evanston, 1953.

——— Soviet National Income and Product in 1937. New York, 1953.

Bergson, Abram, and Lynn Turgeon. Prices of Ordinary Rolled Steel in the Soviet Union. Research Memorandum RM–767, The RAND Corporation, Santa Monica, Jan. 21, 1952.

——— Prices of Quality Rolled Steel in the Soviet Union 1928–1950. Research Memorandum RM–778, The RAND Corporation, Santa Monica, Feb. 8, 1952.

Bergson, Abram, and others. "Postwar Economic Reconstruction and Development in the USSR," *Annals of the American Academy of Political and Social Science,* May, 1949.

Berliner, Joseph. "Comments," in Abram Bergson (ed.), Soviet Economic Growth.

Bienstock, Gregory, Solomon M. Schwarz, and Aaron Yugow. Management in Russian Industry and Agriculture. New York, 1944.

Boylston, H. M. Iron and Steel. London, 1936.

Camp, J. M., and C. B. Francis. The Making, Shaping, and Treating of Steel. Pittsburgh, 1940.

Cherniak, A. O tempakh razvitiia sotsialisticheskoi promyshlennosti (The Tempo of Development of Socialist Industry). Moscow, 1948.

Clark, Colin. The Conditions of Economic Progress. London, 1951.

—— A Critique of Russian Statistics. London, 1939.

Company Testimony before the Presidential Fact-Finding Board. Steel Industry Case, August, 1949.

Conference Board. The Economic Almanac 1951–52. New York, 1951.

Cooper, R. Conrad. Productivity in the Steel Producing Subsidiaries of United States Steel. Brief before the President's Steel Industry Board, Aug. 22, 1949.

Davis, Hiram S. "The Meaning and Measurement of Productivity," in L. R. Tripp (ed.), Industrial Productivity. Madison, 1951.

Davis, John C. "Productivity Trends and Some Economic Implications," in L. R. Tripp (ed.), Industrial Productivity. Madison, 1951.

Deutscher, Isaac. Soviet Trade Unions. London, 1950.

Dunlop, John T. "Productivity and the Wage Structure," in Lloyd Metzler and others, Income, Employment, and Public Policy.

Duzh, P. D. "Proizvoditel'nost' truda v kammenougol'noi promyshlennosti SSSR," in Akademiia Nauk, Institut Ekonomiki, Proizvoditel'nost' truda v promyshlennosti SSSR.

Eason, Warren W. "Population and Labor Force," in Abram Bergson (ed.), Soviet Economic Growth.

—— "Trends and Prospects of the Soviet Population and Labor Force." Paper P-289, The RAND Corporation, Santa Monica, Dec. 17, 1952, p. 49.

Ezhov, A. I. Kurs promishlennoi statistiki (Course in Industrial Statistics). Moscow, 1946.

Fabricant, Solomon. Employment in Manufacturing, 1899–1939. New York, 1942.

Fisher, Douglas A. Steel Making in America. New York, 1949.

Flux, A. W. "Industrial Productivity in Great Britain and the United States," *Quarterly Journal of Economics,* Vol. XLVIII (1933).

Garbutt, P. E. The Russian Railways. London, 1949.

Gerschenkron, Alexander. A Dollar Index of Soviet Machinery Output, 1927–28 to 1937. Report R–197, The RAND Corporation, Santa Monica, April 6, 1951.

Gerschenkron, Alexander, and Nancy Nimitz. A Dollar Index of Soviet Iron and Steel Output. Research Memorandum RM–1055, The RAND Corporation, Santa Monica, March 15, 1953.

Gorelik, I. Metodika planirovaniia chernoi metallurgiia (Methods of Planning Ferrous Metallurgy). Moscow, 1937.

Gornostai-Polskii, A. M. Osnovy ekonomiki kozhevenno-obuvnoi promyshlennosti (Basic Economics of the Leather-Shoe Industry). Moscow, 1947.

Granovskii, E. L., and B. L. Markus. Ekonomika sotsialisticheskoi promyshlennosti (The Economics of Socialist Industry). Moscow, 1940.

Grossman, Gregory. "Some Current Trends in Soviet Capital Formation." National Bureau of Economic Research, New York, 1953.

Gurevitch, S., and S. Partigul. The New Economic Upswing of the USSR in the Postwar Five Year Plan. Moscow, 1950.

Gzovski, Vladimir. "Elements of Soviet Labor Law," *Monthly Labor Review*, March, 1951.

Hassman, Heinrich. Erdöl in der Sowjetunion. Hamburg, 1951.

Hodgman, Donald R. "Industrial Production," in Abram Bergson (ed.), Soviet Economic Growth.

——— "Soviet Machinery Output," *The American Slavic and East European Review*, February, 1953.

Hogan, William T. Productivity in the Blast-furnace and Open-hearth Segments of the Steel Industry. New York, 1950.

International Labor Office. Employment, Unemployment, and Labor Force Statistics. Studies and Reports, New Series, No. 7. Geneva, 1948.

——— Methods of Labor Productivity Statistics. Geneva, 1951.

International Labor Office, Coal Mines Committee, Fourth Session. Productivity in Coal Mines. Geneva, 1951.

Jasny, Naum. The Socialized Agriculture of the USSR. Stanford, 1949.

——— The Soviet Price System. Stanford, 1951.

Kahn, Alfred E. "Investment Criteria in Development Programs," *Quarterly Journal of Economics,* February, 1951.

Kantor, L. M. Osnovnye fondy promyshlennosti i ikh ispol'zovanie (The Basic Funds of Industry and Their Use). Leningrad, 1947.

Kaplan, Norman. "Capital Formation and Allocation," in Abram Bergson (ed.), Soviet Economic Growth.

Kershaw, Joseph. "Agricultural Output and Employment," in Abram Bergson (ed.), Soviet Economic Growth.

Khromov, P. A. Ocherki ekonomiki tekstil'noi promyshlennosti SSSR (Essays in the Economics of the Textile Industry of the USSR). Moscow, 1946.

——— "Proizvoditel'nost' truda v khlopchatobumazhnoi promyshlennosti

SSR," in Akademiia Nauk, Institut Ekonomiki, Proizvoditel'nost' truda v promyshlennosti SSSR.

Klimenko, K. I. "Proizvoditel'nost' truda v mashinostroitelnoi i metalloobrabatyvaiuschei promyshlennosti," in Akademiia Nauk, Institut Ekonomiki, Proizvoditel'nost' truda v promyshlennosti SSSR.

Kukulevitch, I. L., and M. A. Rubin. Planirovanie i analiz trudovikh pokazatelei (The Planning and Analysis of Labor Indexes). Moscow, 1948.

Levin, S. M. Teknicheskoe normirovanie v chernoi metallurgii (Technical Norm Making in Ferrous Metallurgy). Kharkov, 1950.

Maddison, A. "Productivity in an Expanding Economy," *The Economic Journal,* September, 1952.

——— "Productivity in Canada, the United Kingdom, and the United States," *Oxford Economic Papers* (New Series), October, 1952.

Markus, B. L. "The Stakhanov Movement," *International Labor Review,* July, 1936.

Maslova, N. S. Proizvoditel'nost' truda v promyshlennosti SSSR (The Productivity of Labor in the Industry of the USSR). Moscow, 1949.

Medinskii, E. N. Narodnoe obrazovanie v SSSR (Public Education in the USSR). Moscow, 1947.

Metzler, Lloyd, and others. Income, Employment, and Public Policy. New York, 1948.

Nikolayevski, N. "Proizvoditel'nost' truda v neftiannoi promyshlennosti SSSR," in Akademiia Nauk, Institut Ekonomiki, Proizvoditel'nost' truda v promyshlennosti SSSR.

Nimitz, Nancy, and Alexander Gerschenkron. A Dollar Index of Soviet Coal Output. Research Memorandum RM–1042, the RAND Corporation, Santa Monica, Feb. 18, 1953.

Official Report of the Elected Delegation of Trade Unionists to the USSR. Russia: The Truth. London, 1951.

Opatski, L. V. "Proizvoditel'nost' truda v sakharnoi promyshlennosti SSSR," in Akademiia Nauk, Institut Ekonomiki, Proizvoditel'nost' truda v promyshlennosti SSSR.

Pashkov, A. I. Voprosy sotsialisticheskoi ekonomiki (Questions of Socialist Economics). Moscow, 1951.

Phelps-Brown, E. H., and P. E. Hart. "The Share of Wages in National Income," *The Economic Journal,* June, 1952.

Popova, N. Zhenshchiny strany sotsializma (Women of the Land of Socialism). Moscow, 1948.

Rabinowitsch, Ewsey. Die russisch-ukrainische Zuckerindustrie seit dem Weltkriege. Berlin, 1930.

Report of the British Workers' Delegation. Russia with Our Own Eyes. London, 1950.

Report of the Nineteen Americans on Their Visit to the USSR. We Saw for Ourselves. New York, 1951.

Rodin, Nicholas W. Productivity in Soviet Iron Mining. Research Memorandum RM–1116, The RAND Corporation, Santa Monica, July 7, 1953.

Rostas, L. Comparative Productivity in British and American Industry. Cambridge, 1948.

Rotshtein, A. I. Problemy promyshlennoi statistiki v SSSR (Problems of Industrial Statistics in the USSR). Vols. I and III, Moscow, 1947.

Savinskii, D. V. Kurs promyshlennoi statistiki (Course in Industrial Statistics). Moscow, 1949.

Schwartz, Harry. Russia's Soviet Economy. New York, 1950.

Schwarz, Solomon M. Labor in the Soviet Union. New York, 1951.

Shevchenko, A. Stakhanovski rukh i osvoyenya tekhniki v chernoi metallurgii (The Stakhanov Movement and Basic Techniques in Ferrous Metallurgy). Kiev, 1940.

Shimkin, Demitri B. "The Automobile Industry That's Behind the Iron Curtain," *Automotive Industries,* Feb. 15, 1948.

—— Minerals—A Key to Soviet Power. Cambridge, 1953.

Shul'kin, L. P. Potreblenie chernykh metallov v SSSR (The Consumption of Ferrous Metals in the USSR). Moscow-Leningrad, 1941.

Shul'kin, S. I. "Proizvoditel'nost' truda v zhelezorudnoi promyshlennosti SSSR," in Akademiia Nauk, Institut Ekonomiki, Proizvoditel'nost' truda v promyshlennosti SSSR.

Siegel, Irving H. Concepts and Measurement of Production and Productivity. Bureau of Labor Statistics, Washington, D.C., 1952.

—— "Labor Productivity in the Soviet Union," *Journal of the American Statistical Association,* March, 1953.

Snow, E. C. "The International Comparison of Industrial Output," *Journal of the Royal Statistical Society,* Part I, 1944.

Spiridonov, M. Proizvoditel'nost' truda v sotsialisticheskom obshchestve (Labor Productivity in Socialist Society). Moscow, 1951.

Stern, Boris. "Labor Productivity in the Boot and Shoe Industry," *Monthly Labor Review,* February, 1939.

Strumilin, S. G. Chernaia metallurgiia v Rossii i v SSSR (Ferrous Metallurgy in Russia and in the USSR). Moscow, 1935.

Tinbergen, J. "The Influence of Productivity on Economic Welfare," *The Economic Journal,* Vol. LXII (March, 1952).

Turetskii, Sh. Proizvoditel'nost' truda (The Productivity of Labor). Moscow, 1947.

—— Vnutripromyshlennoe nakoplenie v SSSR (Internal Accumulation in Soviet Industry). Moscow, 1948.

United Kingdom, Ministry of Production. Report of the Cotton Textile

Mission to the United States of America. London, March–April, 1944 (The Platt Report).

United Nations, Department of Economic Affairs. Labour Productivity of the Cotton Textile Industry in Five Latin-American Countries. New York, 1951.

United Nations, Economic Commission for Europe. Economic Survey of Europe in 1950. Geneva, 1951.

University of Birmingham. *Bulletins on Soviet Economic Development,* No. 1, May, 1949.

Varga, E. Two Systems. New York, 1939.

Veingarten, S. M. Ekonomika i planirovanie chernoi metallurgii (The Economics and Planning of Ferrous Metallurgy). Moscow, 1939.

Voznesenskii, N. Voennaia ekonomika SSSR v period otechestvennoi voiny (War Economy of the USSR during World War II). Moscow, 1948.

Zobel, Sigmund P. "On the Measurement of the Productivity of Labor," *Journal of the American Statistical Association,* Vol. XLV (June, 1950).

PERIODICALS AND NEWSPAPERS

American Slavic and East European Review
American Statistician
Annals of the American Academy of Political and Social Science
Automotive Industries
Avtomobil'naia promyshlennost' (The Automobile Industry)
Bulletin of the Oxford University Institute of Statistics
Economic Bulletin for Europe
Economic Journal
Gornyi zhurnal (Mining Journal)
Industriia (Industry)
International Labor Review
International Monetary Fund Staff Papers
Journal of the American Statistical Association
Journal of the Royal Statistical Society
Kozhevenno-obuvnaia promyshlennost' (The Leather and Shoe Industry)
Legkaia promyshlennost' (Light Industry)
Monthly Labor Review
Neftianaia promyshlennost' SSSR (The Oil Industry of the USSR)
Neftianoe khoziaistvo (Oil Economy)
New York *Times*
Oxford Economic Papers
Plan
Planovoe khoziaistvo (Planned Economy)
Problemy ekonomiki (Problems of Economics)

Professional'nye Soiuzy (The Trade Unions)
Quarterly Journal of Economics
Review of Economic Progress
Review of Economics and Statistics
Sakhar (Sugar)
Sakharnaia promyshlennost' (The Sugar Industry)
Sovetskaya metallurgiia (Soviet Metallurgy)
Soviet Studies
Stal' (Steel)
Tekstil'naia promyshlennost' (The Textile Industry)
Teoriia i praktika metallurgii (The Theory and Practice of Metallurgy)
Trud (Labor)
Ugol' (Coal)
USSR Information Bulletin
Voprosy ekonomiki (Questions of Economics)

OTHER VOLUMES OF RAND RESEARCH

PUBLISHED BY COLUMBIA UNIVERSITY PRESS, NEW YORK

Bergson, Abram, and Hans Heymann, Jr. *Soviet National Income and Product, 1940–48* (1954).

Hoeffding, Oleg. *Soviet National Income and Product in 1928* (1954).

PUBLISHED BY MCGRAW-HILL BOOK COMPANY, INC., NEW YORK

Leites, Nathan. *The Operational Code of the Politburo* (1950).

Janis, Irving L. *Air War and Emotional Stress* (1950).

Mead, Margaret. *Soviet Attitudes toward Authority* (1950).

Selznick, Philip. *The Organizational Weapon: A Study of Bolshevik Strategy and Tactics* (1952).

McKinsey, J. C. C. *Introduction to the Theory of Games* (1952).

Shanley, F. R. *Weight-Strength Analysis of Aircraft Structures* (1952).

Williams, J. D. *The Compleat Strategyst: A Primer on the Theory of Games of Strategy* (1954).

PUBLISHED BY THE FREE PRESS, GLENCOE, ILLINOIS

Goldhamer, Herbert, and Andrew W. Marshall. *Psychosis and Civilization* (1953).

Garthoff, Raymond L. *Soviet Military Doctrine* (1953).

Leites, Nathan. *A Study of Bolshevism* (1953).

Leites, Nathan, and Elsa Bernaut. *The Ritual of Liquidation, Communists on Trial* (1954).